A Special Issue of
Visual Cognition

Object and Face Recognition

Edited by

Vicki Bruce
University of Stirling, UK

Glyn Humphreys
University of Birmingham, UK

LAWRENCE ERLBAUM ASSOCIATES, PUBLISHERS
Hove (UK)   Hillsdale (USA)

Lawrence Erlbaum Associates Ltd., Publishers
27 Palmeira Mansions
Church Road
Hove
East Sussex, BN3 2FA
U.K.

British Library Cataloguing in Publication Data

A catalogue record for this book is available from the British Library

ISBN 0-86377-930-1

Subject Index compiled by Ingrid Lock
Cover design by Joyce Chester
Typeset by G. Beard & Son, Brighton
Printed and bound by BPC Wheatons Ltd, Exeter

Contents

[*]This book is also a special issue of the journal *Visual Cognition* which forms Issues 2
& 3 of Volume 1 (1994). The page numbers used here are taken from the journal and
so begin on p.137.

VISUAL COGNITION, 1994, *1* (2/3), 137–139

Preface

This Special Issue on Object and Face Recognition presents a series of papers that show how current experimental, neuropsychological, and computational techniques are clarifying the mechanisms involved in processing and recognizing objects and faces, and the relationship between face recognition and the recognition of other kinds of visual object.

The first paper, written by ourselves, presents a selective review of the literature on object and face recognition, focusing on the relationship between the two. We conclude that although there seem to be distinct differences in the visual representations subserving basic level object recognition and face recognition, there are some similarities when the task of object recognition requires discrimination within a basic level category. Moreover, the organization of the higher-level sub-stages of identification, for perceptual classification, semantic description, and naming, appears similar for faces and objects, although the representation of proper names may be distinct from that of common names. However, although there appear major similarities between recognition within categories of objects and faces, neuropsychological evidence does appear to suggest that at least high-level recognition networks may be dedicated to faces distinct from other objects, given the observed dissociations between face and other kinds of object processing.

The second paper, by Rumiati et al., reinforces this suggestion by describing a patient with visual agnosia for objects but without alexia or prosopagnosia (i.e. with good recognition of words and faces as visual objects). It appears that this patient has difficulties confined to the visual and/or semantic representations of objects. This pattern of deficit is one that cannot be easily explained by recent accounts of the visual agnosias in terms of purely perceptual impairments, such as that proposed by Farah (1990). On Farah's model, face recognition involves holistic processing based on non-decomposed visual representations, and word recognition involves parts-based processing, with visual object recognition involving elements of both. While there is evidence for this difference between object and face processing, reviewed by Bruce and Humphreys here, it cannot account for the pattern of deficit in Rumiati et al.'s patient, as any perceptual deficit affecting visual object recognition would have to impair either visual word recognition or face recognition as well. Separation of the systems for representing faces and other objects is also suggested by the masking effects reported here by Costen et al., where recognition of faces is disrupted by masks comprised of other faces, or (to a lesser extent) face-like masks, but not by masks that show other visual objects of roughly similar size and shape. The degree of masking of one face by another does not seem to depend on the specific resemblance between the two depicted individuals, as there was no greater masking between faces similar in overall appearance than between ones dissimilar in appearance.

Holistic or configural processing of upright faces is often cited as the special ingredient of (upright) face recognition which enables so many similar patterns to be discriminated. Papers by Carey and Diamond and by Rhodes and Tremewan investigate this further. Carey and Diamond show a dissociation between the developmental time course of the inversion effect (the reduction in the efficiency of face processing when faces are inverted) and the facial composite effect (where component halves of composite faces are more difficult to recognize upright when the halves are aligned than when they are not). Younger children experience relatively less difficulty with inverted compared with upright faces than do adults, but the composite effect is as strong in the youngest age group as in the adults. This suggests that the relationship between configural or holistic processing and face processing expertise is rather more complex than it seemed. Rhodes and Tremewan explore the relationship between the effects of caricaturing faces—which might seem specifically to involve configural processing—and those of inversion of faces. Although the advantages that occasionally are found for the recognition of caricatured compared with veridical faces do appear confined to upright faces, the more reliable caricature equivalence effect, in which caricatures and veridical representations are recognized equally well but better than anticaricatures, is not affected by inversion. These papers suggest that the effects of inversion, facial composites, and caricature cannot all be attributed to simple disruption of configural information in faces and point to the need to specify in greater detail the nature of the visual information manipulated by these different changes.

In our introductory paper we describe connectionist models separately developed in our different laboratories to describe and explore the activation of different stages of object and person identification. Each of the models described uses localist rather than distributed representations, in the interactive activation with competition (IAC) architecture orginally developed by McClelland, Grossberg, and others. One criticism that is sometimes levelled at such models is that they model the steady state of the adult system rather than modelling the acquisition of new items. Burton's paper here describes an extension of the IAC model of person identification to learn new face patterns by the automatic recruitment of new units for items initially unfamiliar to the system.

Although there are clearly similarities in some of the representational and identification processes involved in face and object recognition, faces clearly differ quite radically from objects in the range of different kinds of meaning to which they give rise. In addition to individual identification, faces allow us to recognize emotional states, contribute to speech recognition, and signal direction of attention, as well as being recognized as belonging to sub-categories of facial appearance (male face, old face, etc.). However, we are able to spell out the relationship between face and object recognition uncontaminated by other uses made of facial information because there is very good evidence from a number of sources that emotional expressions, and probably facial speech, are analysed by neural systems quite independent from those used for facial identification. In this issue, Justine Sergent and colleagues add further evidence for the independent processing of emotional expression and face recognition obtained from PET scanning.

In addition to providing substantive empirical and theoretical contributions to our understanding of object and face recognition, the papers in this Special Issue also demonstrate how studies taking different methodological approaches to visual cognition can converge to provide a richer account of behaviour than would be possible from any approach taken alone.

While we were assembling the final versions of the papers for the issue, we were shocked to hear of Justine Sergent's death. She will be remembered for her many respected and distinguished contributions to cognitive psychology and neuropsychology, and at a personal level for the charm and warmth of her interactions with us and other UK colleagues on her many visits to Europe. Typically, Justine acted as a prompt, constructive, and courteous reviewer of one of the articles in this collection. Her work often focused on the relations between object and face recognition, and it is very appropriate that she was able to contribute to this Special Issue. We will miss very much her scholarship and her good company.

Vicki Bruce and Glyn Humphreys
May 1994

REFERENCE

Farah, M.J. (1990). *Visual agnosia.* Cambridge, MA: MIT Press.

VISUAL COGNITION, 1994, *1* (2/3), 141–180

Recognizing Objects and Faces

Vicki Bruce

University of Stirling, Stirling, U.K.

and

Glyn W. Humphreys

University of Birmingham, Edgbaston, Birmingham, U.K.

We review evidence and theories concerning the processing mechanisms leading to the visual recognition of objects and faces. A good deal of work suggests that identification of objects at a basic level depends on edge-coding, whereas face recognition depends more on representations of surface properties such as colour and shading. Moreover, basic-level object recognition seems to involve a parts-based description, whereas face recognition depends upon more holistic processing. This work distinguishes between the visual processes mediating the recognition of objects and faces. However, when the demands of object recognition are made more similar to those of face recognition, then there appear to be some similarities in the perceptual representations used for objects and faces. Moreover, when we progress beyond the stage of perceptual representation to consider the organization of cognitive stages involved in the full identification of objects and faces, there are marked similarities in the processing of these different kinds of material. We discuss the implications of the results for understanding visual identification, in normality and in pathology.

Classification of the visual world into discrete categories is of fundamental importance for our behaviour. Everyday activities such as chatting with a friend over lunch depend upon our recognition of the friend, a chair, types of food and

Requests for reprints should be sent to V. Bruce, Department of Psychology, University of Stirling, Stirling FK9 4LA, Scotland, U.K.

This paper was supported by independent grants from the Economic and Social Research Council to both authors, from the Science and Engineering Research Council to the first author, and from the Medical Research Council to the second author. We thank Mike Burton, Jon Driver, Rebecca Lawson, Jane Riddoch, and Mel Vitkovitch for their comments, which have helped us to improve the presentation.

items of cutlery, and of the activities that each affords. The effortless achievement of such activities depends on a complex interaction between incoming visual information and stored knowledge of the world in general, and objects and people in particular. Some functions may be specified by quite general aspects of shape (e.g. that a chair, like many other things, can be sat upon or that a spoon can be used as a scoop). Other activities require more specific categorization of an object as a particular type of thing—both a cup and a milk jug may afford drinking from, but in polite company we know which one to pour from and which to drink from. This more specific process we here describe as "basic-level" classification (e.g. Rosch et al., 1976).

Gabriel Garcia Márquez (1967/1978) had a profound insight into the special role that stored knowledge plays in our everyday activities when he described the consequences of a fictional disease of the memory spreading through the inhabitants of the village of Macondo in "One Hundred Years of Solitude". To begin with, the hero attempted to avert the consequences of the disease by labelling each object with its name. This proved a temporary remedy only.

> Little by little, studying the infinite possibilities of a loss of memory, he realised that the day might come when things might be recognized by their inscriptions but that no one would remember their use . . . . The sign that he hung on the neck of the cow was exemplary proof of the way in which the inhabitants of Macondo were prepared to fight against the loss of memory: *This is the cow. She must be milked every morning so that she will produce milk, and the milk must be boiled in order to be mixed with coffee to form coffee and milk* (p.46).

Later in this review we will consider how certain kinds of visual agnosia seem to affect people's knowledge of the meanings of visual objects in a way not dissimilar to that anticipated by Marquez. However, our everyday activities require still further precision in categorization. Most people may "afford" chatting-with, but we need to recognize visually those particular people that we know in order to interact appropriately. We need to recognize not just "a car", but different makes of car and our own car in the car park. Such behaviour involves discriminating within a basic-level category, to classify at a subordinate (different makes of car) or individual (our car) level. The problem of face recognition is the most studied example of this latter kind of activity, although the ability to go beyond basic level classification is also studied in the performance of visual expertise for other stimuli, including, for example, dogs, sheep and particular types of car (see below).

One of the most enduring and intractable problems in visual perception and cognition has been that of how we manage to identify objects and faces across the range of transformations that we usually encounter. Whether we are talking about recognition at the basic or at a more specific level, we can recognize familiar items despite changes in size, location, background, viewpoint, and lighting. Our lack of understanding the means by which recognition procedures succeed across image transformations is one major reason why machine recognition of objects and faces is currently limited to very restricted conditions (e.g. where size, lighting, and background are constant).

Faces vary in ways that are not shared by most categories of object because of their rubbery surfaces; thus, there are dynamic non-rigid changes as faces talk and express. Hairstyles also change, giving rise to shifts in the shape of the overall outline of the object that are more dramatic than those that occur when a person gains or loses weight. Slower, non-rigid changes may also arise during ageing.

The invariance of object and face recognition across changes in size, viewpoint, and so forth severely constrains the theoretical accounts of the representational processes involved. Early theories of recognition were dominated by the problem of two-dimensional (2D) pattern recognition and, particularly, letter recognition, a domain that avoids some of the trickier difficulties associated with changes of viewpoint and lighting. Approaches to the recognition of three-dimensional (3D) objects were reviewed by Ullman (1989), who categorized past accounts into three main classes: (1) Recognition by invariant properties, (2) recognition by object decomposition into parts, and (3) "alignment" methods. The first achieves recognition via the storage of features that are common to all instantiations of the category. This kind of approach may have potential for recognition in restricted domains, as might be required by an industrial robot, for example, and it might be used when we are presented with a limited set of objects repeatedly so that we learn the invariant properties within a specific context (e.g. see Jolicoeur, 1992). However, the approach may have limited application for object recognition more generally, where we encounter many thousands of objects, often unpredictably, yet object recognition still proceeds efficiently and exceedingly rapidly (e.g. Thorpe & Imbert, 1989). The other two approaches differ in that the second suggests that objects are first parsed into parts, and the properties and arrangements of these parts define the object. On such accounts, viewpoint invariance can be achieved by a variety of methods, as we elaborate below. The third approach is based on the use of a more holistic representation, in which the image, or some derived measurements made upon the image, is aligned with one of a number of stored canonical views. On this account, object decomposition into parts need not be posited.

In this paper we first review some of the psychological evidence relevant to the question of what type of representational processes characterize face and object recognition. At first glance, the evidence seems to suggest that basic object recognition is achieved via a part-based decomposition process (at least for many objects) based largely on the analysis of edge features, and face recognition is achieved via a more holistic or "configural" process encompassing more information about surface texture, colour, and shading. However, we will also show that many of the apparent differences between these two processes arise because research has concentrated on either basic-level object categorization or on the within-category identification of individual faces, without considering how object recognition at more specific levels may make demands and involve processes very similar to those involved in face recognition. We will then turn to outline what is currently understood about the way in which visual analysis of an object or face shape leads on to the access of meaning and names, and to review evidence on neuropsychological disorders of face and object recognition. Here again we note similarities as well as differences in the processing of objects and faces.

Edge Features versus Surface Features

Object Recognition

One way in which the recognition of objects and faces may differ is in terms of whether edge-based visual descriptions (i.e. descriptions made on the basis of major discontinuities in image intensity) or descriptions of the surface characteristics of the stimuli (their pigmentation, texture, shading, etc.) are of primary importance. Most recent accounts of object recognition put the representation burden on "edges" rather than on the texture, colour, or shading of an object's surface (e.g. Biederman, 1987; Bulthoff & Edelman, 1992; Ullman, 1989). Several experiments demonstrated that the categorization of objects as, say, living versus non-living seems to be achieved as quickly with line drawings as with coloured photographs of objects (Biederman & Ju, 1988; Davidoff & Ostergaard, 1988; Ostergaard & Davidoff, 1985), though significant advantages for full-colour photographs can be shown when the task requires objects to be named rather than classified (Davidoff & Ostergaard, 1988), unless the stimuli are briefly presented and pattern-masked (Biederman & Ju, 1988). These early studies tended also to find no disadvantage to object classification when stimuli were presented in incongruous colours (e.g. a dog shown in red or an apple in blue). Such results were used by Biederman and associates to support an edge-based theory of object recognition (see below) and by Davidoff and colleagues to argue that colour was not represented in the structural or semantic representation of an object, though it might form part of a lexical system influencing object naming.

Subsequently, Price and Humphreys (1989) re-examined the role played by surface detail, including colour, on object recognition. They revealed advantages for the classification as well as for the naming of objects when they were shown with their usual surface details (shading, texture, and/or colour) compared with simple line drawings, and disadvantages when incongruous colour was presented. However, the effects observed were greater when items were drawn from categories in which many of the exemplars share perceptual features (e.g. animals) compared with those drawn from categories with structurally more dissimilar exemplars (e.g. tools), and they were greater when the tasks required greater differentiation within categories (e.g. deciding whether an item was British or foreign, relative to whether it was living or non-living) (and see Wurm, Legge, Isenberg, & Luebker, 1993, for evidence on the effects of colour on the identification of foodstuffs). The effects with objects thus do not seem confined purely to accessing lexical information about object names but can also influence access to semantic knowledge (for classification). From these results it appears that surface properties can influence object recognition, though the magnitude of the effects increases as a function of the homogeneity of the edge-based structures of object categories. Given this, we might predict that surface features of faces, which are structurally very similar one to another, might play a particularly important role in their recognition.

Face Recognition

The effects of surface detail are, indeed, pronounced for face recognition. Davies, Ellis, and Shepherd (1978) compared the identification of famous faces from photographs and from line drawings created by tracing around the features in the photographs. Even when elaborated line drawings were used, which contained traced wrinkles and surface folds in the face as well as the "features" of eyes, nose, mouth etc., recognition of famous faces averaged only 47% correct from the line drawings, compared with 90% correct from photographs. Bruce et al. (1992) have shown that line drawings of faces can be well recognized but that this requires that, in addition to "edges", the drawings convey information about the pigmentation and shading of the original image by preserving areas of dark and light. This conclusion arose from an evaluation of the efficiency of Pearson and Robinson's (1985) algorithm for computer-drawn "cartoons". The Pearson and Robinson algorithm included a "threshold" operator, which drew as black any region that was darker than a specified level of grey in the original image, in addition to a "valledge" operator, which marked contrast edges and locations where there was an abrupt change in the orientation of the surface with respect to the viewer. Bruce et al. showed that both components combined to produce images that were recognized almost as accurately as original photographs, whereas drawings based on "valledges" alone were recognized rather poorly.

The extreme difficulty of recognizing faces shown in photographic negative may also reflect the importance of pigmentation and/or shading for the face recognition process. Bruce and Langton (in press) showed that presenting images of famous faces as photographic negatives disrupted recognition even more than inverting them did, and that the two manipulations of inversion and negation combined additively, suggesting that they affected different aspects of face image processing (cf. Sternberg, 1969). Hayes (1988; Hayes, Morrone & Burr, 1986) has shown that negation has no effect on the recognition of high-spatial-frequency images. Thus a line-drawn or "edge" representation of a face, although itself a poor representation for recognition, is unaffected by the reversal of brightness values. This result is consistent with the effect of negation, as studied by Bruce and Langton, arising from the reversal of information specifying pigmentation or shading. Further experiments conducted by Bruce and Langton examined effects of negation on images of faces that lacked pigmentation, so that any effect of negation arose solely from effects of the reversal of shading patterns. The images were of the 3D surfaces of faces, which were measured by laser and displayed as smooth surfaces using computer-aided design techniques. Negation had no significant effect on tasks that required identification of these surfaces images, suggesting that the usual effect of negation arises from reversing pigmentation rather than shading patterns. However, in tasks requiring the classification of the sex of these surface images, negation significantly slowed performance, supporting the use of shading patterns in sex classification (cf. Bruce et al., 1993; Burton, Bruce, & Dench, 1993). Here we have one example from the face-classification literature where rather different findings result from different task demands (cf. Roberts & Bruce, 1988), a point to which we return later in this paper.

Although the data from object and face recognition studies are not directly comparable—for example, deriving from different tasks—the findings do suggest that surface properties may play a stronger role in the recognition of faces than they do in the basic level recognition of many common objects. These differences may be a natural consequence of the relative informativeness of different aspects of shape and surface features. Where basic shapes are all very similar, edge-based representations may not differentiate individuals, and additional information about surface features may be essential for identification.

In the next section we describe how theories of object and face recognition propose that edges and/or surface features are analysed and used to provide representations that can mediate recognition across changes in location, size, lighting, and viewpoint.

Part-based versus Holistic Representations

Object Recognition

1. Marr and Nishihara (1978). Marr and Nishihara (1978) were perhaps the first theorists to develop a fully articulated part-based approach to object recognition. They proposed a theory of the representation of natural shapes in terms of the spatial arrangement of generalized cones at different levels of spatial scale. On this theory, the difference between, say, a gorilla's and a person's shape would be given by the arrangement and relative lengths of the axes of the generalized cone shapes approximating the head, body, trunk, and limbs. These axis-based representations were held to be object-centred, being coded relative to the main axis of the object (e.g. the body length, for a person), and derived from, initially, the occluding (silhouette) contour of the image and, secondly, an analysis of the 3D shape of the surfaces of the object, coded via other routes (shading, stereo, and so forth). Little evidence was furnished for the psychological validity of such a scheme, however, and apart from a suggestion that the decomposition into parts was achieved by analysing concavities in the occluding contour, the process of arriving at the full object-centred description was not specified in a way that led to psychological validation.

Evidence for the importance of concavities in the parsing of complex shapes was provided by Hoffman and Richards (1984), who demonstrated geometrically that concavities in the image of an object mark the divisions between the contours of distinct parts. Hoffman and Richards (1984) provided perceptual demonstrations to support the idea that the visual system uses concavities in parsing, by noting that when ambiguous figures such as the faces-goblet or Schroeder staircase reverse, the perceptual interpretation is always such that the parts seen are divided by concavities.

Experimental evidence has also been found for the importance of the axes of elongation and symmetry in setting up reference frames for the internal representation of simple shapes. For example, Palmer (1980) showed that the time to decide the direction of pointing of an equilateral triangle was influenced by the orientation of the axis of symmetry of the configuration of which it was a part. Humphreys and Quinlan (1988) found that the time to decide whether a shape was a square or a triangle was facilitated by precueing the orientation of the main axis of the shapes. Performance was disrupted when subjects were cued with the wrong axis for the shape description needed for the task (e.g. cueing a diagonal axis of symmetry within a square, consistent with the description of a diamond rather than a square). Quinlan and Humphreys (1993) examined classification responses to shapes possessing a single axis of both elongation and symmetry and found that subjects responded in an integral fashion to the orientation of the shape and the orientation of an axis drawn onto the shape (e.g. responses were speeded when the orientation of the shape and the depicted axis were congruent, and they were slowed when they were incongruent). In shapes without a "good" axis of symmetry, responses to the orientation of the global shape and to the orientation of a depicted axis were independent.

Other studies have implicated a role for axis-based descriptions in the recognition of more complex real objects. Humphrey and Jolicoeur (1993) reported that the identification of line drawings was markedly disrupted when the objects were depicted with their main axis oriented directly towards the viewer so that the main axis appeared foreshortened. This disruptive effect of foreshortening occurred even though the main components of the objects were salient at all viewing angles. Lawson and Humphreys (1993) used a matching task with line drawings of objects rotated in depth. With relatively long intervals between the stimuli, there was little effect of the angle between consecutive objects until the to-be-matched stimulus had its main axis foreshortened. Again the effect of foreshortening occurred even when all the main part components were present in the foreshortened images. Using photographs of objects, Palmer, Rosch, and Chase (1981) also found that views in which the main axis is foreshortened were rated as being atypical, and that objects seen from this view were identified very slowly. In neuropsychological studies, Humphreys and Riddoch (1984) found that patients with lesions to the right parietal lobe were abnormally poor at matching photographs of objects in which one object was foreshortened, whereas they were not impaired at matching objects shown in other unusual views but where the main axis was not foreshortened. Also, the performance of the patients was greatly improved when the objects were shown against a perspective background suggesting the orientation of the main axis.

These studies are consistent both with there being some form of parts-based decomposition of objects, and also with the description of the parts being encoded relative to the main axis of the object. However, alternative interpretations are possible. Foreshortened views may be highly unfamiliar and hence lead to major disruptions to recognition. This might occur equally if the representation derived from the image for matching or for recognition is parts-based, or if it is not decomposed into parts.

2. Biederman (1987). A rather different perspective on parts decomposition of objects was proposed by Biederman (1987) who argued that objects are recognized on the basis of the nature and relative locations of their parts, without encoding the positions of the parts in relation to the object's main axis. Biederman argued that the parts of objects are represented as primitive volumetric shapes, which he termed "geons". Object recognition is based on the relationships between a limited set of such geons, much as spoken word recognition is based on the relationships between a limited set of phonemes. Furthermore, he proposed that geons could be recovered in a way that was robust across changes in view, background, lighting, size, and location, according to the presence of particular "non-accidental" features in the image. These features include the presence of parallel and collinear edges, of particular forms of edge junction, and so forth. Thus a "brick" geon can be distinguished from a "wedge" geon because of the different number and arrangement of straight and curved edges, parallel edges, symmetry, and so forth, all of which are image features that can be used as cues to object shape provided that it is assumed that such properties do not arise merely as accidents of particular viewpoint. Thus on Biederman's model, invariance is built into the representational format itself, which is size-, location-, and (largely) viewpoint-independent, except where different viewpoints reveal different geons. Other variations, such as lighting or texture, are ignored by the representational process, which analyses major contours only.

Biederman described experiments in which the perception of degraded and incomplete objects was compared. Line drawings of objects had parts of their contours deleted in ways that either maintained the underlying part structures or rendered them non-recoverable by deleting contour at the regions of concavity, which destroyed the part structure. For equivalent portions of contour deleted, recognition was much more accurate in the recoverable than in the non-recoverable condition, and the identification of non-recoverable versions of objects did not benefit from increases in exposure duration in the way that recoverable objects did.

In other experiments, Biederman and Cooper (1991) investigated how repetition priming is affected by a change in the way a line drawing of an object is depicted. When a picture of an object is presented twice for naming, the naming latency on the second occurrence is much faster than on the first. The difference between the priming given when a quite different exemplar of the category is shown (e.g. an upright piano followed by a grand piano) and that found when the same exemplar is repeated (e.g. the same or a different picture of an upright piano) gives a measure of "visual" priming over and above priming at the level of the meaning or the label of the object category. The magnitude of this visual priming of object identification was unaffected if the second view of the same object exemplar showed the same image components, represented by complementary but non-overlapping edge features. However, visual priming was reduced if the depicted components (geons) themselves were changed from first to second presentation (when different parts of the same object exemplar are shown on the two occasions). Further experiments have shown that priming is invariant over other changes that alter the image but preserve its components, such as size, location, and moderate changes in viewpoint. In contrast, the same manipulations do affect episodic memory for line-drawn pictures (Biederman & Cooper, 1992; Cooper, Schacter, Ballesteros, & Moore, 1992; Humphrey & Khan, 1992), suggesting that variations in object components that are irrelevant for identity may be processed and maintained by other parts of the visual system—perhaps those to do with spatial layout and action. The location of an object in the visual field does not affect its identity but will affect how an observer reacts to it (e.g. if reaching out to grasp it, or ducking to avoid being hit by it).

Cooper, Biederman, and Hummel (1992) furnished other evidence supporting the geon theory. In one study, people were asked to decide whether two successive objects shown were the same or different in name. When objects shared the same name (e.g. both were wine goblets), the two exemplars could differ in terms of the geon shown (e.g. the bowl of the goblet could have rounded or straight sides), or they could differ in a way that did not involve any change in accidental properties and hence geons (e.g. the bowl of the goblet could be stretched in the second view compared with the first). They found that matching was severely affected by a change in geon, but not by other metric changes that left the geons unchanged, suggesting that it is the categorization of the shape parts, rather than holistic or metric properties of shape, that determines ease of matching.

However, other workers have produced evidence that seems to favour more holistic over part-based object description schemes. Cave and Kosslyn (1993) showed that the identification of objects was severely disrupted by the scrambling of the spatial arrangement of the overall shape—a result that would be expected on a part-based as well as a holistic coding scheme. However, they also found that it mattered rather little how the objects were divided into parts. Dividing objects in ways that coincided with natural part boundaries (i.e. ways that kept geons intact) produced little advantage over dividing them in ways that did not maintain natural part boundaries. It was only when exposure durations were extremely short that there was an advantage for the natural over the unnatural part divisions. Cave and Kosslyn suggest that people can use parts such as geons as the building blocks for recognition but that they do not need to do so. A problem with Cave and Kosslyn's study, however, is that naturally parsed geons may serve as "objects" for perceptual identification in their own right and therefore compete for identification, whereas objects divided in other ways (not into natural parts) may not do so.

3. Alignment Methods. Alternative accounts of object recognition include "alignment" methods (Ullman, 1989), in which more *holistic*, pictorial descriptions are stored and accessed by using some kind of spatial transformation. Template-matching models are the oldest and best-known of such methods, but Ullman (1989) describes more sophisticated developments that can cope with 3D and non-rigid objects. On Ullman's (1989) scheme, access to stored representations is based on an "alignment key", which is extracted from prominent spatial landmarks. Scale and location invariance would be achieved by this extraction process, as Ullman claims that the key needed for alignment can be encoded independent of scale and location changes. Related theories of object recognition are those based on the storage of several discrete 2D views of objects (e.g. Poggio & Edelman, 1990; Tarr & Pinker, 1989). According to these theories, invariance of viewpoint, size, and location would be achieved through experience with the 2D views on which object recognition is trained. Currently Poggio and Edelman's theory has been developed to encode simple shapes where the extraction of the features (vertices and lengths of axes, etc.) is assumed.

As a to-be-recognized object must be brought into correspondence with one or more stored forms of that object, alignment and multiple view models predict that recognition should be slower the further the to-be-recognized shapes depart from the stored canonical forms. Linear effects on identification from placing objects at unfamiliar orientations in the plane have been reported (e.g. Jolicoeur, 1985; though see Eley, 1982), and linear effects on recognition memory and matching performance have been shown by changing the sizes of shapes (e.g. Jolicoeur, 1987; Jolicoeur & Besner, 1987). Also, several studies have indicated effects of changing viewpoint on the matching of both familiar (Bartram, 1974; Ellis, Allport, Humphreys, & Collis, 1989) and unfamiliar object shapes (Edelman & Bulthoff, 1992), suggesting that matching requires reorientation of a shape into one of a number of discrete viewpoints that have been stored.

For example, a recent series of studies by Edelman and associates has invest-igated the processes that enable discrimination within a set of unfamiliar objects of similar overall appearance—for example, bent wire shapes (e.g. Bulthoff & Edelman, 1992; Edelman & Bulthoff, 1992). Bulthoff and Edelman (1992) compared the predictions made by theories proposing that recognition is medi-ated by a 3D model (e.g. Biederman, 1987) and those proposing that recognition is mediated by a set of 2D viewer-centred representations (e.g. Poggio & Edelman, 1990). Subjects examined a series of transformations in depth of a to-be-remembered object and later had to discriminate a novel view of a learned object from a distractor object. Novel views could be presented within the same plane of rotation as the "old" objects, or in a plane orthogonal to that of the old exemplars. The authors argued that the experience of the 2D views in motion at training should have induced a 3D representation to which novel viewpoints in the same or a different plane could be compared. Their results, however, showed that generalization to the orthogonal views was very poor, and generalization within the plane was much better to views interpolated between those that had been experienced than to those that involved extrapolating beyond that range of views experienced. Their detailed results were fit rather well by a simulation based on a 2D view approach, with the views encoded as vectors of vertex co-ordinates and segment lengths.

In tasks requiring the matching of drawings of real objects, however, effects of depth rotation on performance are non-linear until objects are foreshortened (Lawson & Humphreys, 1994). This suggests either that linear alignment processes are not required for the matching of real objects in depth, or that multiple views may be stored for common objects, producing effects only when depicted views are highly unusual (as when they are foreshortened).

Although evidence of this kind has been used to support viewpoint-dependent and/or holistic representational models, there are some difficulties in accepting this interpretation of the evidence unequivocally. First, effects of the scale, orientation, or viewpoint of objects might show up in episodic tasks, such as deciding whether an object has been shown earlier, but these tasks may not necessarily tap the description that itself mediates object identification. As we saw earlier, for example, changes in the size or location of an object affect old-new recognition but not the size of the visual repetition priming effect, suggesting that the former effect arises from a different source to the latter. Thus it is very important that the demands that the experimental task might make on different memory systems be considered.

Perhaps more important is that models that suggest that object recognition proceeds via an analysis of parts, with a resulting structural description that is viewpoint-independent, still would predict effects of certain transformations. On Biederman's model, for instance, given that the spatial relationship between geons is critical for the description of an object, and given that such spatial rela-tionships must be defined relative to some thing or other (e.g. so that one part is "on top of" another), effects of rotating the object in the plane would also be expected (as relations such as "top-of" would change with respect to the positions of the geons on the retina; however, whether such changes would be expected to produce linear effects of within-plane rotation on matching and identification performance is perhaps questionable).

Viewpoint-dependent effects would also be expected if different views revealed or obscured more of the defining characteristics of the basic geon sets. Biederman and Gerhardstein (1993) examined effects of changing the orientation in depth on the visual repetition priming of familiar objects and found that rotations in depth that preserved the same visible part structure of objects had only a very small effect on the size of visual priming, whereas those that altered the visible part structure (such that different geons were visible in the views shown in the first and second exposure) had a greater effect. This suggests that at least part of the effect of changes in depicted viewpoint arises because of changes in part structure. Also, although very large effects of change in viewpoint are found in recognition tasks using unfamiliar shapes that have no individuating part structure, such as the "bent paper-clip" shapes used by Edelman and Bulthoff (1992), Biederman and Gerhardstein (1993) showed that these effects were virtually abolished when each of the depicted shapes was given an individuating geon segment. However, against approaches such as Biederman's, which emphasize parts-based recognition, other investigators have found effects of view even when the major parts of the object are visible (e.g. Humphrey & Jolicoeur, 1993). Also, Lawson, Humphreys, and Watson (1994), using a naming task with objects presented briefly in a series of consecutive or randomly-related depth-rotated views, found effects of the angle of disparity between consecutive views irrespective of whether or not parts changed. Apparently the similarity of consecutive views can influence object recognition in addition to any effects based on the part-structure of the objects.

Overall, whereas some recent evidence suggests that holistic transformation processes might be involved in object recognition, there remains a considerable body of evidence for a role of the part-structure of objects in basic level object identification, at least for classes of object with a clearly defined part structure. When we turn to face identification, in contrast, it seems that the evidence more clearly favours a more holistic representation.

Face Recognition

In contrast to the evidence for a part-based representational scheme for objects, face representation seems to be more "holistic". This term may itself have many interpretations, as we examine below.

The main observation favouring the holistic processing of faces is that it seems to be difficult or impossible to encode a particular part or "feature" of an upright face without some influence from other, more distant features. It is not just that the spatial arrangement of face features is important—after all, we have seen that the spatial arrangement of geons is crucial for the definition of an object. For faces, it seems either that the internal description of the parts themselves is influenced by that of other parts (e.g. see Sergent, 1984), or that parts themselves are not made explicit in the description that mediates face identification (Tanaka & Farah, 1993). For example, Young, Hellawell, and Hay (1987) took pictures of famous faces and divided them horizontally across the centre. They showed that subjects were able to identify these halves in isolation. When halves of different faces were recombined, however, it became extremely difficult for subjects to name the people who contributed to the composites if these were aligned—new (and unfamiliar) faces seemed to emerge from the combination of the top half of, say, Margaret Thatcher's face and the bottom half of, say, Princess Diana's. However, when the composite faces were presented upside down, subjects' abilities to identify the halves improved. These results have been replicated by Carey and Diamond (this issue), who extend the findings to children as young as 6 years of age.

The fact that the effect of making "composite" faces decreases when faces are inverted is consistent with several other studies suggesting that upside-down faces cannot benefit from the holistic processing mode that is used for upright ones (Yin, 1969). Interestingly, face identification in young children is not so affected by inversion as in adults (Carey, 1981)—a finding that has been taken to suggest that it takes time for children to develop processes sensitive to holistic facial properties. Yet Carey and Diamond show here that the increasing effects of inversion, as children develop, are independent of the effects of composite faces on identification. This pattern of results suggests a situation somewhat more complex than the simple view that holistic properties either are or are not used, depending upon experience with upright faces. For example, rather than face identification involving non-decomposed facial properties, it might depend on "configural" processing of several parsed features, which are recombined to form new emergent properties. Diamond and Carey (1986) termed these emergent properties "second-order relational features". Here Carey and Diamond propose that children, like adults, encode faces in terms of their configural properties, but that children use many fewer features than do adults. Essentially, children encode an impoverished configural representation. Inversion disrupts the encoding of configural properties of faces, and this particularly affects adults because their formerly rich configural representations become impoverished. A similar proposal concerning the effects of inversion on face encoding has recently arisen in other studies that have examined the effects of various distortions of facial features on judgements made to upright and inverted faces (e.g. Bartlett & Searcy, 1993; Rhodes, Brake, & Atkinson, 1993).

The argument for the specific use of *non-decomposed* facial properties in face identification has been made by Tanaka and Farah (1993). They asked subjects to learn the identities of individuals constructed from an electronic "kit" of face features. After learning the faces, subjects were asked questions such as "Which is Larry's nose?", and they had to choose the nose that went with the face they had learned to identify as Larry. Subjects were much better at making this judgement when the noses were shown in the context of the whole face than when presented in isolation. However, this advantage for presentations of the whole face was not shown when identities had initially been learned for scrambled faces, upside-down faces, or houses (in the latter case, questions about windows, doors, etc. replaced those about face features such as the nose). These results suggest that memory for intact, upright faces is not based upon a representation in which parts are made explicit, in contrast to memory for jumbled or inverted faces. Note, though, that the results do not necessitate the view that facial representations are non-decomposed; indeed, the results are consistent with the idea that memory representations for faces are based on emergent, configural descriptions in which parsed features are no longer represented independently.

So far, we have discussed evidence that suggests that in contrast to basic-level object identification, face recognition is based upon more holistic representations in which surface features are preserved. None of the parts-based schemes of object recognition (e.g. Biederman's) prove very suitable for accommodating evidence from face recognition, and those models of object recognition based upon more holistic, view-specific methods have yet to be specified in a way that includes sensitivity to surface features that as we have seen, are important for identifying faces. Indeed, when we consider models of the analysis and representation of faces for recognition, it seems that a quite different kind of model— based on analysis of low-level image properties—provides a promising alternative account.

Image-based Processing of Faces.   Although several different models of face recognition have been described in the literature, few have been offered as serious accounts of the visual processes mediating performance. Those that have been suggested as having some psychological plausibility have tended to be based on statistical analysis of the face images, with little or no pre-processing or abstraction. Baron's (1981) model stored faces as coarse-quantized image templates, combining templates of whole faces with finer-scale representations of local features. WISARD (e.g. Stonham, 1986) was one of the earliest face classifiers based upon neural network principles, in which the particular recurrent patterns of light and dark image elements that were correlated with specific individuals in the training set would become learned. WISARD could learn to recognize one of several different identities, or to classify faces in some other way (e.g. to discriminate smiling from unsmiling faces), but could only generalize within the range of exemplars present at training and not beyond this range. Moreover, such things as location or lighting invariance were probably impossible given this kind of statistical classifier.

Of somewhat more interest are recent statistical systems based upon Principal Components Analysis (PCA)—again inherently a statistical operation that can be implemented by a neural network. On such schemes, individual pixel values are regarded as a set of correlated measurements, and across a set of faces PCA can extract the significant axes of variation, and any face can be described by its coding in this "face space". Recognition of an old face is achieved by matching derived PCA coordinates with those stored for known faces. Turk and Pentland (1991) described a pre-processing operation that could locate a face-like region of the image, thereby offering a suggestion for how location invariance could be achieved. On their system, scale invariance could be achieved by a scaling transformation, or by having different analyses of images of different sizes. However, extraction of figure from ground, and achievement of size and to some extent viewpoint invariance can be achieved within a face recognition scheme using methods similar to those of alignment theorists. Craw, Aitchison, and Cameron (1992) describe how faces can be normalized by using a set of control points to extract "shape-free" vectors describing each face, and in other work they have implemented a system for the automatic extraction of such control points (Craw, Tock, & Bennett, 1992). Thus there are various ways in which the background, size, and location invariance could be solved. To recognize faces across different viewing positions on such a scheme would require different PCA nets trained to different views, and some way of assigning a given view to a particular network.

The PCA method has some psychological plausibility. For example, O'Toole, Deffenbacer, Valentin, and Abdi (1994) show that there is a very high correlation between recognition memory scores obtained from a set of faces and those predicted on the basis of the distinctiveness of their encoding via a PCA network. However, there remain a number of questions to do with generalization across different kinds of lighting, viewpoint, and expression.

Attempts to provide solutions to the question of invariant recognition have thus tended to posit different processes for faces compared with objects, with some form of principal component analysis (or related statistical analysis) based directly on 2D images mediating view-invariant recognition of faces, compared with abstracted structural descriptions based largely on edge features mediating view-invariant object recognition. Such differences would mesh with the argument for parts-based and holistic encoding procedures, and edge- and surface-based representations, respectively, involved in object and face recognition. However, the contrasts between the different approaches to viewpoint-invariant recognition for objects and faces may be rather less than at first appears.

Identification of Objects beyond the Basic Level

The above evidence and theory suggest that faces may differ quite fundamentally in their representation compared with other object classes. However, when we shift to examine within-category discrimination of objects, using observers who have *expertise* with the class of objects in question, results obtained with non-face objects begin to look more like those obtained with faces. For example, Diamond and Carey (1986) examined the effects of inversion on the recognition of pictures of dogs, by people with expertise with such images (dog judges) compared with novices. The experts, but not the novices, showed effects of inverting dog images like those of inverting face images. Diamond and Carey suggest that this is because expertise with members of a class of objects all sharing the same overall (first-order) configuration leads to sensitivity to second-order configural differences that distinguish one member of the class from another, and it is this configural process that suffers following inversion.

Another study that also suggests that representational processing of faces and other objects can be similar was reported by Rhodes and McLean (1990). They investigated the effects of caricaturing line-drawings of passerine birds— members of which have a similar overall shape but differ in their configural details. Rhodes, Brennan, and Carey (1987) had earlier shown that recognition of line drawings of personally familiar faces was somewhat enhanced when the line drawings were "caricatured" to a moderate extent, via a process that exaggerated differences between a particular face and a representation of an average face (Brennan, 1985). Using the same algorithm for producing caricatures of line drawings, Rhodes and McLean found that bird-watchers similarly recognized members of the passerine family better when the drawing was caricatured. Similar effects were not found with novice observers. This experiment again suggests that some aspect of the holistic and/or configural process that mediates face recognition, a task at which we all have expertise, may develop within other object classes given the appropriate expertise within those classes. As the demands and experience of object recognition become more like face recognition, so the effects appear to converge.

Rhodes and Tremewan (this issue) show that an advantage found (at least for some items) for the identification of caricatured over veridical representations of faces is eliminated when faces are inverted. They distinguish this caricature advantage from another effect, namely the equivalent identification for caricatures and for veridical face representations, relative to the poorer identification of "anti-caricatures", distorted towards rather than further away from the face norm. The "caricature equivalence effect" occurs even with inverted faces. In their study of bird recognition, Rhodes and McLean, too, found a caricature equivalence effect with non-experts, though the caricature advantage was confined to expert bird-watchers. This result suggests that the caricature advantage is related to expertise in discriminating between members of perceptually homogeneous classes. The caricature equivalence effect may still represent use of configural relationships between image features, but these configural relationships appear to be impoverished in comparison to those derived by experts, and which lead to a caricature advantage. Inversion leads to impoverishment of the representations encoded even by experts, rendering performance by experts and non-experts more similar. This fits with Carey and Diamond's (this issue) proposals concerning the effects of inversion on face identification by adults and (in this sense, non-expert) children.

The effects of caricaturing bird outlines observed by Rhodes and McLean show that it can be advantageous for within-category identification if shapes are made more deviant from the norm—that is, if shapes are made more distinctive. Thus the caricature effect may be related to the more general effects of distinctiveness. The effects of typicality and distinctiveness on human performance depend upon whether the task is one of basic-level classification or one of individuation, but the basic patterns are similar for faces and objects. Thus Valentine and Bruce (1986a) showed that there was an advantage for faces that were more typical in appearance in a task of deciding whether a pattern was a face or a non-face (where face features were rearranged), an effect that mirrors the advantage for more typical category members in tasks of category verification. For example, given the task of deciding whether a stimulus is a bird, people are faster when shown a sparrow than a chicken, the sparrow being the more typical of the two birds (see Smith & Medin, 1981). However, when the task is to individuate, there is an advantage for distinctive items. Valentine and Bruce (1986a, 1986b) found that even when faces were highly familiar, those rated as distinctive in appearance could be identified more rapidly than those rated as more typical in appearance. Jolicoeur, Gluck, and Kosslyn (1984) reported a related result with objects. They showed that, in a picture naming task, atypical category members could be assigned their individuating names faster than more typical category members.

In sum, when the recognition of objects begins to make similar demands to face recognition (discrimination within a set of items sharing the same overall shape) and as observers acquire expertise with non-face objects, so the representational processes involved appear more similar for faces and objects. At the level of theory, while image-based theories of face recognition are quite distinct from parts-based theories of basic-level object recognition, there is much more convergence between the image-based analysis of faces and the alignment and other view-based methods described for object recognition. Interestingly, where evidence for the view-based methods of object recognition is strongest, it has been derived from experiments with object shapes from structurally similar sets, such as the bent paper-clip shapes of Bulthoff and Edeleman (1992).

Stage Models of Object and Person Identification

So far, we have concentrated on the process of visual representation of objects and faces but said rather little about the non-visual information derived as a result of such analysis, which mediates our activities and interactions in the world. In this section, we will consider how visual analysis leads to the retrieval of non-visual information about the meaning or name of an object or face. Following on from the successful analysis of visual word recognition into different stages (e.g. Morton, 1969, 1979), a number of people during the 1970s and 1980s developed similar "box-and-arrow" analyses of the key stages of object and person identification (e.g. Hay & Young, 1982; Ratcliff & Newcombe, 1982; Seymour, 1979). As noted by Bruce and Young (1986), there was an overall similarity in the stages that were suggested to mediate between visual perception and naming of objects and people. Several authors suggested that object naming (e.g. Humphreys, Riddoch, & Quinlan, 1988; Ratcliff & Newcombe, 1982; Warrington, 1982) and person identification (e.g. Hay & Young, 1982) involved three main stages: perceptual classification (the process we have already discussed of deriving and matching a visual representation), semantic categorization, and naming. Neither objects nor faces appeared to access their names directly, in contrast to the naming of printed words, where direct links from print to pronunciation seem to exist (Schwarz, Marin, & Saffran, 1979).

Evidence for this sequence of derivation of structural descriptions, semantic descriptions, and, finally, names has been obtained from neuropsychology and from experiments with normal adults. Neuropsychologically, it is observed that deficits in the identification of objects and/or faces are consistent with the access of names via a prior stage of semantic classification. Thus patients are observed who have particular difficulties in naming objects (e.g. Kay & Ellis, 1987) or in accessing names of people (e.g. Semenza & Zettin, 1988), along with preserved ability to describe object uses or to provide information about the personal identity of the stimulus in other ways; however, the converse deficit has never been demonstrated convincingly (i.e. there is not a class of patient who can name objects or faces correctly but who cannot use or describe them in other ways; see Riddoch & Humphreys, 1987a, for a review). Thus there are patients who cannot name a button when they see one but can say that it is used to fasten a coat or shirt, but there are not patients who can label an object "button" but then do not know what to do with one. Similarly, some patients cannot name John Wayne but do know that he used to star in cowboy films, but there are no convincing examples of patients who produce names correctly but do not know why the people are familiar. This contrasts strikingly with studies of reading, where patients can name exception words (which require visual recognition in order for the correct phonology to be retrieved) but still know little about their meaning (Schwarz et al., 1979).

Experiments with normal adults also support the idea that both objects' and peoples' names are accessed via the semantic system rather than directly from the visual patterns of objects or faces. People are generally faster to make decisions to objects about their uses than to access names, though there is difficulty in drawing conclusions from this direct comparison as the task demands are not equivalent. However, Potter and Faulconer (1975) showed that subjects were faster to name a word than to name a picture, but faster to categorize a picture than to categorize a word, supporting the idea that pictures have more direct access to meaning than do words, but less direct access to their names. With faces, people are also faster to categorize than to name. Moreover, even when task demands are equated, so that decisions involving names and those involving other categorical judgements involve the same number of response alternatives, and the faces presented are drawn from controlled sets (e.g. half named John, half named James; half American, half British; etc.), people are faster to make decisions based upon occupation, nationality, or even whether the person is dead or alive than they are to make a decision based upon the name of the person (Johnston & Bruce, 1990; Young et al., 1986). In this last case, fast classification responses cannot be based simply on the detection of diagnostic perceptual characteristics, as people with the same occupation are generally no more physically similar than people from different occupations. Also, with objects, classification responses to pictures from categories with members with quite different perceptual structures are faster than to words corresponding to the category members (Riddoch & Humphreys, 1987a), confirming that objects gain rapid access to semantic information. Furthermore, this rapidly accessed semantic information is revealed when subjects make naming or misidentification errors, because such errors tend to be drawn from the same semantic category as the target. For example, Vitkovitch and Humphreys (1991) had subjects name objects to a deadline time that was faster than usual. Under this circumstance, subjects make a preponderance of semantic errors to objects.

Studies such as these support the idea that for both faces and objects there is direct access to semantic attributes and indirect access to phonologial attributes, compared with the processing of printed words, where access to phonology can be direct (without semantic mediation), following recognition of the visual form of the word. However, this cannot be quite the whole story, because for faces there appears to be a particular difficulty with the retrieval of their proper names, which is not readily explicable in terms of access of output phonology. Thus even when phonological output is not required, decisions involving peoples' names are harder than decisions involving other information about personal identity, and when phonological output is required, the phonology of proper names can be blocked, while that of other information about personal identity may be retrievable (Semenza & Zettin, 1988). Thus access to proper names seems to involve an extra difficulty over and above that of access to any kind of spoken label. We do not have space in this review to go into these additional complexities about proper names but refer the reader to a number of recent articles in a special issue of the journal *Memory* (Cohen & Burke, 1993), where these problems are considered.

Similarities in the major stages involved in object and face recognition have also been supported by studies of priming and interference effects. In the next sections we consider what has been learned about face and object recognition using different kinds of priming technique.

Repetition Priming

We have already mentioned the effect of priming on object identification in considering evidence for Biederman's (1987) theory of the representation of visual objects. Repetition priming of object identification was first demonstrated by Warren and Morton (1982) in a task that examined the threshold exposure duration needed to identify pictured objects as a function of prior identification history. Objects that had previously been identified pictorially were subsequently identified at a lower exposure duration than objects that had not previously been seen. Priming was greater if the earlier exposure was to the same pictured exemplar of the category, but was still significant if the prior exposure was to a different exemplar (e.g. a picture of a different clown). However, prior exposure to the category label (i.e. the word CLOWN) produced no facilitation on the identification of pictured objects.

Warren and Morton's demonstration of priming of basic-level object identification stimulated a similar experiment with identification of famous faces. Bruce and Valentine (1985) investigated the threshold exposure duration needed to identify the faces of famous people who had earlier been identified in the same picture, in a different picture, or as a printed name. Compared to an unprimed control condition, all three conditions of earlier exposure produced facilitation, though the most facilitation was given in the same-picture condition and the least in the name condition. Thus there was an apparent contrast with Warren and Morton's results, as some facilitation of identification was found when names were presented. However, Bruce and Valentine (1985) argued that the facilitation from reading the name earlier could have arisen at the stage of name retrieval. In contrast to naming pictures such as "dog" or "clown", naming faces such as "Bjorn Borg" or "Sean Connery" is highly error-prone, and the recent pronunciation of the name could have facilitated the name retrieval stage over and above facilitation of the visual recognition stage. Indeed, more recent studies have produced evidence demonstrating that, in object naming tasks also, priming can affect the process of mapping from a semantic description of the stimulus to its name (Vitkovitch & Humphreys, 1991; Wheeldon & Monsell, 1992). In a further experiment, Bruce and Valentine (1985) used a face familiarity decision task in the second phase of the experiment, where subjects had to decide whether each of a sequence of familiar and unfamiliar faces was that of a famous person. Decisions were made more quickly to the faces of people who had earlier been seen in the same or different pictures, compared to an unprimed control condition, but there was no priming from earlier exposure to the people's names, a result that was now consistent with that reported in basic-level object categorization. Like Warren and Morton, priming was greatest from identical pictures and less from different pictures of the same "category" (in this case the category was an individual person's identity).

Johnston and Bruce (1994) have shown that the kind of priming obtained is dependent upon the level in the system that mediates the required response.

When a task involving pictures of objects requires that they are *individuated* rather than categorized at the basic level, then other exemplars of the same general category do not give repetition priming. So, when the subjects' task was to judge whether cartoon characters were famous (e.g. Mickey Mouse) or not (a picture of any old mouse), priming of this decision arose when previous experience was with Mickey Mouse, but not when it was a picture of another mouse. This contrasts with Warren and Morton's finding that priming of the basic-level response "mouse" occurred from any pictured exemplar of that category. Thus, when the demands of producing proper names (Bruce & Valentine, 1985, Experiment 1) as opposed to category labels are put to one side, the basic repetition priming effect for objects and faces appears to be the same.

Warren and Morton argued that repetition priming reflected reactivation at the level of the perceptual descriptions subserving object identification. Following on from this, a number of researchers have used priming in order to explore the perceptual primitives that mediate recognition. Biederman's research with objects suggests that provided that the same set of geons is present in first and second occurrence, priming will be the same if image features differ, as if they are identical. However, here there seems to be some contrast with the results obtained with faces. Bruce et al. (1994) examined how repetition priming was affected if there was a change in "format" from full image to line-drawn "cartoon" (see earlier) or vice versa. The linedrawings were obtained using Pearson and Robinson's (1985) algorithm to sketch the images, and thus preserved information about viewpoint, expression, and so forth from the original. Despite this, priming was severely reduced when there was a switch in format from cartoon to photographic image, or vice versa, between presentation and test. This format effect was as great after a one-week interval between prime and test phase as after 10 minutes, suggesting that it did not reflect a temporary memory for item characteristics. To the extent that repetition priming does tap underlying structural descriptions, this suggests that for faces the representations mediating their identification preserve relatively low-level image features. This reinforces our earlier discussion where information about pigmentation, shading, and/or texture seems to be more important for the identification of faces than for basic-level object classification.

However, other research on repetition priming leads us to question the pure perceptual basis of these effects. Repetition priming of faces is extremely long-lasting—even for faces that should have been encountered on numerous occasions between prime and test phase (Flude, 1991). Such observations suggest that repetition priming is more "episodic" in character—that subjects retain the information that a particular face was encountered within a particular laboratory episode. However, face priming does not reflect mere repetition of encoding or response operations (Ellis, Young, Flude, & Hay, 1987), as priming seems to arise whenever a categorical decision at test requires identification of faces, irrespective of the nature of the decision made in the first phase. Thus priming is not found when subjects repeat judgements about the sex of faces between phases, but it is found if a sex judgement in the first phase is followed by a familiarity decision in the second (Ellis et al., 1987). Familiarity but not sex decisions with faces may depend on access to stored face recognition units (cf. Bruce & Young, 1986). Nevertheless, the data suggest that it is difficult to prevent stored recognition units for faces from being activated (even though the priming task—sex decisions—is not dependent on the activation of such units). Similar conditions, however, do not seem to extend to repetition priming of objects. For example, in unpublished research in both of our laboratories, we have found it difficult to produce repetition priming to tasks where objects must be categorized in some way (e.g. as living or non-living; or as living inside or outside the house), even though such categorizations should also involve the reactivation of object structural descriptions. Tasks that require objects to be named, in contrast, produce large and reliable priming effects. The reasons for these differences between objects and faces are currently the subject of investigation.

Semantic Priming and Interference Effects

Effects of priming by categorically or associatively related items ("semantic" priming) are also similar for faces and objects. Following early studies of priming in lexical decision (e.g. Meyer & Schvaneveldt, 1971), it was quickly demonstrated that similar effects hold in picture recognition. Thus Palmer (1975) showed that recognition of an object was facilitated if it was preceded immediately by an appropriate scene. An analogous effect was reported by Schweich, et al. (1991), who showed that famous faces were easier to identify if they were preceded by an associated visual context (e.g. a picture of the White House for an American President). Sperber, McCauley, Ragain, and Weil (1979) found that object naming was facilitated when a picture was preceded by a picture of an associated object, compared with a condition where the picture was unrelated, and Kroll and Potter (1984) found a similar effect in an object decision task, where subjects had to decide whether shapes were real or nonsense objects. No study of face recognition has used a task that is quite the same as either that of Sperber et al. or of Kroll and Potter, but reliable semantic priming of face recognition has been found in a face familiarity decision task (Bruce & Valentine, 1986), which is most closely analogous to a lexical decision task with words. Unlike the similar studies with objects, Bruce and Valentine included a neutral as well as an unrelated condition, in order to provide a baseline measure of performance. They reported that semantic priming of faces was facilitation dominant in that, relative to the neutral baseline, related primes gave an advantage to recognition but unrelated ones gave no disadvantage. Though this is not the only explanation for such a pattern of priming (see Neely, 1991), Bruce and Valentine's result is consistent with activation spreading between recognition units for semantically related faces (perhaps due to feedback from the semantic system to the person recognition system; cf. Burton, Bruce, & Johnston, 1990).

As we noted above, it seems that objects and faces can access semantic descriptions more directly than they access their names. Consistent with this, the semantic classification of names can be interfered with by distracting pictures (Glaser & Dungelhoff, 1984). Conversely, because written names can access spoken names more directly than can pictures, the naming of pictures shows interference from distracting irrelevant names (e.g. Glaser & Dungelhoff, 1984; Rosinski, Golinkoff, & Kukish, 1975). Interference is greater when the word describes an object from the same category as the to-be-named picture than when it describes an unrelated object. Similarly, pictures of faces interfere with the categorization of printed names, and irrelevant names interfere with the naming of pictures (Young et al., 1986), and this effect also seems to be sensitive to the categorical relationship between distractors and target stimuli.

Interference effects may be rather complex. Interference effects with objects may arise from perceptual rather than conceptual structures of categories (Riddoch & Humphreys, 1987a). Here faces provide an interesting test example, however, as there is no necessary perceptual overlap between members of the same conceptual category. Although popstars tend to be young and hairy compared with politicians, there is no perceptual characteristic distinguishing politicians from, say, actors. Young et al. (1986) were able to show that face-name interference arose even when the visual characteristics of the face categories were carefully controlled.

Dynamic Models

Simple "box and arrow" models provide an account of when various forms of priming might occur, according to whether primes pre-activate target representations (e.g. Warren & Morton, 1982). However, they do not provide a detailed framework for understanding the dynamic time-course of priming and interference effects in object and face processing. To provide such a framework, researchers have turned towards connectionist models, which can generate detailed accounts of the time course of activation and inhibition in a range of information-processing tasks.

Humphreys et al. (1988) outlined an account of object recognition and naming using a connectionist framework in which activation values are transmitted continuously between processing units representing different types of stored knowledge—structural descriptions, semantic representations, name representations. According to this "cascade model", object recognition and naming will vary as a function of various factors, including the visual similarity between the target and other members of the same category (e.g. the similarity of their edge-based perceptual structures). Objects from categories in which there are many structurally similar exemplars will activate a number of "neighbour" representations at the structural and semantic levels. This can facilitate their classification as members of their categories, due to increased activation of semantic units when neighbouring units "gang together". However, this same process may also impede naming because objects from categories with many structurally similar exemplars will have many competitors for individual name selection. Furthermore, as competition for name selection will take some time to be resolved for these stimuli, factors affecting the efficiency of this particular process (e.g. the frequency of the name) will play a lesser role in determining the naming time of these objects relative to objects from categories with fewer structurally similar exemplars. This interaction between structural similarity and name frequency was confirmed by Humphreys et al. (1988).

A simple form of the cascade model proposed by Humphreys et al. (1988) has more recently been implemented by Humphreys, Lemote, and Lloyd-Jones (in press) using an interactive activation with competition (IAC) architecture (cf. McClelland, 1981) similar to the architecture used by Burton et al. (1990) to model face recognition (see further on). In their simulation, Humphreys et al. had pools of units at structural, semantic, and name levels, which were competitive (inhibitory) within a level and excitatory between related units at different levels. The structural similarity of objects from different categories was captured by entering input activations that reflected the rated visual similarity between category exemplars. A separate set of semantic units for classification decisions was entered at the same "level" in the model as the name units, to enable comparisons between naming and categorization times for units separated by the same number of connections from the input (see Figure 1; having a separate set of semantic units for super-ordinate classification and for information specific to individual objects also prevented within-level inhibition of general semantic information by specific information, and vice versa). Humphreys et al. confirmed that classification times for objects were faster than naming times (cf. Potter & Faulconer, 1975)—a result that arises because naming but not classification requires that competition at the semantic level be resolved before a response can be successfully achieved. More interestingly, classification was more efficient for objects from structurally similar categories than those from structurally more dissimilar categories, whereas the reverse was true for naming. The model also predicts the differences between categories in the spread of errors produced under "deadline" naming conditions (Vitkovitch, Humphreys, & Lloyd-Jones, 1993), when performance is stopped before asymptotic activation values are reached, and the difficulties found in identifying objects from categories with structurally similar exemplars for patients with impairments to different "levels" within the object processing system (cf. Sartori, Job, & Coltheart, 1993).

Turning to face recognition, Burton et al. (1990) produced an implementation of aspects of person identification previously expressed in terms of a "box and arrow" model (Bruce & Young, 1986), again using an IAC architecture (see Figure 2). Pools of units were deemed to correspond to the visual "features" of faces, to face recognition units (FRUs, activated by appropriate combinations of

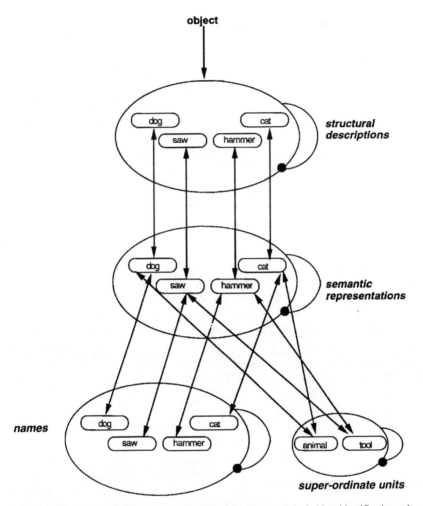

FIG. 1. Framework for the interactive-activation-competition model of object identification, taken from Humphreys et al. (submitted). ➤ indicates excitatory connections; ─● inhibitory connections. The model contains separate "output" units for naming and for semantic classification decisions (animal vs. tool). This was done by Humphreys et al. (in press) to enable response times for naming and semantic classification to be compared directly.

features), to person identity nodes (PINs), and to semantic information units. Related units in different pools were connected by excitatory links, and units within a pool by inhibitory links. This simple architecture was able to produce accounts of the different patterns of effect in repetition priming and semantic priming of faces and was extended to provide novel explanations of covert recognition (Burton et al., 1991), face naming (Burton & Bruce, 1992), and name recognition (Burton & Bruce, 1993).

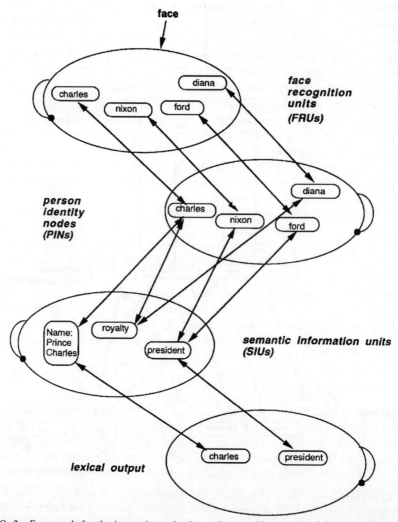

FIG. 2. Framework for the interactive-activation and competition model of face identification, adapted from Burton and Bruce (1993).

In the IAC model of face recognition it was assumed that a familiarity decision could be made to a face, or to any other kind of input such as a voice or written name, when activation at the person identity nodes exceeded some threshold level. The implication of this is that activation from different kinds of input—from face and voice, for example—is combined at the level of the PINs, which act as multi-modal nodes into the semantic system. The IAC model can provide an account of repetition priming by proposing that excitatory links between, say, the FRUs and the PINs become strengthened with use via a simple

Hebb modification of their weights. Thus if a person had been recognized via their face, the link between the FRU and PIN will be strengthened, but this will have no effect on the strength of the link between name input and the PINs, so repetition priming should be within a domain (e.g. between faces) but not across domains (between words and faces). The account of semantic/associative priming is rather different. Although all units within a pool inhibit one another, because the PIN (for Prince Charles, for example) activates semantic units (e.g. Royal Family) that are shared by other associated faces (such as the Queen, or Princess Diana, in this example), this means that activation at one PIN can lead to a rise in activation in the PIN of a semantically related person despite the within-pool inhibition. It follows that a person (e.g. Diana) will be recognized as familiar more easily following the recognition of a related person (e.g. Charles) as less activation will be needed from input units to achieve a threshold level at a PIN that already has a rise in activation from the previously recognized person. However, as the advantage of the preceding context occurs through activation level at the PIN, this advantage will be delivered even if there is a change in the domain between prime and target. Using this implementation, Burton et al. (1991) were able to demonstrate that normal levels of semantic priming could be observed in a "damaged" net where activation from FRUs to PINs was insufficient to produce threshold levels of "familiarity", and thereby offered an account of the covert recognition observed in some prosopagnosic patients. Extensions of this model to allow for the learning of new faces are reported by Burton (this volume).

Comparing the Models

The accounts so far developed to capture the time course of object and face processing (Burton et al., 1990; Humphreys et al., in press) have some noticeable similarities in their architectures, though they have so far been implemented and applied to rather different kinds of experimental data. Some of the differences in the two models may be more apparent than real. For example, Figure 1 shows structural descriptions for objects mapping direct to semantic representations, in apparent contrast to the person model of Figure 2, where the structural description system (FRUs) map to person identity nodes before reaching semantic information units. However, notice that in the object recognition model of Figure 1, there appear to be some similarities in the *role* played by the semantic representation stage and the stage of the PINs of Figure 2. In each case, this stage leads to the access of superordinate information at a separate level in the model.

Although considerable further development of each model will be required to make a more careful analysis of their differences, there would seem to be little reason at present to draw a qualitative distinction between the overall architectures of the face and object identification systems. Unresolved issues remain, however, concerning the overlap between the two processing systems. Do similar or different processes provide the input to the recognition systems for faces and objects? At the different levels of stored representation (structural, semantic, name), are the networks for faces and objects independent?

One approach towards answering this last question is to examine performance when objects and faces require the same responses. This can be done by contrasting the processing of so-called common nouns (e.g. major, nightingale) with those of proper nouns (e.g. John Major, Florence Nightingale). Typically, the recall of proper nouns is much worse than that of common nouns, even when the same items are involved (McWeeny, Young, Hay, & Ellis, 1987), and people seem to enter "tip of the tongue" states more frequently when trying to retrieve proper nouns than when retrieving other nouns (Burke, Mackay, Worthley, & Wade, 1991). This suggests some differences in the retrieval of people's names relative to other lexical items, a result supported by neuropsychological research demonstrating double dissociations between patients with selective deficits and selective sparing for the retrieval of proper nouns (e.g. see papers reported in Cohen & Burke, 1993). However, these differences probably rest either in contrasting forms of semantic representations for the different nouns or in differences in their representation in the name lexicon (cf. Burton & Bruce, 1993; Cohen, 1990), rather than differences in the visual processing of objects and faces or in their stored structural descriptions.

A rather different way to address such issues is to examine the effects of neurological damage on recognition and naming performance. In the next section we briefly review evidence on the relations between neurological impairments of face and object processing.

Neurological Impairments of Face and Object Processing

Selective Impairments of Face or Object Recognition

Neurological impairments of face and object identification have been documented over the past 100 years, from the first reports of selective object processing deficits (agnosia) presented by Lissauer (1890) and selective face recognition impairments (prosopagnosia) presented by Bodamer (1947). The relations between acquired disorders of face and object processing have been, and remain, the matter of some controversy, however. For example, reports of patients with deficits in object recognition but without concomitant problems in face recognition have been noted (e.g. McCarthy & Warrington, 1986), and, likewise, patients have been reported with problems in face identification but without problems in object recognition (e.g. De Renzi, 1986). In some cases, the nature of the dissociations between face and object recognition can be quite fine-grained. For example, Bruyer et al. (1983) and McNeil and Warrington (1993) described cases of farmers who could not recognize faces but who coald recognize, in one case, their own cows and dogs and, in another, their own sheep. In contrast, Assal, Favre, and Anderes (1984) described a farmer who was initially impaired at recognizing both human faces and animals, but who recovered to recognize faces whilst still being unable to recognize his cows. Taking another category of object with considerable visual similarity between category members, Serget and Signoret (1992) reported the case of one prosopagnosic patient who showed a better-than-average ability to identify cars. Such results suggest some differentiation in the recognition of faces and objects.

One problem in making comparative studies of face and object recognition deficits is in equating the tasks for the difficulty of the visual discriminations required. For example, one of the most frequently cited cases of "pure" prosopagnosia (i.e. face recognition impairments without difficulties in object recognition) was reported by De Renzi (1986). De Renzi's patient was able to retrieve his own personal objects (e.g. his wallet) when placed amongst other exemplars from the same category, despite being markedly impaired at face recognition. From this De Renzi proposed that faces engage different visual processes to those engaged by objects, even those belonging to categories with relatively homogeneous perceptual structures. However, Sergent and Signoret (1992) showed that similarly good performance can be found when prosopagnosics are given forced-choice face-processing tasks. For example, they reported 2 cases who were unable to identify photographs of either their own face or the faces of relatives when given photographs one at a time, in isolation; yet both patients pointed unhesitatingly to the familiar faces when they were presented amongst unfamiliar faces. Both patients also showed good discrimination of their own personal belongings, under similar task constraints (cf. De Renzi, 1986). However, in other cases, the contrasts between the patients' object and face recognition skills cannot easily be attributed to different task constraints. McNeil and Warrington's (1993) patient showed good recognition memory and paired-associate face-name learning for sheep, along with poor performance on the same tasks for faces, whereas normal control subjects (even those with similar experience of sheep to the patient) performed better with human than with sheep faces. Rumiati, Humphreys, Riddoch, and Bateman (this issue) report a converse case, in which a patient with impaired visual recognition of simple objects (for which control subjects are at ceiling) performed at a normal level in a relatively difficult test of face identification (for which control subjects are some way below ceiling).

However, it remains difficult to draw conclusions about the relations between face and object processing from studies that merely demonstrate dissociations between recognition of the different types of stimulus. We need to know the nature of the deficits in the different patients, and the functional locus of any impairments within the visual processing system, as disorders of face and object recognition might arise from any of a number of different lesions, from those affecting perceptual encoding to those affecting particular memory systems (e.g. see Humphreys & Riddoch, 1993; Warrington, 1982, for reviews). Farah (1990,

1991), in a historical review of reported cases of prosopagnosia and agnosia, noted that different patterns of association and dissociation had been documented between disorders of face recognition, object recognition, and recognition of a third type of visual stimulus: printed words. She noted that cases of pure prosopagnosia and pure alexia (selective deficits in the recognition of visual words) had been documented, but that cases of pure agnosia had not (i.e. patients with agnosia but without prosopagnosia typically have poor visual word recognition). From this, she concluded that there is a continuum of visual processes that mediate the recognition of visual stimuli, with some stimuli dependent on the parallel representation of multiple parts (e.g. visual word recognition), and others dependent on the representation of non-decomposed perceptual wholes (e.g. face recognition). Object recognition can be determined by both parts-based and more holistic representations, depending perhaps on the objects involved. Visual recognition disorders are linked to difficulties in encoding perceptual wholes, and "pure" alexia to difficulties in encoding in parallel multiple parts of visual stimuli. "Pure" agnosia should not occur.

Perceptual and Memory Impairments

In contrast to Farah's proposals, there are several cases suggesting that prosopagnosia is not always due to poor processing of perceptual wholes. Riddoch and Humphreys (1987b) reported the case of a patient, HJA, with severe prosopagnosia and agnosia. HJA's reading was considerably better than his face recognition, in the sense that he was able to read many words under brief exposure conditions, although he was unable to identify any faces (see Humphreys, 1994; Humphreys, Donnelly, & Riddoch, 1993). Yet, in object decision tasks requiring him to discriminate real from novel object shapes, HJA performed better with silhouettes (lacking internal part information) than with line drawings (which specify the local parts of the object) (Riddoch & Humphreys, 1987b). Riddoch and Humphreys argued that HJA's deficit was linked to a problem in integrating local detail with global shape information; rather than integration taking place, local detail was often used to segment an object into separate representations. Irrespective of the validity of this proposal, HJA's good performance with silhouettes makes it difficult to associate his prosopagnosia with a simple deficit in processing perceptual wholes, because silhouettes ought to stress the processing of global perceptual structures more than line drawings.

Sergent and her colleagues (Sergent & Poncet, 1990; Sergent & Signoret, 1992) had prosopagnosic patients carry out visual similarity ratings of pairs of line drawings of faces that, when they differed, could differ on the basis of 1, 2, or 3 "features". The resulting data were fitted to different multidimensional scaling solutions to capture the underlying similarity metric used by the patients. The data for normal subjects are best fit by a 3-dimensional Euclidian model, in which the features of the faces are not treated independently; such a result is consistent with the use of configural relations between facial features in face judgement tasks. Interestingly, the same result occurred for at least some prosopagnosic patients, suggesting that, in these cases, configural information about faces could be computed.

The patients reported by Sergent and colleagues as being able to process facial configurations also showed some effects of covert face recognition—for instance, being better able to learn correct face-name pairings than incorrect face-name pairings. This indicates that these patients were able to activate stored face memories, at least to some degree. Their deficit may then lie in the process of activating stored face memories to threshold level or in information being transmitted with full weighting from stored face memories to other parts of the processing system (see Burton et al., 1991, for a simulation of such effects; see also Farah, O'Reilly, & Vecera, 1993, for a related account). In such cases there may be a memorial rather than a perceptual impairment (cf. De Renzi, 1986). The distinction between perceptual and associative disorders of visual object recognition dates back to the original study conducted by Lissauer (1890).

Rumiati et al. (this volume) similarly propose a memorial account of the patient they report. As already noted, this patient was able to recognize faces whilst being impaired at recognizing many common objects by sight. He was also able to read aloud both regular and irregular English words with both a normal reading speed and accuracy, demonstrating intact visual recognition of words. Hence, in his case, there is a "pure" agnosia for objects. This runs counter to the idea that all visual recognition impairments are perceptual in nature and due to deficits in computing either parts-based or holistic visual descriptions. This patient was relatively poor at making object decisions and at matching bodies of objects with their heads, both of which might be performed correctly on the basis of access to stored structural knowledge about objects (cf. Riddoch & Humphreys, 1987c). Rumiati et al. suggested that there was a selective loss of stored visual memories for objects, but with stored visual memories for faces and words being spared. Their patient is reminiscent of the inhabitants of Macondo in "One Hundred Years of Solitude" (see the introduction), who were unable to remember a cow from its visual appearance and so had to rely on verbal labels. Note, though, that if this argument about object memories being selectively impaired is valid, it would follow that stored visual memories for faces and objects are functionally isolatable.

As we have already noted, work with aphasic rather than agnosic or prosopagnosic patients has also shown that name (and possibly also semantic) representations, as well as stored visual representations, may be functionally distinct for objects and faces. In particular, some aphasic patients may have selective impairment of name retrieval for proper names (Semenza & Zettin, 1988), whereas others can show a selective sparing of name retrieval for proper names in the context of a global aphasia for names of common objects (e.g.

Cipolotti, McNeil, & Warrington, 1993). This double dissociation between name retrieval deficits for proper and object names suggests that there may be separate name retrieval processes for objects and faces.

Not all cases of prosopagnosia or agnosia seem due to memorial impairments, however. HJA (see above) showed intact stored visual memories for both objects (Riddoch & Humphreys, 1987b) and faces (Young et al., 1994), along with impairments on a range of visual processing tasks not requiring access to stored visual memories (e.g. Humphreys et al., 1992). Sergent (Sergent & Poncet, 1990; Sergent & Signoret, 1992) has found that some prosopagnosics do not show a Euclidian similarity metric when they rate similarity between pairs of faces; rather, they show an abnormal "city-block" metric, in which the individual features of faces seem to be treated independently. In such cases there appears to be a deficit in encoding configural properties of faces.

Can such a "perceptual" impairment be specific for faces? Sergent and Signoret (1992) had patients (and control subjects) carry out a rating task equivalent to that performed with faces, but using cars differing in 1, 2, or 3 subtle features (all models from the Ferrari range). Normal subjects again performed this task using a 3D Euclidian metric. One prosopagnosic patient, RM, appeared to use a city-block metric when judging faces but seemed to use a Euclidian metric when judging cars. RM had a special interest in cars and showed remarkably good recognition of different makes of car; however, this "preserved" similarity metric for cars cannot simply be attributed to his expertise, as he should also have been "expert" for face recognition pre-morbidly. Instead, the results suggest that the perception of facial configurations can be selectively impaired without there being necessarily damage to putatively equivalent processes for objects. Of course this proposal rests on the assumption that the Euclidian similarity space for judging cars is directly equivalent to that for judging faces, and there is no guarantee that this is the case. Judgements about cars may rest on the computation of a few critical local features, whereas judgements about faces may rely on the relations between features that must be computed more globally or that depend on surface- rather than edge-based properties. The more critical question is whether, in such a case, the similarity metric for other kinds of objects would be impaired along with that for faces. RM, like many prosopagnosics, was poor at visually recognizing objects other than faces belonging to relatively homogeneous perceptual categories, such as feline animals and flowers, so it is possible that a common functional impairment caused the deficit across these stimuli. Our conclusion is that, on the question of whether perceptual deficits can in some cases be selective for faces, the jury remains out. What seems more certain is that the perceptual deficits leading to impaired object and face recognition can differ in some cases, as can the memorial deficits that precipitate some disorders. We propose that memorial systems for objects and faces can be functionally separate, even if the perceptual processing of these stimuli may overlap to some degree.

CONCLUDING REMARKS

We have reviewed evidence from (1) the literature on normal object and face recognition, (2) attempts to develop computational models of visual recognition, and (3) neuropsychological impairments of visual recognition. The research we have documented clearly points to there being some differences in the processing of faces and of many objects. In brief, the identification of objects at the basic level seems to be parts-based, whereas face recognition seems more holistic, involving at least the configural processing of facial features. Object recognition also seems more strongly determined by edge-based descriptions than does face recognition, where surface-based information can easily be shown to be important. Face recognition and object recognition impairments can also be functionally separable in brain-damaged patients. Against this, the recognition by experts of individual objects belonging to categories with relatively homogeneous perceptual structures—a task that goes beyond identification at the basic level—can also be shown to depend on the computation of configural relationships between image features. Similarly, surface properties can be important for the recognition of objects under similar circumstances. This suggests that, when the task constraints are more adequately matched and both require individuation beyond basic-level representations, face and object coding can be similar. Also, for both object and face recognition, computational models with relatively simple architectures and assumptions of interactive-competitive visual processing can account for a good deal of the data dealing with access to stored structural, semantic, and name representations. Nevertheless, neuropsychological evidence does suggest some functional independence in the representation of stored memories for faces and objects, and also some differences in the perceptual encoding procedures the different stimuli may evoke. This evidence also points to differences in the nature of our representations of people's names and names for other objects. Such evidence suggests that both the perceptual encoding processes and the stored representations for objects and faces will often differ. Whether there is a functional separation between the processes *typically* used for face encoding and those *sometimes* used for object encoding remains unresolved.

REFERENCES

Assal, G., Favre, C., & Anderes, J. (1984). Nonrecognition of familiar animals by a farmer: Zooagnosia or prosopagnosia for animals. *Revue Neurologique, 140,* 580–584.

Baron, R.J. (1981). Mechanisms of human facial recognition. *International Journal of Man-Machine Studies, 15,* 137–178.

Bartlett, J.C., & Searcy, J. (1993). Inversion and configuration of faces. *Cognitive Psychology, 25,* 281–316.

Bartram, D.J. (1974). The role of visual and semantic codes in object naming. *Cognitive Psychology, 6,* 325–356.

Biederman, I. (1987). Recognition-by-components: A theory of human image understanding. *Psychological Review, 94,* 115–147.

Biederman, I., & Cooper, E.E. (1991). Priming contour-deleted images: Evidence for intermediate representations in visual object recognition. *Cognitive Psychology, 23,* 393–419.

Biederman, I., & Cooper, E.E. (1992). Size invariance in visual object priming. *Journal of Experimental Psychology: Human Perception and Performance, 18,* 121–133.

Biederman, I., & Gerhardstein, P.C. (1993). Recognizing depth-rotated objects: Evidence and conditions for three-dimensional viewpoint invariance. *Journal of Experimental Psychology: Human Perception and Performance, 19,* 1162–1182.

Biederman, I, & Ju, G. (1988). Surface versus edge-based determinants of visual recognition. *Cognitive Psychology, 20,* 38–64.

Bodamer, J. (1947). *Die Prosop-Agnosia. Archiv für Psychiatrie und Nervenkrankheiten, 179,* 6–53.

Bulthoff, H.H., & Edelman, S. (1992). Psychophysical support for a two-dimensional view interpolation theory of object recognition. *Proceedings of the National Academy of Sciences, 89,* 60–64.

Brennan, S.E. (1985). The caricature generator. *Leonardo, 18,* 170–178.

Brennen, T., & Bruce, V. (1991). Context effects in the processing of familiar faces. *Psychological Research, 53,* 296–304.

Bruce, V., Burton, A.M., Carson, D., Hanna, E., & Mason, O. (1994). Repetition priming of face recognition. In C. Umilta & M. Moscovitch (Eds.), *Attention & performance, XV.* Cambridge, MA : MIT Press.

Bruce, V., Burton, A.M., Hanna, E., Healey, P., Mason, O., Coombes, A., Fright, R., & Linney, A. (1993). Sex discrimination: How do we tell the difference between male and female faces? *Perception, 22,* 131–152.

Bruce, V., Hanna, E., Dench, N., Healy, P., & Burton, A.M. (1992). The importance of "mass" in line drawings of faces. *Applied Cognitive Psychology, 6,* 619–628.

Bruce, V., & Langton, S. (in press). The use of pigmentation and shading information in recognising the sex and identities of faces. *Perception.*

Bruce, V., & Valentine, T. (1985). Identity priming in the recognition of familiar faces. *British Journal of Psychology, 76,* 373–383.

Bruce, V., & Valentine, T. (1986). Semantic priming of familiar faces. *Quarterly Journal of Experimental Psychology, 38A,* 125–150.

Bruce, V., & Young, A.W. (1986). Understanding face recognition. *British Journal of Psychology, 77,* 305–328.

Bruyer, R., Laterre, C., Seron, X., Feyereisen, P., Strypstein, E., Pierrard, E., & Rectem, D. (1983). A case of prosopagnosia with some preserved covert remembrance of familiar faces. *Brain and Cognition, 2,* 257–284.

Burke, D.M., Mackay, D.G., Worthley, J.S., & Wade, E. (1991). On the tip-of-the-tongue: What causes word finding failures in young and older adults. *Journal of Memory and Language, 30,* 542–579.

Burton, A.M., & Bruce, V. (1992). I recognise your face but I can't remember your name: A simple explanation? *British Journal of Psychology, 83,* 45–60.

Burton, A.M., & Bruce, V. (1993). Naming faces and naming names: Exploring an interactive activation model of person recognition. *Memory, 1,* 457–480.

Burton, A.M., Bruce, V., & Dench, N. (1993). What's the difference between men and women? Evidence from facial measurement. *Perception, 22,* 153–176.

Burton, A.M., Bruce, V., & Johnston, R. (1990). Understanding face recognition with an interactive activation model. *British Journal of Psychology, 81,* 361–380.

Burton, A.M., Young, A.W., Bruce, V., Johnston, R., & Ellis, A.W. (1991). Understanding covert recognition. *Cognition, 39,* 129–166.

Carey, S. (1981). The development of face perception. In G. Davies, H. Ellis, & J. Shephard (Eds.), *Perceiving and remembering faces.* New York: Academic Press.

Cave, C.B., & Kosslyn, S.M. (1993). The role of parts and spatial relations in object identification. *Perception, 22,* 229–248.

Cipolotti, L., McNeil, J.E., & Warrington, E.K. (1993). Spared written naming of proper nouns: A case report. *Memory, 1,* 289–312.

Cohen, G. (1990). Why is it difficult to name faces? *British Journal of Psychology, 81,* 287–297.

Cohen, G., & Burke, D.M. (1993). *Memory for proper names.* Hove: Lawrence Erlbaum Associates Ltd.

Cooper, E.E., Biederman, I., & Hummel, J.E. (1992). Metric invariance in object recognition: A revew and further evidence. *Canadian Journal of Psychology, 46,* 191–214.

Cooper, L.A., Schacter, D.L., Ballesteros, S., & Moore, C. (1992). Priming and recognition of transformed three-dimensional objects: effects of size and reflection. *Journal of Experimental Psychology: Learning, Memory and Cognition, 18,* 43–57.

Craw, I., Aitchison, A., & Cameron, P. (1992). Principal component analysis of face images. *Technical Report, University of Aberdeen.*

Craw, I., Tock, D., & Bennett, A. (1992). Finding face features. Lecture notes in computer science – ECCV92, *S88,* 92–96.

Davidoff, J.B., & Ostergaard, A.L. (1988). The role of colour in categorical judgements. *Quarterly Journal of Experimental Psychology, 40A,* 533–544.

Davies, G.M., Ellis, H.D., & Shepherd, J.W. (1978). Face recognition accuracy as a function of mode of representation. *Journal of Applied Psychology, 63,* 180–187.

De Renzi, E. (1986). Current issues in prosopagnosia. In H. Ellis, M.A. Jeeves, F. Newcombe, & A.W. Young (Eds.), *Aspects of face processing,* Dordrecht: Martinus Nijhoff.

Diamond, R., & Carey, S. (1986). Why faces are and are not special: An effect of expertise. *Journal of Experimental Psychology: General, 115,* 107–117.

Edelman, S., & Bulthoff, H.H. (1992). Orientation dependence in the recognition of familiar and novel views of three-dimensional objects. *Vision Research, 32,* 2385–2400.

Eley, M.G. (1982). Identifying rotated letter-like symbols. *Memory and Cognition, 10,* 25–32.

Ellis, A.W., Young, A.W., Flude, B.M., & Hay, D.C. (1987). Repetition priming of face recognition. *Quarterly Journal of Experimental Psychology, 39A,* 193–210.

Ellis, R., Allport, D.A., Humphreys, G.W., & Collis, J. (1989). Varieties of object constancy. *Quarterly Journal of Experimental Psychology, 41A,* 775–796.

Farah, M.J. (1990). *Visual agnosia: Disorders of object recognition and what they tell us about normal vision.* Cambridge, MA:MIT Press.

Farah, M.J. (1991). Patterns of co-occurrence among the associative agnosias: Implications for visual object recognition. *Cognitive Neuropsychology, 8,* 1–19.

Farah, M.J., O'Reilly, R., & Vecera, S.P. (1993). Dissociated overt and covert recognition as an emergent property of lesioned attractor networks. *Psychological Review,* *100,* 571–588.

Flude, B. (1991). *Long-term repetition priming of faces.* Paper presented at the International Conference on Memory, University of Lancaster, July 1991.

Glaser, W.R., & Dungelhoff, F.J. (1984). The time course of picture-word interference. *Journal of Experimental Psychology: Human Perception and Performance, 10,* 640–654.

Hay, D.C., & Young, A.W. (1982). The human face. In A.W. Ellis (Ed.), *Normality and pathology in cognitive functions.* London: Academic Press.

Hayes, A. (1988). Identification of two-tone images: Some implications for high- and low-spatial frequency processes in human vision. *Perception, 17,* 429–436.

Hayes, T., Morrone, M.C., & Burr, D.C. (1986). Recognition of positive and negative bandpass-filtered images. *Perception, 15,* 595–602.

Hoffman, D.D., & Richards, W.A. (1984). Parts of recognition. *Cognition, 18,* 65–96.

Hummel, J.E., & Biederman, I. (1992). Dynamic binding in a neural network for shape recognition. *Psychological Review, 99,* 480–517.

Humphrey, G.K., & Jolicoeur, P. (1993). An examination of the effects of axis foreshortening, monocular depth cues and visual field on object identification. *Quarterly Journal of Experimental Psychology, 46A,* 137–160.

Humphrey, G.K., & Khan, S.C. (1992). Recognizing novel views of three-dimensional objects. *Canadian Journal of Psychology, 46,* 170–190.

Humphreys, G.W. (1994). Cognitive neuropsychology of visual object recognition: A hierarchical analysis of visual agnosia. In B. Weekes (Ed.), *Proceedings of the 5th Australian Society for the Study of Brain Impairments.* Canberra: Australian National University Press.

Humphreys, G.W., Donnelly, N., & Riddoch, M.J. (1993). Expression is computed separately from facial identity, and it is computed separately for moving and static faces: Neuropsychological evidence. *Neuropsychologia, 31,* 173–181.

Humphreys, G.W., Lemote, C., & Lloyd-Jones, T.J. (in press). An interactive activation-competition model of object naming: Effects of object category, priming and simulated lesions on object identification. *Memory.*

Humphreys, G.W., & Quinlan, P.T. (1988). Priming effects between two-dimensional shapes. *Journal of Experimental Psychology: Human Perception and Performance, 14,* 203–220.

Humphreys, G.W., & Riddoch, M.J. (1984). Routes to object constancy: Implications from neuropsychological impairments of object constancy. *Quarterly Journal of Experimental Psychology, 36A,* 385–415.

Humphreys, G.W., & Riddoch, M.J. (1993). Object agnosias. In C. Kennard (Ed.), *Balliere's clinical neurology: Visual perceptual deficits.* London: Balliere Tindall.

Humphreys, G.W., Riddoch, M.J., & Quinlan, P.T. (1988). Cascade processes in picture identification. *Cognitive Neuropsychology, 5,* 67–103.

Humphreys, G.W., Riddoch, M.J., Quinlan, P.T., Price, C.J., Donnelly, N. (1992). Parallel pattern processing in visual agnosia. *Canadian Journal of Psychology, 46,* 377–416.

Johnston, R., & Bruce, V. (1990). Lost properties? Retrieval differences between name codes and semantic codes for familiar people. *Psychological Research, 52,* 62–67.

Johnston, R., & Bruce, V. (1994). Who primed Roger Rabbit? An investigation of priming between individual items. *British Journal of Psychology, 85,* 115–130.

Jolicoeur, P. (1985). The time to name disoriented natural objects. *Memory and Cognition, 13,* 289–303.

Jolicoeur, P. (1987). A size-congruency effect in memory for visual shape. *Memory and Cognition, 15,* 531–543.

Jolicoeur, P. (1992). Identification of disoriented objects: A dual-system theory. In G.W. Humphreys (Ed.), *Understanding vision.* Oxford: Blackwells.

Jolicoeur, P., & Besner, D. (1987). Additivity and interaction between size ratio and response category in the comparison of size-discrepant shapes. *Journal of Experimental Psychology: Human Perception and Performance, 13,* 478–487.

Jolicoeur, P., Gluck, M., & Kosslyn, S.M. (1984). Pictures and names: Making the connection. *Cognitive Psychology, 16,* 243–275.

Kay, J., & Ellis, A.W. (1987). A cognitive neuropsychological case study of anomia: Implications for psychological models of word retrieval. *Brain, 110,* 613–629.

Kroll, J.F., & Potter, M.C. (1984). Recognising words, pictures and concepts: A comparison of lexical, object and reality decision. *Journal of Verbal Learning and Verbal Behavior, 23,* 39–66.

Lawson, R., & Humphreys, G.W. (1994). View-specificity in object processing: Evidence from picture matching. *Journal of Experimental Psychology: Human Perception and Performance.*

Lawson, R., Humphreys, G.W., & Watson, D.G. (1994). Object recognition under sequential viewing conditions: Evidence for viewpoint-specific recognition procedures. *Perception, 23,* 595–614.

Lissauer, H. (1890). Ein Fall von Seelenblindheit nebst einem Beitrage zur Theorie derselben. *Archiv fur Psychiatrie und Nervenkrankheiten, 21,* 222–270.

Lowe, D.G. (1987). Three-dimensional object recognition from single two-dimensional images. *Artificial Intelligence, 31,* 355–395.

Márquez, G.G. (1967/1978). *One hundred years of solitude.* Translated from Spanish by Gregory Rabassa. 1978 Picador edition, London: Pan Books Ltd.

Marr, D., & Nishihara, H.K. (1978). Representation and recognition of the spatial organization of three-dimensional shapes. *Proceedings of the Royal Society of London, B200,* 269–294.

McCarthy, R.A., & Warrington, E.K. (1986). Visual associative agnosia: A clinico-anatomical study of a single case. *Journal of Neurology, Neurosurgery and Psychiatry, 49,* 1233–1240.

McClelland, J.L. (1981). Retrieving general and specific information from stored knowledge of specifics. *Proceedings of the Third Annual Meeting of the Cognitive Science Society,* 170–172.

McNeil, J. & Warrington, E.K. (1993). Prosopagnosia: A face-specific disorder. *Quarterly Journal of Experimental Psychology, 46A,* 1–10.

McWeeny, K.H., Young, A.W., Hay, D.C., & Ellis, A.W. (1987). Putting names to faces. *British Journal of Psychology, 78,* 143–149.

Meyer, D.E., & Schvaneveldt, R.W. (1971). Facilitation in recognizing pairs of words: Evidence of a dependence between retrieval operations. *Journal of Experimental Psychology, 90,* 227–234.

Morton, J. (1969). Interaction of information in word recognition. *Psychological Review, 76*, 165–178.

Morton, J. (1979). Facilitation in word recognition. Experiments causing change in the logogen model. In P.A. Kolers, M. Wrolstad, & H. Bouma (Eds.), *Processing of visible language, Vol. 1*. New York: Plenum Press.

Neely, J.H. (1991). Semantic priming effects in visual word recognition: A selective review of current findings and theories. In D. Besner & G.W. Humphreys (Eds.), *Basic processes in reading: Visual word recognition*. Hillsdale, N.J. : Lawrence Erlbaum Associates, Inc.

Ostergaard, A.L., & Davidoff, J.B. (1985). Some effects of color on naming and recognition of objects. *Journal of Experimental Psychology: Learning, Memory and Cognition, 11*, 579–587.

O'Toole, A., Deffenbacher, K.A., Valentin, D., & Abdi, H. (1994). Structural aspects of face recognition and the other race effect. *Memory and Cognition, 22*, 208–224.

Palmer, S. (1975). The effects of contextual scenes on the identification of objects. *Memory and Cognition, 3*, 519–526.

Palmer, S.E. (1980). What makes triangles point: Local and global effects in configurations of ambiguous triangles. *Cognitive Psychology, 12*, 285–305.

Palmer, S.E., Rosch, E., & Chase, P. (1981). Canonical perspective and the perception of objects. In J. Long & A.D. Baddeley (Eds.), *Attention and performance, IX*. Hillsdale, NJ : Lawrence Erlbaum Associates Inc.

Pearson, D.E., & Robinson, J.A. (1985). Visual communication at very low data rates. *Proceedings of the IEEE, 73*, 795–811.

Poggio, T., & Edelman, S. (1990). A network that learns to recognise three-dimensional objects. *Nature, 343*, 263–266.

Potter, M.C., & Faulconer, B.A. (1975). Time to understand pictures and words. *Nature, 253*, 437–438.

Price, C.J., & Humphreys, G.W. (1989). The effects of surface detail on object categorization and naming. *Quarterly Journal of Experimental Psychology, 41A*, 797–828.

Quinlan, P.T. (1991). Differing approaches to two-dimensional shape recognition. *Psychological Bulletin, 109*, 224–241.

Quinlan, P.T., & Humphreys, G.W. (1993). Perceptual frames of reference and two-dimensional shape recognition: Further examination of internal axes. *Perception, 22*, 1343–1364.

Ratcliff, G., & Newcombe, F. (1982). Object recognition: Some deductions from the clinical evidence. In A.W. Ellis (Ed.), *Normality and pathology in cognitive functions*. London: Academic Press.

Rhodes, G., Brake, S., & Atkinson, A. (1993). What is lost in inverted faces? *Cognition, 47*, 25–57.

Rhodes, G., Brennan, S., & Carey, S. (1987). Recognition and ratings of caricatures: Implications for mental representation of faces. *Cognitive Psychology, 19*, 473–497.

Rhodes, G., & McLean, I.G. (1990). Distinctiveness and expertise effects with homogeneous stimuli: Towards a model of configural coding. *Perception, 19*, 773–794.

Riddoch, M.J. & Humphreys, G.W. (1987a). Picture naming, In G.W. Humphreys & M.J. Riddoch (Eds.), *Visual object processing: A cognitive neuropsychological approach*. Hove: Lawrence Erlbaum Associates Ltd.

Riddoch, M.J., & Humphreys, G.W. (1987b). A case of integrative visual agnosia. *Brain, 110*, 1431–1462.

Riddoch, M.J., & Humphreys, G.W. (1987c). Visual object processing in optic aphasia: A case of semantic access agnosia. *Cognitive Neuropsychology, 4*, 131–185.

Roberts, T., & Bruce, V. (1988). Feature saliency in judging the sex and familiarity of faces. *Perception, 17*, 425–426.

Rosch, E., Mervis, C.B., Gray, W.D., Johnson, D.M., & Boyes-Braem, P. (1976). Basic objects in natural categories. *Cognitive Psychology, 8*, 382–439.

Rosinski, R.R., Golinkoff, R.M., & Kukish, K.S. (1975). Automatic semantic processing in a picture-word interference task. *Child Development, 46*, 247–253.

Sartori, G., Job, R., & Coltheart,M. (1993). The organization of object knowledge: Evidence from neuropsychology. In D.E. Meyer & S. Kornblum (Eds.), *Attention & performance, XIV*. Cambridge, MA:MIT Press.

Schwarz, M.F., Marin, O.S.M., & Saffran, E.M. (1979). Dissociations of language function in dementia: A case study. *Brain and Language, 7*, 277–306.

Schweich, M., Schreiber, A.C., Rousset, S., Bruyer, R., & Tiberghien, G. (1991). Effects of the meaning of visual context on semantic processing of famous faces. *European Bulletin of Cognitive Psychology, 11*, 55–71.

Semenza, C., & Zettin, M. (1988). Generating proper names: A case of selective inability. *Cognitive Neuropsychology, 5*, 711–721.

Sergent, J. (1984). An investigation into component and configural processes in face recognition. *British Journal of Psychology, 75*, 221–242.

Sergent, J., & Poncet, M. (1990). From covert to overt recognition of faces in a prosopagnosic patient. *Brain, 113*, 989–1004.

Sergent, J., & Signoret, J.-L. (1992). Varieties of functional deficits in prosopagnosia. *Cerebral Cortex, 2*, 375–388.

Seymour, P.H.K. (1979). *Human visual cognition*. London: Collier MacMillan.

Smith, E.E., & Medin, D.L. (1981). *Categories and concepts*. Cambridge, MA.: Harvard University Press.

Sperber, R.D., McCauley, C., Ragain, R.D., & Weil, C.M. (1979). Semantic priming effects on picture and word processing. *Memory and Cognition, 7*, 339–345.

Sternberg, S. (1969). The discovery of processing stages: Extensions of Donder's method. In W.G. Koster (Ed.), *Attention & performance, II*. Amsterdam: North Holland.

Stonham, J. (1986). Practical face recognition and verification with WISARD. In H. Ellis, M.A. Jeeves, F. Newcombe, & A.W. Young (Eds.), *Aspects of face processing*. Dordrecht: Martinus Nijhoff.

Tanaka, J., & Farah, M.J. (1993). Parts and wholes in face recognition. *Quarterly Journal of Experimental Psychology, 46A*, 225–246.

Tarr, M.J., & Pinker, S. (1989). Mental rotation and orientation dependence in shape recognition. *Cognitive Psychology, 21*, 233–283.

Thorpe, S.J., & Imbert, M. (1989). Biological constraints on connectionist models. In R. Pfeifer, Z. Schreter, & F. Fogelman-Soulie (Eds.), *Connectionism in perspective*, Elsevier Science: Amsterdam.

Turk, M., & Pentland, A. (1991). Eigenfaces for recognition. *Journal of Cognitive Neuroscience, 3*, 71–86.

Ullman, S. (1989). Aligning pictorial descriptions: An approach to object recognition. *Cognition, 32*, 193–254.

Valentine, T., & Bruce, V. (1986a). The effects of distinctiveness in recognising and classifying faces. *Perception, 15*, 525–536.

Valentine, T., & Bruce, V. (1986b). Recognising faces: The role of distinctiveness and familiarity. *Canadian Journal of Psychology, 40*, 300–305.

Vitkovitch, M., & Humphreys, G.W. (1991). Perseverative responding in speeded naming to pictures: It's in the links. *Journal of Experimental Psychology: Learning, Memory and Cognition, 17*, 664–680.

Vitkovitch, M., Humphreys, G.W., & Lloyd-Jones, T.J. (1993). On naming a giraffe a zebra: Picture naming errors across different categories. *Journal of Experimental Psychology: Learning, Memory and Cognition, 19*, 243–259.

Warren, C., & Morton, J. (1982). The effects of priming on picture recognition. *British Journal of Psychology, 73*, 117–129.

Warrington, E.K. (1982). Neuropsychological studies of object recognition. *Philosophical Transactions of the Royal Society, London, B298*, 15–33.

Wheeldon, L.R., & Monsell, S. (1992). The locus of repetition priming of spoken word production. *Quarterly Journal of Experimental Psychology, 44A*, 723–762.

Wurm, L., Legge, G.E., Isenberg, L.M., & Luebker, A. (1993). Color improves object identification in low and normal vision. *Journal of Experimental Psychology: Human Perception and Performance, 19*, 899–911.

Yin, R.K. (1969). Looking at upside-down faces. *Journal of Experimental Psychology, 81*, 141–145.

Young, A.W., Ellis, A.W., & Flude, B.M. (1988). Accessing stored information about familiar people. *Psychological Research, 50*, 111–115.

Young, A.W., Ellis, A.W., Flude, B.M., McWeeny, K., & Hay, D.C. (1986). Face-name interference. *Journal of Experimental Psychology: Human Perception and Performance, 12*, 466–475.

Young, A.W., Hellawell, D.J., & Hay, D.C. (1987). Configural information in face perception. *Perception, 16*, 747–759.

Young, A.W., Humphreys, G.W., Riddoch, M.J., Hellawell, D.J., & de Haan, E.H.F. (1994). Recognition impairments and face imagery. *Neuropsychologia, 32*, 693–705.

Revised Manuscript received 1 May 1994

VISUAL COGNITION, 1994, *1* (2/3), 181–225

Visual Object Agnosia without Prosopagnosia or Alexia: Evidence for Hierarchical Theories of Visual Recognition

Raffaella I. Rumiati, Glyn W. Humphreys,
M. Jane Riddoch, and Andrew Bateman

University of Birmingham, Edgbaston, Birmingham, U.K.

A single case study is presented of a patient, Mr. W, with a selective deficit in recognizing pictures and real objects, linked to impaired stored visual knowledge about objects. Despite this, Mr. W maintained a preserved ability both to read aloud printed words and to recognize famous faces, when compared with age-matched control subjects. In addition, his access to semantic information from words was superior to that from pictures. The data provide evidence that visual agnosia can occur without alexia or prosopagnosia, contrary to recent proposals (Farah 1990, 1991). This finding is consistent with a hierarchical model of visual object recognition in which agnosia can reflect impaired stored knowledge of objects without accompanying perceptual deficits. The selective recognition deficit for objects further indicates that stored knowledge concerning different classes of visual stimuli (common objects, faces, and words) is separately represented in the brain.

Requests for reprints should be sent to Glyn W. Humphreys, School of Psychology, University of Birmingham, Edgbaston, Birmingham, B15 2TT, U.K., e-mail G.W. HUMPHREYS @ UK.AC.BHAM.

This work was supported by a grant from the Italian Ministry of University and Scientific Research to the first author, and by grants from the Medical Research Council of Great Britain and from the Human Frontier Science Programme to the second and third authors. We thank Andy Ellis and Andy Young for helpful comments on an earlier version of the paper.

Apperceptive and Associative Agnosia

Visual agnosia is a clinical impairment in the recognition of visually presented objects, in the presence of normal visual sensation.despite the potential importance of cases of visual agnosia for understanding visual object recognition, up until the relatively recent past, the very existence of the syndrome was doubted (Bender & Feldman 1972). For instance, Bay (1953) argued that visual agnosia is not a visual recognition impairment *per se* and suggested instead that the selective deficit in visual recognition always occurs along with impaired elementary visual functions and general intellectual impairment. Arguments such as this in part reflected the rarity of the syndrome but also, we believe, the lack of tests able to tap the different stages of the object recognition process. Despite early scepticism, over the past two decades detailed case studies have convincingly demonstrated that visual agnosia is not necessarily contingent on intellectual decline and sensory loss (see Etcoff, Freeman, & Cave, 1992; Humphreys & Riddoch, 1993, for recent reviews). For example, patients have been shown to have impaired object recognition (in the sense that they are unable to demonstrate knowledge of object functions or inter-object associations), while showing good discrimination between real objects and non-objects constructed by inter-changing parts of real objects to form perceptually good, but unfamiliar figures (e.g. Riddoch & Humphreys, 1987a; Sheridan & Humphreys, 1993). In such cases, perceptual processing seems sufficient for patients to access stored visual knowledge about objects, even though visual recognition remains impaired. Such patients can also have good verbal knowledge about the objects they fail to recognize visually, indicating that their visual recognition problems are not due to general intellectual impairment (Riddoch & Humphreys, 1987a). Rather, the cases support a distinction between the stored representation of visual knowledge about objects and stored semantic knowledge about object functions and inter-object associations. Patients can have impaired recognition due to poor access to stored semantic knowledge, even though access to stored visual knowledge can be good.

Since Lissauer (1890). theoretical accounts of agnosia have generally been discussed in terms of the two-stage framework he offered for visual object recognition. These two stages he termed (1) "apperception"—the construction of a perceptual representation from vision; and (2) "association"—the use of the perceptual representation to access stored knowledge of the object's functions and associations. Thus, impairments in these two processes give rise to two basic classes of agnosia: apperceptive and associative agnosia, respectively. Other neuropsychological and computational accounts of the recognition process, extending Lissauer's view, have been proposed, which divide both the apperception and the association stages into further sub-stages (Marr, 1982; Humphreys & Riddoch, 1987a; Warrington, 1982, 1985). For example, apperceptive processes may span from the encoding of the primitive dimensions of shape to the segmentation of figure from ground; associative processes may include access to stored visual knowledge about objects, followed by access to stored associative and functional (semantic) knowledge (cf. Humphreys & Riddoch, 1993; see above). Following brain damage, each of the sub-stages of apperception and association may be selectively impaired, and it may be possible for patients previously classed as either apperceptive or associative agnosics to be damaged at only some particular sub-stage (Riddoch & Humphreys, 1987b). Note that in Lissauer's (1890) scheme, and in those that have followed in the course of further sub-dividing his framework, a distinction is drawn between perceptual and memorial forms of agnosia. In particular, these schemes hold that associative forms of agnosia are possible in which patients have impaired recognition but intact perception. Also within these schemes, the recognition of certain classes of visual stimuli can be spared or jointly impaired, depending on the degree to which their recognition relies on common perceptual and memorial processes. Thus, to the extent that object, word, and face recognition all rely on functionally and anatomically separate memorial systems (and see Sergent & Signoret, 1992, for evidence from PET studies), it becomes possible to account for isolated word and face recognition disorders (without associated object recognition problems) in terms of selective losses of stored representations for particular stimuli (and see De Renzi, 1986, and Warrington & Shallice, 1980, respectively, for cases of apparently pure face and visual word recognition impairments). In contrast, impairments that occur across these classes of stimuli may be due to impaired perceptual processes that are needed for deriving descriptions of all visual stimuli, including words, objects, and faces (e.g. see Humphreys & Riddoch, 1987b).

Perceptual Theories Revisited

Recently, Farah (1990, 1991) has argued that, rather than reflecting a memorial deficit affecting the stored representations needed for visual object recognition, associative agnosia is due to an impairment in the high-level perceptual representation of shape. On this account, no distinction is drawn between memorial and perceptual processes; rather, all disorders are held to be perceptual in nature, and the line between association and apperception reflects different degrees of visual perceptual impairment in different patients.

Linked to the above argument, Farah rejected the proposal that visual recognition procedures for faces, words, and common objects are neurally separated, as some, but not all, patterns of dissociation have been observed between these three classes of stimulus. In particular, Farah argues that there have been no convincing reports of patients with *visual object agnosia without alexia or prosopagnosia*, or with *prosopagnosia and alexia but without visual object agnosia*. The failure to find these two patterns of problems suggests that instead of there being separate recognition processes (e.g. reflecting independent memorial representations for faces, words, and objects), there may be a continuum of recognition processes characterized at one end by the encoding of non-decomposed perceptual wholes and at the other by the encoding of multiple perceptual parts. Faces and words differ in the degree to which their recognition is dependent on these visual encoding procedures. Faces depend primarily on being encoded as non-decomposed perceptual wholes for their recognition (e.g. Rhodes, Brake, & Atkinson, 1993; Tanaka & Farah, 1993); words depend primarily on the encoding of multiple parts (their letters) (see Humphreys & Bruce, 1989, for a review of the evidence for word recognition being dependent on letter coding). Object recognition will be determined by either encoding procedure, depending on the perceptual characteristics of the objects, their similarity to other objects, and so forth. Brain damage may affect either encoding procedure to varying degrees; hence patients may have impaired encoding of non-decomposed perceptual wholes or of multiple parts. These two impairments will, respectively, result in (in their most selective manifestations) problems in face recognition and in visual word recognition (i.e. "pure" prosopagnosia and "pure" alexia). However, as object recognition depends also on the same encoding procedures, it should not be possible for object identification either to be selectively spared or impaired without there also being concomitant sparing or impairment of either face or word recognition. Thus Farah (1991, p. 8) states that "this hypothesis, that two main types of representational capacity underlie the range of associative agnosias, ... would be falsified by a case of object agnosia without either prosopagnosia or alexia". In this paper we report evidence of one such case, Mr W, a patient with a selective impairment in recognizing both pictorially presented and real objects, but without problems in either reading printed words or visual face recognition (i.e. without either alexia or prosopagnosia). Mr W's case supports the argument that visual recognition procedures for objects are differentiated from those for faces and words. We present detailed evidence on the case, before going on to consider the implications for theories of visual object, face, and word recognition.

CASE REPORT

The patient, Mr W, born in 1905, was a retired solicitor and a part-time writer of popular songs. He was first seen in June 1992, three weeks after he had gone to hospital following a fall. A CT-scan (18–6–1992) revealed generalized cerebral and cerebellar atrophy, but no indication of a focal lesion. He had no sensory impairment and no limb weakness; however, he showed impaired control of fine hand movements. When he was first tested on the BUNS (the Birmingham University Neuropsychological Screen: Bateman, Riddoch & Humphreys, in preparation), he named 10 pictures correctly out of 15 (age-matched control group, $n = 20$: mean correct naming $= 14.14$; $SD = 1.26$), making 5 semantic errors. His ability to read written letters or words appeared unaffected. He read

18/18 irregular words correctly (age-matched control group, n = 20: mean correct naming: 16.15; SD = 1.87) and 8/8 pronounceable non-words correctly (age-matched control group, n = 20: mean correct naming = 6.85; SD = 2.4). His digit span was slightly below normal, being 5 forwards (age-matched control group, n = 20: mean span = 6; SD = 1.2) and 2 backwards (age-matched control group, n = 20: mean span = 3.9; SD = 0.8). When asked to recall verbally an address given earlier in the test session, he retrieved 2 items out of 6 (age-matched control group, n = 20: mean correct retrieval score = 3.7; SD = 1.6). Hence there was some indication of a memorial deficit. He showed no neglect on a line-cancellation task. He had no apparent expressive or receptive speech problems, and his spontaneous language was fluent and accurate. The present investigation was carried out between the beginning of June 1992 and the end of August 1992. Although during this time Mr W's performance was relatively stable, there was an indication in some tests that performance was deteriorating over time (in particular, see Experiment 1). For this reason, attempts were made to ensure that all crucial comparisons involved tests conducted within the same sessions.

EXPERIMENTAL INVESTIGATION

SECTION A

Object Naming

To determine the nature of the problems in naming that were apparent when we first saw him, we asked Mr W to name objects presented in different formats, either as line drawings, real objects, or toy models. In addition to this, we assessed Mr W's ability to produce a name to auditory definitions, in order to evaluate whether his naming problems were general and independent of the modality of stimulus presentation.

Experiment 1: Naming Line Drawings

Method

Mr W was given a set of 76 black-and-white pictures from Snodgrass and Vanderwart (1980), with each picture presented separately on a card. He was asked to name each picture without time restriction. The complete set was presented twice in two different sessions separated by 8 weeks, in order to establish whether there was consistency in his performance. The pictures were drawn from categories of stimulus in which there were either many exemplars with similar perceptual structures ("structurally similar" objects, mainly objects from biological categories) or relatively few exemplars with similar perceptual structures ("structurally dissimilar" objects, mainly artefacts). Within each general class of object, half had relatively high-frequency names (above 10 occurrences per million in the Kucera & Francis, 1967, word count) and half had low-frequency names (below 10 occurrences per million). Stimuli were taken from Humphreys, Riddoch, and Quinlan (1988), who also provide a more detailed discussion of the distinction between the classes of structurally similar and structurally dissimilar objects). Items from the different structure and name frequency groups were matched for name agreement and image agreement, using measures taken from Snodgrass and Vanderwart (1980). However, structurally dissimilar objects tended to be more familiar than structurally similar objects, and objects with high name frequencies tended to be more familiar than those with low name frequencies (using the ratings supplied by Snodgrass & Vanderwart, 1980, the rated familiarities for each stimulus set were: 3.79 for structurally dissimilar, high name frequency items; 3.37 for structurally dissimilar, low name frequency items; 2.93 for structurally similar, high name frequency items; 2.53 for structurally dissimilar, low name frequency items, where 1 = low familiarity and 5 = high familiarity). Structurally similar items tended also to be more complex than structurally dissimilar items (average rated complexity: structurally similar, 2.73; structurally dissimilar, 2.66; 1 = low complexity, 5 = high complexity). Effects of variables additional to whether the pictorial stimuli belonged to structurally similar or dissimilar classes, or whether they had relatively frequent or infrequent names, were assessed in Section E, using data collected across the complete set of picture- and object-naming tests used in the study.

Results

Mr W's performance is summarized in Table 1. His picture naming was poor on both occasions, and it tended to be worse on the second relative to the first test occasion, though the items that were named correctly were also consistent across sessions, $\chi^2(1) = 36.13$, $p < 0.0001$, Consistency Coefficient = 0.57. In Test Session 1, Mr W named 48/76 pictures (63%); in Test Session 2, he named 39/76 (51%). Errors were classified using a modification of the criteria set out by Hodges, Salmon, and Butters (1991) (see Appendix A)—(these criteria were followed throughout the study). On both occasions Mr W made mainly semantic errors [e.g. CHISEL→"a garage tool"; CELERY→"cabbage"; 27 out of 28 (96%) errors in Session 1; 36 out of 37 (97%) in Session 2]. The only other errors were visual in nature [e.g. BUTTON→"a circle"; ASHTRAY→"a seat"; 1/28 (0.4%) in Session 1; 1/37 (0.3%) in session 2]. There was no significant difference between the naming of objects from structurally similar and structurally dissimilar categories, and there was no effect of name frequency on his performance [both $\chi^2(1) < 1.0$]. He named correctly 42/76 structurally similar relative to 45/76 structurally dissimilar objects, and 42/76 items with high name frequencies relative to 45/76 items with low name frequencies. We discuss the effects of structural similarity in Section E.

TABLE 1
Number of Correct Naming Responses by Mr W to Visually Presented Line
Drawings, Real Objects, and Definitions (Section A)

		Number correct	Percentage correct
Experiment 1 line drawings	Test 1	48/76	63
	Test 2	39/76	51
Experiment 2 real objects		23/36	64
Experiment 3 animals (toys)		5/15	33
Experiment 4 auditory definitions		10/10	100

Experiment 2: Naming Real Objects

Method

Mr W was given a set of common objects in two different sessions (17 in Session 1, 19 in Session 2, spaced 7 weeks apart and conducted between the two sessions reported in Experiment 1), and he was asked to name them one at a time. Some objects were the same (13) for both sessions, the others were different.

Results

Mr W named correctly 10 objects out of 17 during the first session (59%) and 13 out of 19 during the second one (68%). On the first occasion he made 5 semantic as well as 2 visual/semantic errors (e.g. PAINTBRUSH→"hairbrush"); on the second occasion he made 3 semantic errors (e.g. CAN OPENER→"a domestic thing") and 3 visual/semantic errors (e.g. MEASURING JUG→"cup"). His performance was consistent on the items that he identified across the two sessions: (Fisher exact probability, $p = 0.007$; Consistency Coefficient $= 0.65$). Mr W was unable to make correct gestures to any of the real objects he failed to name correctly; he showed no indication of having recognized those objects correctly.

Experiment 3: Naming Animals (Toys)

Method

Mr W was presented with 15 small toy animals of different colours and asked to name the toys without touching them and without time restriction. This took place during the first session of Experiment 2.

Results

Mr W named 5/15 (33%) of the animals correctly. All of his errors (67%) were either semantic in nature (e.g. PENGUIN→"a bird of some kind"; HIPPO→"prehistoric animal") or visual/semantic (e.g. COW→"kangaroo"). (Note that it is difficult to separate pure semantic errors from errors that are visual and semantic in nature with this class of stimulus.) Five of the animals used here were also used in Experiment 1 (as line drawings). Two animals recognized in Experiment 1 were also recognized here; two not previously recognized were not recognized here, and one item, which had not been recognized before, was recognized in this experiment.

Experiment 4: Naming Auditory Definitions

Method

A set of 10 definitions was derived (see Appendix B), containing visual and functional information about objects. Mr W was asked to give the names of the objects after each definition had been read aloud by the examiner. This took place during the second session for the naming of line drawings, reported in Experiment 1.

Results

Mr W's performance was at ceiling, scoring 10/10 correct responses.

Summary and Discussion, Section A

The above results clarify that Mr W had a deficit in naming pictures, models of objects, and real objects. In addition, in Experiments 1 and 2 the pattern of impairment was consistent across items: Objects that Mr W could not identify during the first session were likely not to be identified during the second session. The vast majority of his naming errors were either semantic or visual/semantic in nature, suggesting that he could gain access to general information about the semantic field to which the target object belonged (e.g. CELERY→"cabbage", or PLIERS→"screwdriver"). In contrast to his poor naming of visually presented objects, Mr W showed good naming of auditory definitions. Given that the naming failure in anomia tends to affect all modalities (Goodglass, Barton, & Kaplan, 1968; Kay & Ellis, 1987; Lesser, 1978), preserved naming to auditory definitions conventionally suggests that anomia is not involved.

A problem in naming visually presented objects could arise from deficits at any of a number of locations within the object-processing system, prior to name retrieval (e.g. Humphreys & Riddoch, 1987a, 1993). Interestingly, nearly all of Mr W's naming errors were either semantically related or both semantically and visually related to the target object. From this it is tempting to infer an impairment in either stored visual or semantic knowledge about objects, which precipitates semantic or visual/semantic errors (and see Vitkovitch, Humphreys, & Lloyd-Jones, 1993, for evidence with normal subjects). However, this may not be conclusive. Recent modelling work, for example, has shown that the same errors can arise from simulated lesions at a number of different locations within a complex information-processing system (see e.g. Hinton & Shallice, 1991; Humphreys, Freeman, & Müller, 1992; Plaut & Shallice, 1993a, 1993b). Consequently, it is difficult to judge the functional location of damage from the nature of the errors that arise in tasks such as object naming (Shallice, 1988). Another approach is to use tasks that attempt to tap different levels of object-processing system directly—for example, by requiring decisions to be made on the basis of particular types of knowledge. Accordingly, we sought to assess Mr W's access to stored semantic and visual knowledge of objects, both when pictorial representations of objects and when words were used as stimuli, by using matching tasks requiring access to stored knowledge to take place in order for a correct decision to be made. In Section B, we assessed access to semantic knowledge about object functions and inter-object associations from visual objects. In Section C we assessed access to semantic knowledge from words. In Section D, we assessed access to stored visual knowledge about objects from both pictures and words.

SECTION B

Access to Semantic Knowledge from Vision

Access to semantic knowledge from objects was tested in four matching tasks. Experiment 5 required Mr W to point to a named picture and used distractors that were either semantically related, visually related, or unrelated to the target (Kay, Lesser, & Coltheart, 1992). Experiment 6 used the same pictures, but Mr W was asked to point to the picture that was semantically related to a reference picture. Two further tests required matching based on whether two pictorially presented stimuli belonged to the same category (Experiment 7) or whether two such stimuli were associatively related (Experiment 8). All of these tests were conducted in the period between the two test sessions reported in Experiment 1.

Experiment 5: Picture–Word Matching

Method

Mr W was given 40 trials. On each trial he was presented with an A4 page containing one printed word and five line-drawings of objects. One object (the target) corresponded to the word, the others were distractors. One distractor was semantically close to the target (e.g. HAMMER for the target AXE), one was semantically more distant (e.g. SCISSORS), one was visually similar (e.g. FLAG), and one was unrelated to the target (e.g. KITE). Stimuli were taken from the PALPA test battery (Kay et al., 1992). Mr W was asked to point to the picture corresponding to a word spoken by the experimenter on each trial. Across trials the target pictures were rotated across the positions on the page.

Results

Mr W matched correctly 25 targets out of 40 (62%). Of the 15 errors he made, 14 were "close" semantic, choosing the distractor semantically most related to the picture target (e.g. AXE→"hammer"), and 1 was visual (e.g. STAMP→ "picture"). This picture-word matching task is trivially easy for non-brain-damaged control subjects. Kay et al. report a mean of 39.5/40 correct ($SD = 1.01$ error) for 40 control subjects. Mr W was clearly impaired at the task.

Experiment 6:   Picture-Picture Matching for Semantic Relations

Method

Mr W was given the same stimuli as those used in Experiment 5, except that the word was removed and the target picture placed in the centre of each page. The central target picture was surrounded by four other pictures, one of which was semantically close to the target, one was semantically distant, one was visually close, and one was unrelated (the pictures were the distractors from Experiment 5). Mr W was asked to point to the picture that was most related in its use and meaning to the target picture. As this task used only pictures, Mr W's performance is less likely than in Experiment 5 to be confounded by any problems in verbal access to semantic knowledge. The picture-picture version of this test was actually conducted within the same sessions as a word-word version of the same task (reported here as Experiment 11), with the two versions of the test balanced in an ABBA design. This was done to facilitate comparisons between access to semantic knowledge from words and pictures. However, for clarity of presentation here, we report each version separately.

Results

Mr W scored 22/40 (55%) correct (scored as trials on which he pointed to the stimulus closely semantically related to the target object). He made errors on 6 trials by pointing to the semantically distant distractor, on 11 trials by pointing to the visually related distractor, and 1 error by pointing to the unrelated distractor. For comparison purposes, the same test was given to a non-brain-damaged, age-matched control, who scored 38/40 (95%) correct. Mr W was again impaired on this matching task. Indeed, he made visual as well as semantic errors, suggesting that on some occasions he failed to gain access to even broad semantic information from the pictures.

Experiment 7: Category Matching with Pictures

In Experiment 7, Mr W was given a somewhat simpler matching task, requiring him to decide which two of three pictures belonged to the same category. No attempts were made to control for there being higher levels of visual similarity between the reference object and its matching category member than between the reference object and the distractors, which were drawn from different categories. Hence visual similarity may be used to facilitate decision making.

Method

There were 40 trials. On each trial, Mr W was presented with three pictures: A reference picture at the top of an A4 page and two others placed lower on the page, one to the left and one to the right of centre (the target and the distractor, positioned randomly). Mr W was asked to point to the target item that came from the same category as the reference object. He was also asked to name the pictures on each trial, after matching was completed.

Results

Mr W matched 33/40 items correctly (82.5%). This matching task was considerably easier than that used in Experiment 6; nevertheless, Mr W performed below ceiling. He named 70/120 of the pictures correctly (58%). Of the 50 naming errors, 19 were semantically related (e.g. LLAMA→"an animal"); 6 were visually related to the target (e.g. ASHTRAY→"toilet"; ROLLER SKATE→"a toy motor car"), and 25 were visual/semantic (PLIERS→"screwdriver"). Mr W named all 3 items correctly on 10 trials (9 correct matches; 1 wrong match), 2 of the 3 items correctly on 13 trials (12 correct matches; 1 wrong match), 1 item correct out of the 3 on 14 trials (12 correct matches, 2 wrong matches), and none of the items correctly on 3 trials (he made incorrect matches on all 3 of these trials).

Experiment 8: Associative Matching between Pictures

In the final picture-picture matching experiment, Mr W was required to match pictures on the basis of whether the objects depicted were associatively related. In this case, distractors were chosen to be as visually similar to the reference objects as the target objects were. Visual similarity should not facilitate performance.

Method

There were 41 trials. On each trial, Mr W was given three pictures: one reference object at the top of the page (e.g. tennis racket) and a target and a distractor object placed randomly on the left or right, below the target (e.g. tennis net and football goal). Mr W was asked to point to the distractor that was associated to the target. After matching the stimuli on each trial, he was asked to name the pictures shown.

Results

Mr W made 20/41 (4%) correct matching responses. He named correctly 62/123 (51%) of the pictures correctly. Of the 61 naming errors, 10 were semantically related to the picture, 8 were visually related, and 27 were visual/semantic. For 16 of the 61 items that he failed to name, Mr W appeared not to access any stored information (e.g. DRILL→"no idea"). On 6 trials (4 correct matches; 2 wrong matches), Mr W named all 3 items on the page; on 15 trials (8 correct matches; 7 wrong matches), he named 2 of the 3 items; on 14 trials (6 correct matches; 8 wrong matches), he named 1 item out of 3; and on 6 trials he did not name any of the items (2 correct matches, 4 incorrect matches). Mr W performed at chance on the matching task, although he tended to perform more accurately when he could name the majority of items present.

Summary and Discussion, Section B

Mr W was impaired on each of the tests used to assess access to semantic information from pictures (see Table 2). He scored at chance when matching visually dissimilar but associatively related objects, and he performed substantially below control levels on picture-word matching and picture-picture matching for semantically related items. He performed somewhat better at a category-matching task with pictures, but he may then have been facilitated by visual similarity between the to-be-matched stimuli. Overall, the data indicate that Mr W achieved, at best,

TABLE 2
Summary of Tests Assessing Access to Semantic Information from
Vision (Section B)

Experiment 5	
picture-word matching	impaired
Experiment 6	
picture-picture matching for semantic relations	impaired
Experiment 7	
picture-picture category matching	impaired
Experiment 8	
picture-picture associative matching	impaired (chance)

access to only general semantic information about objects. We should note that Mr W's poor associative matching with pictures occurred on some occasions even when he was able to name correctly all the stimuli present (though he tended to perform better when he could name the majority of stimuli present than when he failed to name any). This last result suggests that there may be some deficit in accessing semantic information from object names as well as from visual presentation of objects. This was assessed more formally in Section C.

SECTION C

Access to Semantic Knowledge from Words

In order to assess Mr W's ability to access semantic knowledge from words, we tested his ability to judge whether auditorily presented words were synonyms (Experiment 9), to provide verbal definitions, and to answer probe questions to auditorily presented words (Experiment 10) and carry out a word-word matching text analogous to the picture-picture matching test used in Experiment 6 (Experiment 11, using printed words). These tests were again conducted between the two tests reported in Experiment 1, and the word-word matching test was counter-balanced across the same sessions as the picture-picture matching test (Experiment 6), to allow appropriate comparisons to be made.

Experiment 9:   Synonym Matching

Method

Mr W was given 64 word pairs, each read aloud by the experimenter, and he was asked to judge whether each word pair was similar or differed in meaning. The stimuli were taken from PALPA (Kay et al., 1992). Half the pairs were similar in meaning, half were dissimilar, and half the words referred to high-imageability stimuli, half to low-imageability concepts (e.g. "lie" and "falsehood" vs. "ship" and "boat"). The high-imageability stimuli were not necessarily concrete (e.g. story/tale).

Results

Mr W scored at ceiling: 62/62 (100%) correct. He carried out the task efficiently and with no apparent problems.

Experiment 10:   Verbal Definitions

Method

Mr W was asked to provide a verbal definition for 22 auditorily presented names of objects taken from the set used in Experiment 1 (picture naming).

Following his spontaneous definition (and depending on the specificity of his definition), Mr W was asked a series of probe questions concerning the object's colour, size, use, and (if an animal) whether it lived in the United Kingdom or abroad.

Results

In Appendix C we report in full the definitions given by Mr W. The definitions were scored using the criterion adopted by McCarthy and Warrington (1988)—namely, that the definition indicated knowledge of the core concept of the object as decided by a set of independent judges. Judges were told that the definitions were provided by someone with a naming problem, and they were asked to decide whether the patient knew what the object was or whether they had a good idea of the basic concept of the item being represented (see also Sheridan & Humphreys, 1993). The definitions were given to a set of five independent judges. There was agreement between the judges that Mr W provided the core concept for 13/22 of the stimuli; of the remaining 9 stimuli, there was unanimity for 3 (Mr W did *not* provide the core concept) and disagreement over the remaining 6 definitions. Of the 13 items for which Mr W provided the core concept, 5 had been named correctly and 5 had been named incorrectly in both sessions of Experiment 1, and 3 had been named on one occasion in Experiment 1. Of the 3 items for which there was unanimity that Mr W did not provide the core concept, 2 had been named correctly in both sessions of Experiment 1, and 1 on just one occasion. Of the 6 items for which there was disagreement over whether Mr W provided the core concept, 2 had been named correctly and 3 had been named incorrectly in both sessions of Experiment 1, and 1 had been named correctly on one occasion. There was no evidence of consistency between his ability to provide verbal definitions of the objects and his ability to name objects correctly from visual presentation on at least one of the two test occasions in Experiment 1 [collapsing together the cells for which Mr W named objects correctly on one and on two occasions, and the cells for which there was some doubt over whether his verbal definition of the item was correct with those where it was agreed that he failed to retrieve the core concept, $\chi^2(1) < 1.0$] (see Table 3).[1]

On 19 probe questions concerning either the use of objects and animals or their habitat (in the United Kingdom or abroad), Mr W scored 14 correct (10/14 on probe questions concerning the use of animals and objects, 4/5 on questions concerning their habitat). In contrast, he scored 0/12 on probe questions

---

[1]Note that by collapsing together items that Mr W named correctly at least once in Experiment 1, any differences between his ability to name objects from line drawings (in Experiment 1) and his ability to produce accurate verbal definitions (in Experiment 10) cannot be attributed to his performance deteriorating over time between the tests of visual naming and of giving verbal definitions, as the sessions in Experiment 1 spanned the test of verbal definitions in Experiment 10.

TABLE 3
The Relations between Mr W's Visual Object Naming[a] and His Ability to
Define the Core Concept of the Object From Its Name[b]

	Core Definition Provided	
Items Named Correctly[a]	Yes	? or No
1 or more occasions	8	6
0	5	3

[a]In Experiment 1.
[b]In Experiment 10.

concerning the size and colour of animals. He performed worse on the tests probing visual knowledge than on those probing functional and encyclopaedic knowledge (such as habitat) (Fisher exact probability, $p = 0.0085$).

Experiment 11: Matching Printed Words for Semantic Relations

Method

As already noted, Mr W was asked to carry out an analogous word-word-matching task to the picture-picture-matching task used in Experiment 6. The two versions of the task were performed across two sessions in an ABBA design. In the word version, a word was placed at the centre of the page on each trial, and it was surrounded by four flanking words: One closely related, one more distantly semantically related, one visually related, and one unrelated. He was asked to point to the stimulus that was most similar in meaning to the central reference word.

Results

Mr W scored 28/40 (70%) correct (where he pointed to the flanking word closest in meaning to the central reference word). An age-matched control scored 38/40 (95%) correct. Mr W made 8 errors by pointing to the distant semantic distractor, 3 by pointing to the name of the distractor that would be visually similar to the reference stimulus, and 1 by pointing to the name of the unrelated distractor.

Mr W was impaired on this task relative to the control subject. Nevertheless, he performed better in the word-word version than in the picture-picture version of the same task: 28/40 vs. 22/40; $\chi^2(1) = 6.23$, $p < 0.02$, McNemar test of change. His better performance with words indicates that his poor performance with pictures cannot just be attributed to a problem in understanding the task. His access to semantic information was most impaired for pictures, though it was imperfect also for words.

Summary and Discussion, Section C

The evidence on Mr W's ability to access semantic information from verbal input is somewhat mixed. He performed at ceiling on synonym judgements to auditorily presented words. In contrast, his verbal definitions to some items were vague and non-specific, though he was better at answering forced-choice questions about functional characteristics of objects (when given their names) than he was at answering forced-choice questions about visual characteristics of objects. In addition, he was impaired at matching written words according to whether the corresponding objects were semantically related or not (Experiment 11), though even here his performance was better with written words than with pictures (Experiment 6). The data suggest that Mr W's access to semantics from printed words was better than his ability to access corresponding information from pictures, though in both cases it was far from perfect.

Mr W's very good performance in the synonym judgement task may be due to several factors. It could be because words were presented auditorily rather than in print. Against this, he was given auditory names to define in Experiment 10, yet there were problems in his defining some stimuli. A second possibility is that many of the stimuli in the synonym judgement task were abstract; it could be that Mr W has preserved knowledge of abstract relative to concrete concepts. Patients with preserved knowledge of abstract relative to concrete concepts have been reported by Warrington (1975, patient A. B.). However, not all the items in the synonym task were abstract, yet Mr W scored 100% correct. A third possibility is that synonym judgements did not require access to visual properties of objects, and Mr W's problems may be most pronounced when access to stored visual knowledge is required. Consistent with this, Mr W was very poor at answering questions that probed his knowledge about the visual properties of objects (Experiment 10).

One other point to note here is that there was no consistency between Mr W's ability to provide accurate verbal definitions when given the name of objects and his ability to name the same objects from line drawings (in Experiment 1). At the very least, this suggests that there were different constraints on Mr W's performance in the two tasks (see Riddoch, Humphreys, Coltheart, & Funnell, 1988, for this argument). For example, his visual object identification might be affected by factors such as the visual similarity of the stimulus relative to other members of the same category (see Section E); his ability to provide verbal definitions might be affected by the strength of verbal association between a name and the distinct associative properties linked to the object (e.g. camel→Egypt; bee→honey). As these constraints might vary across objects, contrasting effects with objects and words might emerge even if there is a single common impairment affecting Mr W's performance with both visual objects and their names. A rather different view would be that there are two separate impairments involved. These different impairments can also be conceptualized in at least two different ways. One possibility is that semantic knowledge is differentiated according to the modality of the input (e.g Warrington, 1975). According to this view, Mr W may have separate impairments affecting (1) the semantic knowledge system accessed by auditory words (leading to poor verbal definitions) and (2) the semantic knowledge system accessed by visual objects (leading to poor visual object identification). The items affected within each system are not correlated, and hence his performance is inconsistent across the test modalities (while at the same time being consistent for visually presented stimuli; Experiment 1). A second possibility is that Mr W has separate impairments to a central, polymodal semantic system and to stored visual knowledge about objects (cf. Riddoch & Humphreys, 1987a). This second account differs from the first in stressing that (1) the visual knowledge store does not contain information about object function or inter-object associations, which are represented in the semantic system, and (2) the systems representing visual and semantic knowledge about objects can be accessed from different input modalities, depending on the nature of the information required for the task. Visual object identification necessarily requires access to stored visual knowledge in order that semantic information is subsequently accessed. Verbal definitions, however, may either be made on the basis of functional and associative knowledge or they may require access to stored visual knowledge (perhaps according to the nature of the stimulus; for example, animate objects are typically defined in terms of their perceptual characteristics, whereas artefacts are defined in terms of their functional properties; see Warrington & Shallice, 1984). Given separate impairments of stored visual and semantic knowledge, there need not be a necessary correlation between performance across modalities if there is retained functional and associative knowledge about items for which stored visual knowledge is impaired, and vice versa. In fact, inspection of Mr W's verbal definitions indicates that nearly all the accurate information was functional or associative in content, and visual details, when present, were incorrect in nearly all cases (e.g. bee: "It is an insect; it buzzes; it is unpleasant, and it makes honey; it is black"). This suggests that he found it difficult to retrieve almost any stored visual knowledge about objects from their names, a proposal confirmed by his poor performance on forced-choice questions about visual rather than functional properties of objects. Items that are defined correctly may well then be those with distinctive functional or associative characteristics. These items may not necessarily be easy to identify visually, however, if their visual forms overlap others from the same category (e.g. as in the case of a bee). In Section D we attempt to assess in greater detail Mr W's ability to access stored visual knowledge about objects.

SECTION D

Access to Stored Visual Knowledge of Objects

Experiment 12:   Object Decision

Riddoch and Humphreys (1987a) first used object decision tasks to assess whether neuropsychological patients could access stored knowledge of objects from vision. Such tasks require discrimination between real objects and (in their case, and also here) non-objects formed by interchanging the parts of real objects (to create stimuli that are perceptually "good" but visually unfamiliar). Riddoch and Humphreys (1987a; see also Sheridan & Humphreys, 1993) reported data from a patient showing that object decision was preserved even though recognition of the functions of objects and inter-object associations was impaired. They suggested that this pattern of performance reflects good visual access to stored knowledge about the structural characteristics of objects, along with poor access to functional, semantic knowledge. We conducted a similar test with Mr W, to assess whether his visual access to structural knowledge of objects was intact, despite his recognition impairment (Section B).

Method

The stimuli were taken from the BORB test battery (OD A Easy: Riddoch & Humphreys, 1993). There were 16 line drawings of real objects and 16 of non-objects formed by interchanging parts of real objects. Mr W had to judge whether the drawings depicted real or meaningless objects. There were no time limits.

Results

Mr W made 25/32 correct matches. Four real objects were classed as non-objects, and 3 non-objects were classed as objects. Riddoch and Humphreys (1993) report that 14 non-brain-damaged, age-related controls scored in the range of 22-32 (mean of correct responses = 28.9; SD = 2.4) in this test. Mr W's performance fell just within the range of normal subjects, but some way beneath the mean.

Experiment 13:   Colour-Object Decision

Method

In a variation on Experiment 12, Mr W was given a colour-object decision task. On each trial he saw two coloured line-drawings of the same object, one depicted in the correct colour and one in colours that were clearly incorrect (e.g.

A PURPLE FROG). He was asked to point to the correctly coloured drawing. There were 13 trials, each using an object with diagnostic colour. The same set of stimuli was given to 9 non-brain-damaged, age-matched control subjects (with ages ranging between 70 and 89).

Results

Mr W scored 8/13 (61%). The 9 non-brain-damaged, age-related controls scored between 11 and 13 correct (mean number correct = 11.5; SD = 2.4). Mr W's performance fell outside the range of the normal subjects. His poor performance on the colour-object decision task is consistent with him having a deficit in accessing stored visual knowledge about objects. From this test alone, however, we do not know whether it is access to all visual knowledge or access only to colour knowledge that is impaired. Riddoch et al. (1988) noted that their patient, J. B., was poor at colour-object decisions despite being good at object decisions tapping knowledge about the structure of objects. Experiment 14 assessed stored visual knowledge about object structure more directly.

Experiment 14:   The "Heads" test

Method

Twenty-seven stimuli were taken from Riddoch and Humphreys (1987a). On each trial, Mr W was presented with a card containing the body of an animal or of an object positioned in the lower half, and four heads of animals or objects located on the upper half. Of the four heads, one was the correct head for the "body", and the others were both visually similar to the target head and belonged to stimuli from the same category. The position of the correct head was varied across trials. The stimuli were presented one at a time to Mr W, who was told to point to the appropriate head for each body. For the last 21 stimuli, Mr W was asked to name the items from their bodies, after matching had been completed. The same set of stimuli was given to 8 non-brain-damaged, age-matched control subjects (with ages ranging between 70 and 88).

Results

Mr W made 12/27 correct responses. The 8 non-brain-damaged, age-matched controls scored in the range of 24–25 (mean number of correct responses = 24.75; SD = 0.5). Mr W's performance again fell outside the range of the normal subjects. Mr W was impaired at this task. Overall, he named 10/21 of the bodies correctly. Of the 10 correctly named, 7 were also matched to the correct head; on the other hand, of the 11 that he failed to name, only 3 were matched to the correct head. When Mr W succeeded in naming the stimulus body, he tended to be more accurate at matching (Fisher exact probability, p < 0.0861). Mr W's performance on the "heads" test confirms his relatively poor score on the object-decision task in Experiment 12 and its coloured variant in Experiment 13. Taking these data together, the results suggest that he has impaired access to stored visual knowledge of objects. Experiment 14 tested further his ability to retrieve visual knowledge of objects from their names.

Experiment 15: Tails Test

Method

Mr W was auditorily presented with 27 names of animals. For each of them, he was asked to say whether the animal had a long or a short tail relative to its body; 13 were judged by the experimenters to have relatively short tails and 14 to have relatively long tails. There were no time limitations. The same set of stimuli was given to 5 non-brain-damaged, age-matched control subjects (with ages ranging between 72 and 89).

Results

Mr W made 14/27 (52%) correct responses: Chance level of performance; 5 age-matched control subjects scored a mean of 24.6 correct responses ($SD = 2.2$). Mr W was impaired relative to the control subjects.

Summary and Discussion, Section D

In the four tests used to assess access to visual knowledge about objects, Mr W performed at a level below that expected from non-brain-damaged control subjects (see Table 4 for a summary). He was more than 1.5 SDs below the mean of the control subjects on the object-decision task (Experiment 12). He performed at chance (and outside the control range) on the colour-object decision test (Experiment 13). He was above chance but impaired relative to the controls on the "heads" test (Experiment 14). He was also at chance at deciding whether animals had long or short tails relative to their bodies, when given their names (when controls were considerably above chance—Experiment 15). The results suggest that Mr W had impaired access to visual knowledge about

TABLE 4
Summary of Tests Assessing Access to Stored Visual
Knowledge of Objects (Section C)

Experiment 12 object decision	Bottom of control range (1.5 SDs below control mean)
Experiment 13 colour-object decision	impaired (chance)
Experiment 14 heads test	impaired
Experiment 15 tails test	impaired (chance)

objects, and this held whether this knowledge was accessed by pictures or auditory words and whether knowledge about the colour of objects or about their form was assessed.

SECTION E

Stimulus Properties Affecting Object Naming

Across the matching and naming experiments reported in Sections A-D, Mr W attempted to name 292 objects on 532 occasions in total. These naming attempts provide a substantial data-base from which we can assess the potential factors affecting his object identification. This was done by assessing Mr W's naming as a function of the category to which the object belonged (in particular, whether it came from a category with structurally similar or dissimilar exemplars), the frequency of its name, its rated familiarity, complexity, name agreement, and the age of acquisition of the picture name (using the measures supplied for these last 5 variables by Snodgrass & Vanderwart, 1980). The full data are given in Appendix D. On 532 occasions he attempted to name objects belonging either to categories with structurally similar exemplars or to categories with structurally dissimilar exemplars. For the structurally similar items he named 92 objects correctly out of 204 occasions, for the structurally dissimilar items he named 196 objects correctly out of 328 occasions. Identification performance was better with structurally dissimilar than with structurally similar items ($\chi^2(1) = 10.89$, $p < 0.001$). However, the structurally similar and dissimilar items compared here were not matched, and so any effects could be due to differences in a correlated factor, such as item familiarity (Funnell & Sheridan 1992). The effects of the other variables (excluding structural similarity) were examined in the following way. First, the pictures were divided according to whether they had high or low values along each variable, and comparisons were made between the number of items named correctly in the groups with high or low values. There were reliable positive effects only of name frequency and familiarity (see Table 5 for the data). Pictures with high-frequency names were more likely to be named correctly than pictures with low-frequency names ($t(187) = -2.16, p < 0.02$). Highly familiar pictures tended to be named correctly more often than pictures with low familiarity ($t(187) = 1.44, p < 0.08$). Pictures for which there was higher name agreement were also more likely to be named correctly than those for which there was low name agreement ($t(187) = 3.08, p < 0.001$).

Second, a multiple regression analysis was conducted on the percentage of correct responses, relative to the number of attempted responses, for each picture against 7 predictor variables (structural similarity, name frequency, familiarity, complexity, name agreement, image agreement, and age of acquisition). The only reliable predictor of Mr W's identification performance was name agreement ($t(187) = -2.06, p < 0.05$). No other factors accounted for a significant amount of the variance.

TABLE 5
The "Split" Analyses on Mr W's Picture and Object
Naming Performance.

	High		Low	
	N	*% Correct*	*N*	*% Correct*
familiarity	141	61	47	50
complexity	123	58	65	58
frequency	50	79	138	54
name agreement	133	65	55	43
image agreement	126	61	62	52

Note: Familiarity, complexity, and name agreement values were taken from Snodgrass and Vanderwart (1980). In each case, a 5-point rating scale was used, with 1 as a low score and 5 as a high. Median split analyses involved comparisons of all items with scores of between 1–2.5 with those with scores between 2.5–5. Name agreement scores are based on the percentage of subjects in Snodgrass and Vanderwart's (1980) study who gave objects the same name. Here items were divided according to whether their name agreement scores were above or below 0.72 (high being below 0.72). Name frequencies were taken from Kucera and Francis (1967). Items were scored as having a high name frequency if their name occurred above 40 times per million. For each variable, a one-tailed *t*-test was carried out for unrelated samples.

These analyses suggest that structural similarity (in the overall analysis), frequency and/or familiarity (in the item-split analyses), and name agreement (in the item-split and regression analyses) may have contributed to Mr W's object-naming performance. However, to the extent that Mr W had a visual recognition rather than a naming problem (Section A and B), it is unlikely that name frequency played a predominant role. Studies with normal subjects suggest that effects of name frequency, when they occur, are due to name retrieval processes rather than to visual recognition processes (Humphreys et al., 1988; Oldfield & Wingfield, 1965).[2] Effects of familiarity and name agreement are also difficult to separate, as familiar items tend also to have high name agreement (Snodgrass & Vanderwart, 1980); nevertheless, the regression analysis indicated that when these two variables were compared directly, the effects of name agreement were dominant. Name agreement can itself represent either of two factors. One is whether an object has a number of potential names—for example, a "cooker" can be named alternatively as a "stove" or an "oven". A second factor is whether the object can be consistently visually identified from its form. Objects from structurally similar categories, such as an "apricot" or a "plum", have low levels of name agreement in the Snodgrass and Vanderwart (1980) norms *not* because they have alternative names, but because they are visually confusable with other items. For Mr W, it may be that visual confusability plays a dominant role in his

---

[2] We note in passing that effects of name frequency, even on name retrieval, may themselves be contingent on the age at which the name was acquired (Morrison, Ellis, & Quinlan, 1992).

visual object identification: Such a factor would correlate with whether the object belongs to a category with structurally similar or dissimilar exemplars. To assess whether there were effects of structural similarity even when factors such as familiarity and name agreement were controlled for, a set of 88 items (44 from structurally similar and 44 from stucturally dissimilar categories) was derived with objects from the two general categories pairwise matched for familiarity and name agreement (averaged across the items, the mean familiarity and name agreement values for the structurally similar and structurally dissimilar items were 2.94, 0.5, and 2.95, and 0.42, respectively). Even with matched items, there remained an advantage for objects from categories with structurally dissimilar exemplars over those from categories with structurally similar exemplars; for the structurally similar items, Mr W named 61 correctly out of 121 occasions; for the structurally dissimilar items, he named 59 correctly out of 91 occasions, $\chi^2(1) = 4.398$, $p < 0.05$. Over and above effects of familiarity and name agreement, Mr W was selectively impaired at identifying items from categories with structurally similar exemplars. The failure to find this effect in Experiment 1 can be attributed to the slightly smaller number of items in that study and the failure to match pairwise across all potentially important factors (though items were then pairwise matched for name frequency).

SECTION F

Face Recognition

In our clinical testing of Mr W, we failed to observe any noticeable problems in face recognition. For example, he always identified us from our faces, and he could identify members of the ward staff. In view of his impaired visual object recognition, his good face recognition was striking. We examined his face recognition more systematically in two tests of face identification.

Experiment 16: The "Nostalgia" Test

Method

Mr W was presented with a set of 40 black-and-white photographs (from the "Nostalgia" set of stimuli: Holden, 1986) of people who achieved fame between the years 1920 and 1960. The photographs included some paraphernalia (hats, uniforms, etc.), in addition to the faces of the famous people. The faces were presented in random order. Mr W was asked to name each face, and there were no time limitations.

This task was chosen for initial testing because 4 control subjects, aged between 62 and 72, were shown to have some problems in naming the faces (see Table 6). Hence normal performance was some way below ceiling.

Results

Mr W named 21/40 of the faces correctly, a level of performance that is close to the average of the controls and easily within the control range. For 8 of the faces for which he failed to give the correct name, he provided appropriate (and quite detailed) semantic information. For instance, for Harold MacMillan he stated that he was "the conservative politician who became prime minister after Suez". Mr W's responses were fluent and certain, when correct identification occurred.

Experiment 16 suggests that Mr W's face recognition was at least as good as that of the younger control subjects. However, one difficulty with the "Nostalgia" stimuli is that the photographs include dress information as well as faces. Mr W may have benefited by using paraphernalia to boost a faulty face-recognition process. To overcome this problem, and to provide more data on Mr W face-recognition capabilities, Experiment 17 used a set of photographs in which only face information was shown.

Experiment 17: Face Identification

Method

There were 16 coloured photographs, each showing just the face of a famous person. Mr W was asked to name each one without time limits.

Results and Discussion

Mr W named 15/16 (94%) of the faces correctly. The faces were given to the same control subjects as were used in Experiment 16. The mean of the correct responses for the controls was 13.5/16 (see Table 6 for the full data). Mr W showed normal face identification. There was no evidence of prosopagnosia.

Mr W's ability to identify faces from visual presentation stands in contrast to his ability to identify many common objects from visual presentation (Sections A–E). If all associative visual object agnosias are due to degrees of perceptual

TABLE 6
Correct Responses on Face Naming Tests by Mr W and Four
Non-brain-damaged Control Subjects.

	Mr W	Controls			
		1	2	3	4
Test 1 (Experiment 16)					
number correct	21/40	26/40	16/40	22/40	18/40
percentage correct	(52%)	(65%)	(40%)	(55%)	(45%)
Test 2 (Experiment 17)					
number correct	15/16	13/16	11/16	15/16	15/16
percentage correct	(94%)	(81%)	(69%)	(94%)	(94%)

impairment, then the perceptual impairment affecting object but not face recognition is likely to disrupt the encoding of objects with multiple perceptual parts (cf. Farah, 1990, 1991). This follows because visual face recognition, which is preserved for Mr W, is thought to depend on the computation of non-decomposed perceptual wholes, not on the parallel encoding of their parts. In this respect it is interesting that Mr W was worse at identifying objects from categories with structurally similar exemplars (such as natural, biological objects) than objects from categories with structurally dissimilar exemplars (such as artefacts). Many artefacts have similar parts, and a priori we might expect the visual identification of such items to involve visual coding of the relations between these parts (see Biederman, 1987). If the visual routines for encoding such relations were disrupted, we would expect artefacts to be particularly difficult to identify. The data contradict this. However, as noted by Farah (1991), a stronger test of the hypothesis would be to use the stimuli most typically thought to rely on the coding of their multiple parts for recognition, namely printed words. If Mr W has difficulty encoding in parallel multiple visual parts, we expect his reading to be impaired; in particular, there should be alexia.

SECTION G

Naming Printed Words

In our initial clinical screening of Mr W, there was no indication that he was alexic. He appeared to process words fluently and not to have recourse to letter-by-letter reading, as apparent in many alexic patients. Experiments 18–20 tested his visual word-processing more formally by requiring him to name aloud words with either regular or irregular spelling-sound correspondences. Regular and irregular words were chosen because many models of reading assume that irregular words may only be named by the use of a visual recognition route, by which a word makes contact with a stored orthographic entry in the reader's internal lexicon (e.g. Coltheart, 1985; though see Seidenberg, 1992, for an alternative view).

Experiment 18: Naming Regular and Irregular Words (Varying in Frequency)

Method

Mr W was given 42 regular and 39 irregular words, half having high and half low frequencies of occurrence in written English (using a cut-off of 60 occurrences per million in the Kucera & Francis, 1967, word count), and he was asked to read each aloud. The words were printed in size 9 Geneva font and presented in random order, one at a time, for Mr W to read from table height.

Results

In all, Mr W read 78/81 (96.3%) of the words correctly. He made 3 (3.7%) visual errors (e.g. *poet*→"post"), one with a high-frequency irregular word and two with low-frequency irregular words. There was no significant difference between reading regular (42/42) and irregular (36/39) words (Fisher exact probability, $p = 0.12$).

Experiment 19: Naming Low-Frequency Regular and Irregular Words

Seidenberg, Waters, Barnes, and Tanenhaus (1984) showed that regularity effects vary with frequency, with the effects of regularity being most pronounced on low-frequency words. Similar effects have also been found with surface dyslexic readers, who may be assumed to have poor visual access to lexical information (Bub, Canceliere, & Kertesz, 1985). Hence, effects of regularity on Mr W's naming of words might only be expected to emerge with low-frequency stimuli. This would also be consistent with his object recognition being worse for low-familiarity items. To provide a stronger test of Mr W's ability to access the visual lexicon, we explored his naming of a larger set of regular and irregular words.

Method

Mr W was given 42 regular and 42 irregular words, all having low frequencies of occurrence in written English (under 10 per million, Kucera & Francis, 1967), and he was asked to read each aloud. The words were printed in size 12 Geneva font, upper case. Regular and irregular words were presented in random order.

Results

Mr W read correctly 78/84 words (93%) (see Table 7). He misread 1 regular word, making a visual error (e.g. *pour*→"four") and 5 irregular words, making 1 visual error (e.g. *comb*→"come") and 4 regularizations (e.g. *plaid*→"played"). There was no significant difference between his reading of regular and irregular words (41/42 regular vs. 37/42 irregular words, Fisher exact probability, $p = 0.11$). Even when only low-frequency words were presented, there were few signs that Mr W had difficulty accessing the visual lexicon; his word naming was generally accurate, and there was no regularity effect. However, Experiments 18 and 19 used unlimited presentation times, and Mr W's naming responses were not timed. It is possible that he could have read regular and irregular words correctly by using a letter-by-letter identification process followed by recognition of the words from their spelling (e.g. Price & Humphreys, 1992; Warrington & Shallice, 1980). If this had occurred, Mr W's reading responses

TABLE 7
Number of Correct Responses by
Mr W on Tests of Reading Aloud (Section F)

	Number correct	Percentage correct
Test 1 (Experiment 18) Regular/Irregular Words (Low and High Frequency)	78/81	(96%)
Test 2 (Experiment 19) Regular/Irregular Words (Low Frequency)	78/84	(93%)

would be slow and directly related to word length. In Experiment 20, we measured word-naming latencies as well as accuracy.

Experiment 20: Word Naming Latencies

Method

Mr W read aloud regular and irregular words taken from Seidenberg et al. (1984). The words had either high or low frequencies of occurrence and varied between 3 and 6 letters in length. They were presented one at a time, centred on the screen of a Macintosh Classic microcomputer. Mr W named each word as fast as he could. Responses were timed by an examiner tapping a key as soon as Mr W responded. Five control subjects (with ages ranging from 70 to 99 years) without any history of brain damage were also run under equivalent circumstances.

Results

Mr W made only one error, which was with the high-frequency irregular word "*were*" (pronounced as "we're"). His overall mean naming latency was 1517 msec, and RTs varied between 450 and 2200 msec. Mean RTs in each Frequency x Regularity group are given in Table 8.

There were no effects of either regularity or frequency and no Regularity × Frequency interaction on Mr W's word-naming latencies (all $Fs < 1.0$). Importantly, there was no sign of a correlation between naming times and word length ($r = 0.01$). Mean RTs for each word length are given in Table 9. The latencies for the control subjects are also shown in Tables 8 and 9. For the controls there was a tendency for regular words to be named faster than irregular words, $F(1, 4) = 4.66, 0.10 > p < 0.05$, over subjects, but neither the main effect of word frequency nor the Frequency × Regularity interaction approached significance (both $Fs < 1.0$).

It is not clear why we did not observe on elderly control subjects either a main effect of name frequency with the present items, or an interaction between name

TABLE 8
Mean Naming Latencies and Number of Correct Responses for Regular
and Irregular Words Varying in Frequency of Occurrence for Mr W and Five
Non-Brain-Damaged Controls (Experiment 20)

	Mr W			Control Data (Five Subjects)		
	Mean RTs	SD (RTs)	Accuracy	Mean RTs	SD (RTs)	Mean Accuracy
Regular						
high	1551	297	13/13	1252	488	12.8/13
low	1501	229	13/13	1403	868	12.4/13
Irregular						
high	1562	255	12/13	1420	682	12.2/13
low	1462	383	13/13	1420	674	11.8/13

Note: Naming latencies given in msec.

frequency and regularity, as has been observed previously (e.g. Seidenberg et al., 1984). It should be noted, however, that the regular and irregular words used here were closely matched for orthographic regularity; in other studies of word naming, effects of spelling-to-sound regularity have been shown to be weak for orthographically matched items (e.g. Balota & Ferraro, 1993). Balota and Ferraro (1993) have reported that, although older subjects show no greater effects of regularity than do young subjects, they do show increased effects of name frequency on word-naming latencies, and these frequency effects are particularly marked with dementing subjects. Frequency effects may become marked in dementing subjects if there is a breakdown in visual access to stored lexical knowledge, with low-frequency words suffering most. Note, though, that, if anything, Mr W showed a reverse word-frequency effect (Table 8), contrary to there being any disruption to his visual processing of printed words. Also, despite being older than four of the controls, Mr W was only 100 msec slower than the mean control RT, and his RTs comfortably fell within 1 SD of the

TABLE 9
Word Naming RTs as a Function of Word Length for Mr W and
Five Non-brain-damaged Control Subjects (Experiment 20)

	Mr W	Control Subjects	
Word Length	Mean RTs	Mean RTs	SDs
3 letters	1579	1435	720
4 letters	1503	1347	905
5 letters	1527	1425	716
6 letters	1527	1750	1152

Note: Naming RTs given in msec.

control means. He was also just as accurate as the controls, and showed no effects of word length on his reading times. We conclude that Mr W was neither alexic nor surface dyslexic.

Summary and Discussion, Section G

Tests of Mr W's face and visual word recognition have failed to reveal either prosopagnosia or alexia. Mr W recognized famous faces as accurately as did control subjects (Experiments 16 and 17). He showed no effect of regularity on either his naming accuracy (Experiments 18–20) or latency (Experiment 20), even with low-frequency words. Also, there were no effects of word length on reading times, and his naming latencies were inseparable from those of control subjects. We conclude that Mr W did not have difficulties in visually processing either faces or words.

GENERAL DISCUSSION

We have reported data from a single patient, Mr W, who was impaired at recognizing visually presented objects (Sections A–E), but who could both effortlessly identify photographs of famous faces (Section F) and read aloud printed words (Section G). In addition, he experienced greater difficulties in (1) retrieving semantic information from visually presented objects than from printed words (Experiments 6 and 11), and (2) retrieving visual relative to functional knowledge about objects from their names (Experiment 10). His ability to perform synonym judgements to auditorily presented words was particularly good (Experiment 9). There was no indication of a general anomia, as Mr W showed a relatively spared ability to retrieve the names of objects from verbal definitions. These results suggest that Mr W had a selective visual agnosia for objects, along with spared visual processing for faces and words—that is, there was agnosia without either prosopagnosia or alexia. This is the first experimental case report of such a selective impairment.

Accounts that stress that visual agnosia is in all cases due to an underlying impairment in visual perception have difficulty in explaining these results, as the visual processes mediating object recognition should also be utilized in the processing of faces and words if processing varies along a continuum from the encoding of non-decomposed perceptual wholes to the encoding of multiple perceptual parts. Faces are encoded as non-decomposed perceptual wholes and words as multiple perceptual parts. Hence an impairment to this continuum of perceptual processes, sufficient to disrupt the recognition of common objects, ought also to affect either face or word processing. Visual agnosia for objects should necessarily co-occur with either prosopagnosia or alexia. The case of Mr W demonstrates that this does not hold.

Separate Neural Processes for Objects, Words and Faces?

Rather than a two-process account of visual recognition, involving the coding of non-decomposed perceptual wholes and multiple parts, the data favour there being some differentiation within the neural structures subserving the recognition of particular types of visual stimuli in the brain; for example, recognition processes for objects can be separated from those for faces and printed words. This proposal meshes with recent results emerging from PET studies of visual processing. For example, Sergent and Signoret (1992) had subjects perform a number of tasks while blood flow was measured using PET techniques. In one task, subjects categorized familiar faces as being politicians or actors; in another they categorized objects as being either living or non-living. Subtracting the activity in the object categorization task from that in the face categorization task, they found significantly increased activity associated with the face identification task in the right fusiform gyrus, the right hippocampal gyrus, and the anterior temporal lobes of both hemispheres. For the object categorization task, there was enhanced activity in the lateral temporo-occipital region and the middle temporal gyrus of the left hemisphere. These data suggest substantial differences in the neural areas involved in face and object processing. In studies of visual word processing using PET, Petersen, Posner, and colleagues (e.g. Petersen et al., 1988, 1989; Posner, Petersen, Fox, & Raichle, 1988) have shown enhanced activity in the medial extrastriate visual cortex of the left hemisphere when subjects view words (over and above activity produced in a fixation-alone condition). This area is not activated by nonsense strings of letters (Petersen, Fox, Snyder, & Raichle, 1990), nor is it activated by auditory presentations of words (Petersen et al., 1988). Petersen et al. (1990) propose that the medial extrastriate cortex contains representations that respond differentially to letter strings that are orthographically regular—that is, according to some stored memory of the structural properties of the letter strings. Note that this region, presumably involved in visual access to lexical representations of words, is separate from the more lateral and anterior left-hemisphere regions subserving object categorization and from the right hemisphere systems mediating face identification, in Sergent and Signoret's (1992) study.

The PET studies indicate some degree of anatomical specialization in object, face, and visual word processing. However, the tasks that have been used so far have been relatively limited, as they may differ both in terms of their visual processing requirements as well as the types of stored knowledge stimuli need to access (e.g. living/non-living categorization of objects may be based on a relatively small set of visual features, whereas face identification may require processing of the relations between a range of visual features, in addition to differences in the knowledge sources involved). It is not clear whether the neural structures supporting the encoding of objects, faces, and words differ, or whether the differences are confined to accessing stored knowledge.

The data from Mr W extend these PET studies by clarifying that (at least) the memorial processes for visual recognition are separated for particular classes of stimuli. In particular, Mr W's difficulties were most strikingly apparent when stored visual knowledge about objects had to be contacted (Sections A and D). We have suggested that he had special difficulties in retrieving stored visual knowledge about common objects, and this held both when that knowledge had to be accessed from pictures and when it had to be accessed from words (e.g. as in the "Tails test", Experiment 15). However, he did not have difficulties gaining access to stored visual knowledge about words or faces, given his good on-line visual naming of these stimuli. From this, we argue that stored visual representations mediating object, face, and visual word recognition differ, so that a patient (such as Mr W) can have degenerate visual knowledge about objects while still showing good access to stored visual memories for faces and words, from visually presented faces and from print. Furthermore, it appears that the same visual knowledge for the particular class of stimulus (for objects, faces, or words, respectively) needs to be contacted both for on-line visual recognition and for many "off-line" tasks involving visual imagery and recall of the visual characteristics of objects (Riddoch et al., 1988). Hence patients with impaired stored visual knowledge will fail on tasks such as the "tails" test (Experiment 15) and when asked forced-choice questions about the visual characteristics of objects when given the object name (Experiment 10), when stored visual information needs to be retrieved from auditory input to support decision making.

Stored Visual and Stored Semantic Knowledge

In addition to a problem in accessing stored visual knowledge, from both vision and audition (object names), Mr W was also impaired at retrieving stored semantic knowledge about object function and inter-object associations from object names. For example, he performed at a subnormal level on semantic matching tests even with word stimuli (Experiment 11), and he was often unable to give precise verbal definitions about stimuli from their names. Semantic matching tests with word inputs do not necessarily require visual knowledge to be retrieved. For example, Riddoch and Humphreys (1987a) reported a patient who, like Mr W, had impaired access to stored visual knowledge from audition, but who nevertheless (and unlike Mr W) was able to carry out semantic matching tests with words. Mr W's problems with such tests points to there being a semantic impairment. However, there are three pieces of evidence indicating that this semantic impairment is not the sole cause of Mr W's problems in visual object recognition. (1) He showed a small but reliable advantage for semantic matching between printed words over that between pictures (Experiments 6 and 11). (2) His ability to retrieve visual knowledge from an object's name was worse than his ability to retrieve functional knowledge (Experiment 10). (3) There was no consistency between the items that he named when they were presented as line drawings (in Experiment 1) and the items he was able to define from their names (in Experiment 10), even though there was consistency between the items that were named when presented as line drawings on two different test occasions. This last result points to there being two different problems affecting Mr W's performance, with (for example) associative and functional knowledge for some objects being preserved even when stored visual knowledge is impaired. The data support the case for there being separate representations for stored visual knowledge and for stored semantic (associative and functional) knowledge about objects (e.g. Humphreys & Riddoch, 1993).

An extension of the above argument, for different forms of stored knowledge about objects, is the proposal that these forms of stored knowledge are differentiated according to the modality of input, as well as according to the nature of the information being represented (e.g. Warrington, 1975). For instance, stored visual knowledge may be separately represented for on-line visual object recognition and for memory retrieval from object names, if visual knowledge exists within an auditory-verbal semantic system as well as within a functionally independent visual semantic system. According to this account, Mr W has as many as three separate deficits. One is in stored visual knowledge within the visual semantic system, which differentially affects his on-line recognition of objects relative to when words are presented (Experiment 6, cf. Experiment 11). A second affects his retrieval of functional and associative knowledge from verbal input, given his below-normal performance when required to match semantically related words (Experiment 11). A third deficit affects his retrieval of stored visual knowledge within the auditory-verbal semantic system and is observed in his poor performance when given forced-choice questions about the visual characteristics of objects from their names (Experiment 10). The separation between stored visual semantic knowledge and auditory-verbal semantic knowledge is also supported by the lack of consistency between the items Mr W identified from vision and those he was able to define from their names.

This last—multiple semantics—account of Mr W's case is clearly less parsimonious than the account maintaining a distinction between stored visual and semantic knowledge, though the two accounts cannot be distinguished from the present data. For our present purposes this does not matter; the important point is that Mr W has impaired stored visual/visual-semantic knowledge about objects, which is additional to his impaired functional and associative/verbal-semantic knowledge, and which contributes to his poor visual object identification. This contrasts with his good visual processing of faces and printed words, indicating that stored visual/visual-semantic knowledge is differentiated according to the nature of the object, for objects, faces, and words.

Consistency, Category Specificity, and Hierarchical Theories

We have argued that Mr W had impaired stored visual knowledge about objects. In line with such an impairment to stored knowledge, Mr W showed item consistency in his visual identification performance; for instance, he tended to misidentify the same objects on different occasions (Experiment 1). Item consistency has been remarked on in several previous studies of patients with degenerative brain disease (e.g. Hodges, Salmon, & Butters, 1992) and has been attributed to loss of stored knowledge representations (Shallice, 1988; though see Humphreys et al., 1988, for an alternative account). Here we suppose that Mr W has suffered degenerative loss of stored visual and semantic representations for particular objects, which impairs recognition of those objects when they are visually presented on different test occasions.

Interestingly, Mr W also showed signs of category specificity within the classes of object that he failed to recognize visually. There are now numerous reports of patients having specific deficits in the recognition of some classes of visual object. Most typically, patients have difficulties in recognizing living things relative to non-living artefacts (e.g. Riddoch & Humphreys, 1987a; Sartori & Job, 1988; Sheridan & Humphreys, 1993; Silveri & Gainotti, 1988; Warrington & Shallice, 1984), though cases where patients have difficulty recognizing artefacts relative to living things have also been reported (Hillis & Caramazza, 1990; Sacchett & Humphreys, 1992). Amongst patients with cerebral atrophy, however, such cases are apparently rare (Hodges et al., 1992; though see McCarthy & Warrington, 1988, for one case). In Mr W's case, there is a consistent impairment, which tended to be larger for objects from categories with structurally similar exemplars; nevertheless, his good face recognition indicates that the effects of structural similarity were unlikely to be due to the visual complexity of the stimuli involved. An alternative possibility is that, in his case, degenerative changes have added "noise" to the process of retrieval from his visual memories for objects (but not to his retrieval of visual memories of faces). The addition of noise might be expected to disrupt memory retrieval most for objects with highly similar representations—for example, for stimuli belonging to categories with many visually similar exemplars (see Humphreys et al., 1988).

A final point concerns the distinction between "perceptual" and "memorial" disorders of visual object recognition, dating back to Lissauer (1890). We have argued that Mr W's impaired visual object recognition cannot be attributed to perceptual loss, given his good lexical identification of words and his intact face recognition. Rather, we suggest the presence of a memorial impairment that is selective to objects. This case, then, supports the hierarchical view of visual recognition that distinguishes apperceptive from associative disorders. Mr W has an associative disorder that prevents the retrieval of stored visual knowledge for some common objects.

REFERENCES

Balota, D.A., & Ferraro, F.R. (1993). A dissociation of frequency and regularity effects in pronunciation performance across young adults, older adults, and individuals with senile dementia of the Alzheimer Type. *Journal of Memory and Language, 32,* 573–592.

Bateman, A., Riddoch, M.J. & Humphreys, G.W. (in preparation) *Birmingham University neuropsychological screen (BUNS).*

Bay, E. (1953). Disturbances of visual perception and their examination. *Brain, 76,* 515–551.

Bender, M.B., & Feldman, M. (1972). The so-called "visual agnosias". *Brain, 95,* 173–186.

Biederman, I. (1987). Recognition by components: A theory of human image understanding. *Psychological review, 94,* 115–145.

Bub, D., Canceliere, A., & Kertesz, A. (1985). Whole-word and analytic translation of spelling to sound in a non-semantic reader. In K.E. Patterson, J.C. Marshall, & M. Coltheart (Eds.), *Surface dyslexia: Cognitive and neuropsychological studies of phonological reading.* Hove: Lawrence Erlbaum Associates Ltd.

Coltheart, M. (1985). Cognitive neuropsychology and the study of reading. In M.I. Posner & O.S.M. Marin (Eds.), *Attention and performance, XI.* Hove: Lawrence Erlbaum Associates Ltd.

De Renzi, E. (1986). Current issues in prosopagnosia. In H.D. Ellis, M.A. Jeeves, F. Newcombe, & A. Young (Eds.), *Aspects of face processing.* Dordrecht: Martinus Nijhoff.

Etcoff, N.L., Freeman, R., & Cave, K.R. (1992). Can we lose memories of faces? Content specificity and awareness in prosopagnosic. *Journal of Cognitive Neurosciene, 3* (1), 25–41.

Farah, M.J. (1990). *Visual agnosia: Disorders of object recognition and what they tell us about normal vision.* Cambridge, MA: MIT Press.

Farah, M.J. (1991). Patterns of co-occurrence among the associative agnosias: Implications for visual object representation. *Cognitive Neuropsychology, 8,* 1–19.

Funnell, E., & Sheridan, J. (1992). Categories of knowledge? Unfamiliar aspects of living and nonliving things. *Cognitive Neuropsychology, 9,* 135–153.

Goodglass, H., Barton, M.I., & Kaplan, E. (1968). Sensory modality and object naming in aphasia. *Journal of Speech and Hearing Research, 2,* 488–496.

Hillis, A., & Caramazza, A. (1990). Category-specific naming and comprehension impairment: A double dissociation. *Brain, 114,* 2081–2094.

Hinton, G.E., & Shallice, T. (1991). Lesioning an attractor network: Investigations of acquired dyslexia. *Psychological Review, 98,* 74–95

Hodges, J.J., Salmon, D.P., & Butters, N. (1991). The nature of the naming deficit in Alzheimer's and Huntingdon's disease. *Brain, 114,* 1547–1558.

Hodges, J.J., Salmon, D.P., & Butters, N. (1992). Semantic memory impairment in Alzheimer's disease: Failure of access or degraded representation? *Neuropsychologia, 30,* 301–314.

Holden, U.P. (Ed.) (1986). *Nostalgia: Famous faces.* Winslow: Winslow Press.

Humphreys, G.W., & Bruce, V. (1989). *Visual cognition: Computational, experimental and neuropsychological persepectives.* Hove: Lawrence Erlbaum Associates Ltd.

Humphreys, G.W., Freeman, T.A.C., & Müller, H.J. (1992). Lesioning a connectionist model of visual search: Selective effects on distractor grouping. *Canadian Journal of Psychology, 46,* 417–460.

Humphreys, G.W., & Riddoch, M.J. (1987a). The fractionation of visual agnosia. In G.W. Humphreys & M.J. Riddoch (Eds.), *Visual object processing: A cognitive neuropsychological appraoch.* Hove: Lawrence Erlbaum Associates Ltd.

Humphreys, G.W., & Riddoch, M.J. (1987b). *To see but not to see: A case study of visual agnosia.* Hove: Lawrence Erlbaum Associates Ltd.

Humphreys, G.W. & Riddoch, M.J. (1993). Object agnosias. In C. Kennard (Ed.), *Baillière's clinical neurology, Vol. 2.* London: Baillière Tindall.

Humphreys, G.W., Riddoch, M.J., & Quinlan, P.T. (1988). Cascade processes in picture identification. *Cognitive Neuropsychology, 5,* 67–103.

Kay, J., & Ellis, A.W. (1987). A cognitive neuropsychological case study of anomia: Implications for psychological models of word retrieval. *Brain, 110,* 613–629.

Kay, J., Lesser, R., & Coltheart, M. (1992). *PALPA.* Hove: Lawrence Erlbaum Associates Ltd.

Kucera, H., & Francis, W.N. (1967). *Computational analysis of present-day American English.* Providence RI: Brown University Press.

Lesser, R. (1978). *Linguistic investigation of aphasia.* London: Edward Arnold.

Lissauer, H. (1890). Ein fall von seelenblindheit nebst einem Beitrage zur Theorie derselben. *Archiv für Psychiatrie und Nervenkrankheiten, 21,* 222–270.

Marr, D. (1982). *Vision.* San Francisco, CA: W.H. Freeman.

McCarthy, R.A., & Warrington, E.K. (1986). Visual associative agnosia: A clinico-anatomical study of a single case. *Journal of Neurology, Neurosurgery and Psychiatry, 49,* 1233–1244.

McCarthy, R.A., & Warrington, E.K. (1988). Evidence of modality-specific meaning systems in the brain. *Nature, 334,* 428–430.

Morrison, C.M., Ellis, A.W., & Quinlan, P.T. (1992). Age of acquisition, not word frequency, affects object naming, not object recognition. *Memory and Cognition, 20,* 705–714.

Oldfield, R.C., & Wingfield, A. (1965). Response latencies in naming objects. *Quarterly Journal of Experimental Psychology, 17,* 273–281.

Petersen, S.E., Fox, P.T., Posner, M.I., Mintum, M., & Raichle, M.E. (1988). Positron emission tomographic studies of the cortical anatomy of single word processing. *Nature, 331,* 585–589.

Petersen, S.E., Fox, P.T., Posner, M.I., Mintum, M., & Raichle, M.E. (1989). Positron emission tomographic studies of the processing of single words. *Journal of Cognitive Neuroscience, 1,* 153–170.

Petersen, S.E., Fox, P.T., Snyder, A.Z., & Raichle, M.E. (1990). Activation of extra-striate and frontal cortical areas by visual words and word-like stimuli. *Science, 242,* 1041–1044.

Plaut, D.C., & Shallice, T. (1993a). Deep dyslexia: A case study of connectionist neuropsychology. *Cognitive Neuropsychology, 10,* 377–500.

Plaut, D.C., & Shallice, T. (1993b). Perseverative and semantic influences on visual object naming errors in optic aphasia: A connectionist account. *Journal of Cognitive Neuroscience, 5,* 89–117.

Posner, M.I., Petersen, S.E., Fox, P.T., & Raichle, M.E. (1988). Localization of cognitive operations in the human brain. *Science, 240,* 1627–1631.

Price, C.J., & Humphreys, G.W. (1992). Letter by letter reading? Functional deficits and compensatory strategies. *Cognitive Neupsychology, 9,* 427–457.

Rhodes, G, Brake, S., & Atkinson, A. (1993). What's lost in inverted faces? *Cognition, 42,* 25–57.

Riddoch, M.J., & Humphreys, G.W. (1987a). Visual object processing in optic aphasia: A case of semantic access agnosia. *Cognitive Neuropsychology, 4,* 131–185.

Riddoch, M.J., & Humphreys, G.W. (1987b). A case of integrative visual agnosia. *Brain, 110,* 1431–1462.

Riddoch, M.J. & Humphreys, G.W. (1993). *BORB: The Birmingham Object Recognition Battery.* Hove: Lawrence Erlbaum Associates Ltd.

Riddoch, M.J., Humphreys, G.W., Coltheart, M., & Funnell, E. (1988). Semantic systems or system? Neuropsychological evidence re-examined. *Cognitive Neuropsychology, 5* (1), 3–25.

Sacchett, C., & Humphreys, G.W. (1992). Calling a squirrel a squirrel but a canoe a wigwam: A category-specific deficit for artefactual objects and body parts. *Cognitive Neuropsychology, 9,* 73–86.

Sartori, G., & Job, R. (1988). The oyster with four legs: A neuropsychological study on the interaction of visual and semantic information. *Cognitive Neuropsychology, 5,* 150–132.

Seidenberg, M.S. (1992). Beyond orthographic depth in reading: Equitable division of labour. In R. Frost & L. Katz (Eds.), *Orthography, phonology, morphology, and meaning.* Amsterdam: Elsevier Science.

Seidenberg, M.S., Waters, G.S., Barnes, M.A., & Tanenhaus, M.K. (1984). When does irregular spelling or pronunciation influence word recognition? *Journal of Verbal Learning and Verbal Behavior, 23,* 383–404.

Sergent, J., & Signoret, J.L. (1992). Functional and anatomical decomposition of face processing: Evidence from prosopagnosia and PET study of normal subjects. In V. Bruce, A. Cowey, A.W. Ellis, & D.I. Perrett (Eds.), *Processing the facial image.* Oxford: Oxford University Press.

Shallice, T. (1988). *From neuropsychology to mental structure.* New York: Cambridge University Press.

Sheridan, J., & Humphreys, G.W. (1993). A verbal-semantic category-specific recognition impairment. *Cognitive Neurpsychology, 10,* 143–184.

Silveri, M.C., & Gainotti, G. (1988). Interaction between vision and language in category specific semantic impairment. *Cognitive Neurpsychology, 5,* 677–709.

Snodgrass, J.G., & Vanderwart, M. (1980). A standardised set of 260 pictures: Norms for name agreement, image agreement, familiarity and visual complexity. *Journal of Experimental Psychology: Human Perception and Performance, 6,* 174–215.

Tanaka, J.W., & Farah, M. (1993). Parts and wholes in face recognition. *Quarterly Journal of Experimental Psychology, 46A,* 225–245.

Vitkovitch, M., Humphreys, G.W., & Lloyd-Jones, T. (1993). On naming a giraffe a zebra: Picture naming errors across different object categories. *Journal of Experimental Psychology: Learning, Memory, and Cognition, 19,* 243–259.

Warrington, E.K. (1975). The selective impairment of semantic memory. *Quarterly Journal of Experimental Psychology, 27,* 635–657.

Warrington, E.K. (1982). Neuropsychological studies of object recognition. *Philosophical Transactions of the Royal Society of London, B298,* 15–33.

Warrington, E.K. (1985). Neuropsychological studies of object recognition. In G.W. Bruyn & H.L. Klawans (Eds.), *Handbook of clinical neurology.* Amsterdam: Elsevier Science.

Warrington, E.K., & Shallice, T. (1980). Word-form dyslexia. *Brain, 103,* 99–112.

Warrington, E.K., & Shallice, T. (1984). Category-specific semantic impairments. *Brain, 107,* 829–854.

Revised manuscript received 1 May 1994

APPENDIX A

We used the following criteria for classifying naming errors, adapted from the set of criteria used by Hodges et al. (1991) (essentially the criteria were the same, except that we collapsed over different categories of semantic naming error which were distinguished by Hodges et al.).

1. *Nonresponse:* includes don't knows and non-responses.
2. *Visual errors:* (a) responses that are visually similar to the target and from a different category (e.g. spear→snake); (b) whole-part responses, where subjects name part of the object as the whole (e.g. pyramid→block).
3. *Visual/semantic errors:* responses that are visually similar to the target and from the same category (e.g. donkey→horse).
4. *Semantic:* responses that were from the same category as the target but were clearly not visually similar (e.g. asparagus→lettuce); superordinate errors (dog→animal); associative errors (e.g. camel→desert; paintbrush→painting); circumlocutions (e.g. igloo→Eskimo's snow house).
5. *Phonemic:* mispronunciations or distortions of the target name sharing at least one syllable (e.g. igloo→iglow).
6. *Perseverations:* reutterances of a response (correct or incorrect) that had previously been used to name one of the previous five pictures.
7. *Unrelated:* where there was no clear connection between the target and the response.

APPENDIX B

Definitions of common objects used in Experiment 4 (naming auditory definitions).

1. A huge flying vehicle that carries a large number of people. [AEROPLANE]
2. A small, usually round, bit of bone or metal, for fastening, found on an article of clothing. [BUTTON]
3. A large four-footed animal with horns which moos and is used to produce milk. [COW]
4. A farmyard bird which makes a clucking noise and lays eggs. [CHICKEN]
5. A large African or Indian animal with a trunk and tusks. [ELEPHANT]
6. An appliance with a door found in the kitchen and used to keep the food cold. [FRIDGE]
7. A tool, with a wooden handle and an iron head, used to knock a nail into wood. [HAMMER]
8. An item of clothing, made of wool or felt, worn on the head out of doors. [HAT]
9. A thin tool with a pointed end used for writing with ink. [PEN]
10. A device, usually rounded and worn on the wrist, which measures time. [WATCH]

APPENDIX C

Verbal auditory definitions given by Mr W for 22 objects (Experiment 10).

Objects	*Responses*
NECKLACE	An article of adornment for a woman.
AXE	An item which might be found in the garage and used to chop anything.
CHISEL	A domestic article; a sculptor uses it.
GIRAFFE	It is not an English animal. I don't know what it looks like.
LIPS	You find them on the mouth.
TELEVISION	It is a thing that everyone has got and you see a picture on the screen.
FLY	An insect. You don't see very much of them these days.
ASHTRAY	For smokers to put ash on.
LION	It is not an English animal. It is ferocious and wild, as it is said in the poem.
CAMEL	It is not an English animal. It lives in Egypt and it is used to transport men and animals. I don't know what it looks like.
BEE	It is an insect; it buzzes, it is unpleasant and it makes honey. It is black.
BED	You go to sleep in it.
BLOUSE	It is a woman's article of clothes.
SQUIRREL	It is a domestic animal found in this country. It is very agile. I don't know what it looks like.
PLIERS	It is a domestic thing. I don't know what it is used for.
TIGER	It is an animal which does not live in this country, it lives in Egypt or in... . I forgot the name. It is a big dog.
AEROPLANE	It flies. It is used for flying. It looks like an aeroplane.
LEG	It is part of the body attached to the foot.
FOX	It is an animal which doesn't have a good reputation. It is whitish.
CORN	The breath of life. It is made into bread. It is yellow.
BOWL	It is for various uses. I don't know what it looks like.
BUTTON	It is a thing on clothes.

APPENDIX D

In this appendix we summarize Mr W's naming responses. The icon V means a correct response, the icon X an error. Here no distinction is made between different types of errors (i.e. semantic, visual, etc.).

	Experiment								
	1		2						
	I	II	I	II	3	6	7	8	14
aeroplane	V	V					V		
anchor						V	V		
ant							X		
apple						V			
armchair							V		
arrow						X			
artichoke							X		
ashtray	X	X					X		
asparagus							X		
axe	X	X					X		
baby carriage							X		
badger							X		
ball							X		
balloon							V		
barber wire								X	
barrel							V		
basket						V	V		
bath							V		
battery							X		
beacon							X		
bear	V	V			X		V		
bed	V	V					V		
bee	X	X					X		
beetle	V	X					V		
bell							V		
belt						X	V		
blouse	V	X					X		
boar							X		
book							V		
boot						X			
bottle							V		
bow						X	V		
bowl	V	V					V		
box								V	
bread								V	
bridle						X			
broom	V	V					V		
brush							V		
bus							V		
butterfly							V		
button	X	X				X	X		
cage								X	

	Experiment								
	1		2						
	I	II	I	II	3	6	7	8	14
cake								V	
camel	X	X					V		V
can opener			X	X					
candle						V			
canoe						X			
canon								X	
cap							V		
car battery								X	
carrot	V	V				V	V		
cat	V	V					V		
caterpillar							X		
celery	X	X					X		
cheese								V	
cherry								X	
chicken	V	X					V		
chimney								X	
chimpanzee							X		
chin							X		
chisel	X	X					X		
church								V	
clock	V	V					V		
coat						X	V		
coconut								X	
coffee pot								X	
comb						V	V		
corn	X	X					X		
cow	X	X			X	X	X		X
crab						X		X	
crocodile					X				
crown						X			
cup	V	V	X				V		
daffodil								X	
dancer								V	
dart								X	
deer	X	X					X		X
desk								V	
dice				V					
dinosaur I					X				
dinosaur II					X				
doctor								X	
dog	V	V					V		X
donkey									X
door							V		
doorknob	X	X					X		
dress							V		
drill								X	

| | Experiment | | | | | | | | |
| | 1 | | 2 | | | | | | |
	I	II	I	II	3	6	7	8	14
drum	V	V					V		
duck									X
ear							V		
elephant	V	V			V		V		
envelope							V		
eye						V		V	
finger								X	
fireworks								X	
flowerpot						X			
fly	V	V					X		
foot								V	
football							V		
fork							X		
fox	X	X					X		
French horn							V		
fridge	X	X						V	
frying pan								X	
garbage can								V	
giraffe	V	X					X		X
girl								X	
glass				V			V		
glasses						V	V		
glove							V		
goat									X
goldfish-bowl								X	
gorilla	X	X					X		
gown						X			
grandfather clock									V
grasshopper							X		
green house								X	
guinea pig							X		
guitar							V		
gun								V	
hairbrush				V		V			
hammer			V	V					
hammock						V			
hat						V			
hedgehog							X		
helicopter	X	X					V		
hinge								X	
hippopotamus					X				
hoe						X			
horse	V	V			V	V	V		V
horseshoe						V		X	
hose						X			
house						V		V	

| | Experiment | | | | | | | | |
| | 1 | | 2 | | | | | | |
	I	II	I	II	3	6	7	8	14
hutch								V	
ironing board							X		
jelly								X	
jug								V	
kangaroo	V	V					V	V	V
kettle	V	V					V	V	
key			V	V					
kite	V	V				X	V	V	
knife			V	V		V		V	
ladder						V			
ladybird							X		
lamp							V		
leek							X		
leg	V	X				V	V	V	
lemon	X	X				X	V	V	
leopard							X		
lettuce	X	X					X	X	
light bulb								V	
lighter				X					
lion	X	V					X	X	X
lips	V	V					V	V	
lipstick						X		X	
llama							X		
lobster						X			
lock	X	X						X	
logs						X			
lorry							V		
matches								V	
measuring jug			X	X					
mirror			V	V					
mitten							X		
mole							X		
monkey							V		
motorcycle							V		
mountain							X		
mouse	V	V						V	
mug						X			
mushroom	V	V						V	
nail	V	V						V	
nail file							X		
necklace	V	V						V	
needle						X			
nest								X	
nose								X	
notepad								V	
nut	X	X						X	

| | *Experiment* | | | | | | | | |
| | 1 | | 2 | | | | | | |
	I	II	I	II	3	6	7	8	14
octopus							X		
onion	X	X						X	
orange	V	V				V		X	
otter							X		
owl	V	V						V	
oyster								X	
paintbrush			X	X		X			
palm tree						X			
panda					X		X		
paper clip			X						
parachute						X			
peach							X		
peacock							V		
peanut								X	
pear	X	X						X	
pen				V					
pencil	V	X						V	
penguin					X				
pepper	X	X						X	
picture						V			
pie								X	
pig					V		V		V
pipe	V	V		V		V		V	
plane								X	
plate								X	
pliers	X	X						X	
plug								X	
poodle							V		
potato	V	X						V	
pram						V			
pumpkin							X		
rabbit	V	X						V	X
radio						X			
rake						V			
razor			V	X			V		
rhino	X	X			X			X	
rifle								V	
ring	X	V						V	
ring master								X	
roast chicken								X	
rocking chair								V	
roller skate							X		
rolling pin							X		
ruler	V	V						V	
safe								X	
salt cellar	V	X	V	V				V	

| | Experiment | | | | | | | | |
| | 1 | | 2 | | | | | | |
	I	II	I	II	3	6	7	8	14
sandwich								V	
saucepan						V			
saw							V		
scissors	V	V	V	V					V
screw	V	X				X		X	
screwdriver				V					X
sea horse							X		
seal					X				
sheep	V	V			V			V	X
shoe	V	V				V		V	
skirt							V		
slipper								V	
snail							V		
snake						V	V		V
snowman							V		
sofa						V	V		
spider	V	V				X		V	
spoon			V	V				V	
squirrel	V	V						V	V
stamp						V			
steps						V			
stirrup						X			
stool	V	V				V		V	
stove	X	X						X	
strawberry	V	V						V	
suitcase								V	
swan									V
sweater								X	
sword						V	V		
table							V		
tap								X	
television	V	V				V		V	
thimble	V	X							
thistle								X	
thumb						V		X	
tie								V	
tiger	V	V						V	X
toaster	X	X						X	
toe								X	
tomato								X	
toothbrush			V	V					
toothpaste								X	
torch			X	X					
tortoise					V				V
traffic light								X	
train							V		

| | \| Experiment | | | | | | | | |
| | I | | 2 | | | | | | |
	I	II	I	II	3	6	7	8	14
trousers								V	
trowel								X	
trumpet							V		
turtle								X	
underpants						X			
vase	V	V						V	
violin							X		
wall						V			
watch								V	
watering can								V	
watermelon								X	
web								X	
well							V		
wheel						X	V		
whistle			X				X		
window							V		
wine glass								V	
wool						X		X	
zebra	V	V						V	V
zip							X		

VISUAL COGNITION, 1994, *1* (2/3), 227–251

Masking of Faces
by Facial and Non-facial Stimuli

Nicholas P. Costen and John W. Shepherd

University of Aberdeen, Aberdeen, U.K.

Hadyn D. Ellis

University of Wales College of Cardiff, Cardiff, U.K.

Ian Craw

University of Aberdeen, Aberdeen, U.K.

A visual masking technique was used as a tool to study the recognition of well-known faces. Famous faces, but unknown masks were used. The visual relation between target and mask was varied; the effect was measured in terms of the thresholds for reports of "familiarity" and the ability to name the target. Three experiments are reported, all of which employed a backward-masking paradigm. The target and mask had equal display times, and there was no interstimulus interval. Significant masking was found with face masks but none from either object or noise masks. Intermediate levels of masking were found from faces that were inverted, jumbled, or had their inner features removed. The third experiment found that face masks that were similar to the targets had an effect equal to dissimilar ones. In all three experiments no interaction was found between the type of mask and the thresholds for the familiarity and naming criteria. The results are

Requests for reprints should be sent to Ian Craw, Department of Mathematical Sciences, University of Aberdeen, Aberdeen AB9 2TY, U.K.

The research was supported by ESRC / MRC / SERC Joint Council Initiative in Cognitive Science and Human-Computer Interaction: 9002054 to Dr. I.G. Craw, Professor H.D. Ellis and Mr. J.W. Shepherd.

This work arose from the ESRC Face Recognition Programme (XC15250001 to Vicki Bruce at Nottingham University; XC15250002 to Ian Craw at Aberdeen University; XC15250003 to Hadyn Ellis at University of Wales College of Cardiff; XC15250004 to Andy Ellis and Andy Young at Lancaster University; XC15250005 to David Perrett at St Andrews University).

discussed in terms of information-processing models of face recognition, suggesting that masking occurs within the visual coding system but after categorization as a face. They also suggest that symbolic description as faces occurs rather later than has been sometimes assumed.

A considerable amount of effort has been put into decomposing the face recognition process into a number of sub-processes, with most emphasis upon the determination of identity once a representation of the face has been obtained. A number of models of these processes have been constructed (e.g. H. Ellis, 1983, 1986; Hay & Young, 1982; Rhodes, 1985a), that proposed by Bruce and Young (1986) being the most widely used. In terms of recognition, this model proposes three major stages. The first is the structural encoding of the face, in which a particular view of a face is converted into a generalized representation. The second stage consists of the face recognition units, which, by signalling the similarity of the input face to the set of known faces, allows familiarity judgments to be made. The third level, that of the person identity nodes, connects the knowledge of familiarity of the *face* derived from the face recognition units with other sources of information (biographical episodic information) to allow the retrieval of information about the person; and, finally, the retrieval of the person's name takes place.

Although a number of techniques have been used to test this model, surprisingly little use has been made of the method of visual masking—the phenomenon observed when the recognition threshold for a perceptual object is raised by the presence of another (Kolers, 1983). Although it offers one of the most effective ways of studying the nature of the representations as well as the types of processing that occur at different stages within the face recognition system, it has been notably neglected as a tool for the investigation of these processes in recent years. Although priming of faces has been used to consider similar issues (Bruce & Valentine, 1985; A. Ellis, Young, Flude, & Hay, 1987), masking has the advantage, perhaps, of allowing one to observe factors that immediately interact. It is unlikely that these problems of the nature of representation and processing could be so easily studied using the longer time-spans necessary for priming. This paper attempts to show that useful information can be determined on such processing characteristics by a study of the amount of masking induced by different types of mask and argues that the masking seen between faces reflects the operation of a face-specific process, separate from the general object recognition system.

Although masking in face recognition has been relatively neglected, a small number of papers have used this technique and most experiments were performed before the advent of formal models of face recognition. Calis, Sterenborg, and Maarse (1984) showed pairs of faces, each of which was known to the subject. The faces varied in identity, pose (right or left three-quarter view), and the features present (spectacles or no spectacles). The subject chose which face to identify on each trial. It was found that there was a significant tendency to identify the second picture over the first one (referred to as *recency*), and this tendency was increased when the poses of the faces were the same and when the stimulus onset asynchrony (SOA) was longer. More importantly, the interaction between pose, recency, and SOA was significant, as was the four-way interaction among all the factors. When the pose of the two faces was identical, there was a greater tendency to identify the second image with increasing SOA, and this was further enhanced when the images either both wore or did not wear spectacles.

These results were interpreted in terms of a perceptual model involving "microgenesis", suggesting that the first picture activated a schema for face recognition that gave the pose of the head, and that processing of the second picture then started from the latest stage the first picture had reached. One consequence of this putative process was that the underlying tendency to shift from identifying the first face to identifying the second face with increasing SOA was enhanced when the faces had the same pose. Bachmann (1989) confirmed this by displaying pairs of frontal faces drawn from a set of eight photographs normalized so that the features overlapped, for 3 msec, with a SOA of between 20 and 160 msec. A highly symmetric forward- and backward-masking function was found, with the first stimulus being preferred at short SOAs and the second at long SOAs.

This method has also been exploited by Moscovitch and Radzins (1987; see also Bruyer, 1988; Moscovitch, 1988) in attempting to discover the nature of the visual information used to recognize faces and the laterality of the process. They used backward masking with either a jumbled face, random dots, or random dots clustered to form stripes of different spatial frequencies. Right-handed subjects were shown the targets (for between 2 and 16 msec), and the mask (50 msec) in each visual field and the inter-stimulus interval (ISI) was altered until a threshold was reached. With the jumbled face mask, responses to stimuli falling in the left visual field were 8 msec faster than to those in the right visual field, and the relationship between ISI and target duration indicated interrupt masking for the face mask. In contrast, the relationship for noise masks indicated integrative masking and revealed no hemispheric difference. This pattern of results was taken as evidence that whereas the early, energy-dependent stages of face-processing are hemispherically symmetric, the later, information-specific stages are asymmetric with a preference for the right hemisphere. This confirmed the results of Moscovitch, Scullion, and Christie (1976), who found a right-hemisphere advantage when matching judgements between faces that could not be made on a purely visual basis.

Moscovitch and Radzins (1987) also used different spatial frequencies to mask faces. No interaction between mask spatial frequency and hemisphere was found, and the relationship between threshold ISI and the target duration indicated integration masking. However there was a small, consistent, effect of visual field. The findings of Keenan, Witman, and Pepe (1989) appeared to contradict this when faces were shown with spatial-frequency masks. They found significant main effects on correct identification rate due to spatial frequency and visual field, with the right visual field having fewer errors. There was also a significant interaction between these effects, with the highest number of errors for the left visual field at 1.6 cycles/face, and the largest number of errors for the right visual field at 38.4 cycles/face. Keenan et al. (1989) suggested that the differences between these results could be explained by reference to the higher intensity of mask used by Moscovitch and Radzins (1987), which might be inducing intensity masking rather than pattern masking.

The major problem with these previously gathered results is that they can be fitted into a model such as Bruce and Young (1986) at almost any level. Consider the situation investigated by Calis et al. (1984) where two faces are presented together, each of which was known to the subject, spatially overlapping, and with a range of temporal relationships. A reduction in the amount of identification was obtained, but it is not apparent from the result at which level the traces are interacting. At the lowest "contour" level all that is important are the local overlaps of intensity changes in the image. Within the Bruce and Young (1986) model, a change in identification could be due to interference at the structural encoding level. Alternatively, face recognition units could be mutually interfering. Here the faces would be interacting as faces rather than as collections of parts. The presence of two face traces could stop one predominating and forming an unequivocal input to the person identity nodes. A third option is that interference occurs later, at the level of person identity nodes. According to the Burton, Bruce, and Johnston (1990) interactive activation (IAC) version of the model, this interference operates via the semantic information nodes associated with the face, which have bi-directional excitatory connections with the person identity nodes but inhibitory connections between each other. As a consequence, the faces may be fully represented, but the persons may not be recognized and named. At any of these levels, altering the relationship between the faces may alter the tendency to recognize the first or second face. Much the same can be said for the results published by Moscovitch et al. (1976) and Keenan et al. (1989); these data may suggest the presence of a distinction between energy-dependent and object processing of faces, but it is not clear exactly how this interacts with the distinctions derived from cognitive models.

This difficulty in interpreting previous results in terms of the theories currently used to explain face recognition can be attributed to at least four major difficulties that arise in these studies. The first concerns the number of images used, which is small. It is known that repetition priming of faces is extensive (A. Ellis, 1992), long-lasting, and may exhibit pattern completion (Brunas, Young, & A. Ellis, 1990; Brunas-Wagstaff, Young, & A. Ellis, 1992). As a consequence, it is possible that the repeated use of a small set of faces, as employed by Calis et al. (1984), Bachmann (1989), and Moscovitch and Radzins (1987), will potentially alter the manner or amount of processing of the masking faces. In particular, it is possible that under conditions where a small set of faces is repeatedly presented, the subject will move from recognizing the face by the configuration of features present to recognizing the image by a particular set of features it may exhibit. These problems can best be addressed with facilities to run a tachistoscope experiment with several hundred different distracting stimuli; the required equipment, however, has only recently become readily available. Second, apart from the explicitly face-masking studies (Calis et al., 1984; Bachmann, 1989), the only use of non-simultaneous masking, or paracontrast, is by Moscovitch and Radzins (1987). As an asymmetric, interrupt masking curve is likely to show little or no masking at a zero SOA (Breitmeyer, 1984), this procedure will predispose the studies to find integration masking alone. As a consequence, these studies may well have over-estimated the importance of non-specific intensity masking and underestimated the importance of masking by objects. Third, none has entailed full comparative tests of the different effects of types of masks. At most, two or three have been used; as such, it is not possible to say with confidence that the masking demonstrated reflects face processing, rather than image or object processing. A fourth difficulty is the type of response used to measure recognition; the subjects "identified" faces or did two-alternative forced-choice tasks. Thus it is not clear to which processing level these responses could be attributed.

In this paper, we attempt to demonstrate that, despite these problems, it is possible to localize the masking of a face to a particular level in the face-processing system—most probably the structural encoding level. This would suggest that the processing of faces is a separate system from that which is used for recognizing other images. To do this, we need to compare the masking effect of faces with that of well-known objects that are not faces. Subjects were run with a variety of types of masks comprising a face, an object other than a face, an unstructured noise mask, and no mask. Apart from the last two conditions, the subjects never saw the same masking slide twice, so they were not primed by them to behave in an abnormal manner, although there may have been some effect upon overall thresholds. A variable-SOA, constant-ISI design was used, with a feedback system in which SOA was varied in order to ensure an accuracy of 50%. As the system will move to a position where 50% recognition occurred, this ensured that, independent of the shape of the graph relating the degree of masking and the SOA, both interrupt and integration masking would be detected should they occur. Separate thresholds were found both for the recognition of the targets and for their names.

EXPERIMENT 1

Method

Subjects

A total of 28 subjects was used. All the subjects were undergraduate or postgraduate students at the University of Aberdeen. They were paid for their time.

Equipment

Images of faces were captured using an Imaging Technology FG100V framegrabber card fitted to a Sun 3/160M. The framegrabber had a 1024 × 1024-pixel frame buffer that was 12 bits deep, with a maximum of 512 × 512 pixels accessible or visible at any one time. A monochrome Hitachi CCTV camera was used to collect the images used in the experiment; the video source was digitized to 8 bits in frame time. The images were displayed on a Phillips 35cm fast-phosphor monitor. A device driver was implemented for the framegrabber, allowing it to be used as both an input and output device. In particular, it was possible to digitize, store, and manipulate images of faces and then display them on the monitor screen for precise amounts of time, in multiples of 20 msec. This lower limit was provided by the refresh rate of the monitor, and to achieve it the image-display times were manipulated in half-scans. The monitor had an interlaced display, alternately scanning odd- and even-numbered rows. To allow the manipulation of the display in 20 msec units, only the odd or the even rows were scanned on a single frame. The minimum time for which images were displayed was 20 msec, and thus at this level the time to draw the image was the same as the measured display time. The experiment was administered and controlled from a Sun workstation using a combination of compiled C programs and executable shell scripts under Sun UNIX.

Stimuli

Targets. The camera and the framegrabber were used to digitize six target photographs, which were selected from a variety of magazines. Steps were taken to ensure that these pictures were as similar as possible to those previously collected at Aberdeen University for work on the construction of the facial retrieval and matching equipment (FRAME) database of face measurements and ratings (Shepherd, 1986; H. Ellis et al., 1989). The parameters standardized were pose, expression, and clothing, and we also ensured that there were no physical cues to indicate which were targets and which distractors; in particular, the mean and range of luminance values were controlled. The matching of the nature of the images was helped by the relatively low quality induced by the small size of the images. The images used for the experiment were in black and white and reduced to a resolution of 64 × 64 pixels at 8 bits per pixel. The images were placed within a black background of 128 × 128 pixels, thus effectively halving the monitor size. This was carried out to ensure that the whole image could be perceived at one glance. The targets' names are listed in Appendix A.

Masks. More than 600 full-face, high-quality colour photographs of male faces bearing neutral expressions were digitized as grey-scale images. These faces were standardized for the position and spacing of the eyes and then stored on disk at a resolution of 256 × 256 pixels at 8 bits per pixel. The photographs came from the FRAME database. These photographs had been taken some ten years before the date of the experiment, and steps were taken to exclude individuals with whom the subjects might have come into contact.

More than 120 pictures of non-face objects were taken from a variety of magazines and books, and the same precautions operated as with the target faces. Care was taken to ensure that the images came from a range of basic categories (e.g. furniture, household ornaments, and clocks) and that they were all approximately the same size and brightness as the heads used as the other distractors. A total of 96 non-face images were used, as were 96 different face masks; the subject only saw each mask once. In the no-mask condition the place of the mask was taken by a grey field of the same brightness as the mean of the target images. This was constructed artificially, using the HIPS image-processing package (Landy, Cohen, & Sperling, 1984). The noise mask was constructed with HIPS, using random pixel values across the whole field. It had the same mean brightness as the targets and also the same mean contrast as the targets but no structure. A set of examples of the masks used is provided in Figure 1.

Procedure

The images were presented in randomly selected pairs, with stimulus-on time as the controlled variable and no ISI. Mask display time was equal to target display time and thus varied across trials. The thresholds for recognition and then naming were determined by a double-random staircase (Cornsweet, 1962; Rose, Teller, & Rendleman, 1970). This essentially employs the methods of ascending and descending limits in a random order. Thus it starts by displaying

FIG. 1.   Examples of masks used in Experiment 1 (from left to right): No mask, Noise Mask, Non-Face Object (a locket), and Face Mask.

stimuli at a sub-threshold and a supra-threshold level—in this case with stimulus duration times of 20 msec and 140 msec, respectively—and increases the stimulus strength following incorrect responses and decreases this following correct responses. In this case, 20 msec was either added or subtracted from the stimulus duration. There were 12 trials on each staircase, so each target was displayed twice. There was an equal number of "catch" trials, which were identical to the target trial (including the appropriately calculated display times), except that an unknown image was substituted for the target. The order of presentation of the targets, the staircase from which each trial was drawn, and whether the catch trial on each trial preceded or followed the target trial were all set randomly for each subject.

Subjects were randomly assigned to the conditions from the order in which they presented. Each started by checking a list of names, which included the targets as well as similar well-known men. They were asked to tick the name of each person they would recognize if they met in the street. The subjects were then told that the experiment concerned how long it took to recognize faces, and that they would be seeing pairs of faces (or as appropriate), and that some of the faces first in each pair should be known to them, being drawn from the list. The subjects were asked to say when someone was displayed whom they found familiar. The distinction between this ("a sense that you have seen this person before") and naming was stressed. The presence (but not the number) of catch trials was made clear, as was the chance of not seeing a trial if they blinked or failed to fixate at the critical moment. They were told that if this happened, they could have the trial repeated. The subjects were then seated 1 m from the monitor screen, and a short practice session was run, which involved recognizing a woman (Anneka Rice, a television presenter), among other pictures of women or the mask appropriate to the condition. The threshold for familiarity was then determined. Each trial started when the subjects acknowledged that they were ready and was triggered by the experimenter. The subjects first saw a blank, white screen, then a black fixation point on a white background for 1 sec, a blank screen for 1 sec, the target or catch stimulus and its mask, and then the blank white screen again. The subject then gave a verbal response. This sequence of images, from a representative trial, is shown in Figure 2.

After the determination of the familiarity threshold, the subjects had a short rest, in which the second half of the experiment, involving naming the target, was explained. This ran in the same way, with the same targets and distractor-types, but positive responses were scored when the subjects either gave the name of the target or provided some alternatively unique semantic identification (i.e. a piece of information that would identify the target as accurately as his name would). As an example, the subjects were told that "John Major" and "the Prime Minister" were equally acceptable alternatives. This procedure accepts the Burton and Bruce (1992) suggestion that there is no structural difference between the process of naming someone and that of retrieving other information

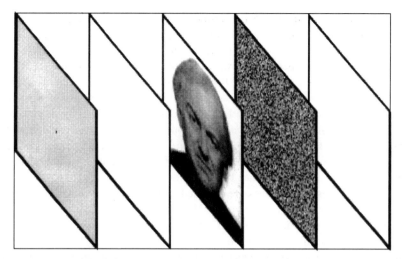

FIG. 2.   A representative trial: Fixation point, blank, target (John Thaw), noise mask, blank shown until next trial.

about him. The name threshold was then run and the false alarms of the subject recorded, with the stimulus that had given rise to them. The subjects were then paid and debriefed.

Results

The use of a staircase technique ensures that the mean or median value display times for the later part of the data will correspond with the threshold for recognition. The negative-feedback response of the system ensures that the subject will converge to the 50% recognition point (Cornsweet, 1962). One problem with this method is that there is inevitably confounding between the number of the targets known to the subject and the threshold for recognition that is found: Subjects who know few people will have higher thresholds than those who know many. This was partly reduced by only testing those individuals who marked three or more of the targets' names as known to them in the pre-testing questionnaire. To reduce this effect further, it was decided to remove those data referring to targets who were never named or recognized by the subject. As the display time will have had to be increased during the periods when such individuals are displayed, this manipulation reduces the measured recognition threshold in those cases where a number of targets were not recognized at all, while not affecting those cases where they were all recognized at some point. This was done individually for the two criteria and reduced the total number of available observations from 1344 to 1039. Thus each threshold for each subject contains approximately 3 observations of each target after the removal of targets that the subject consistently failed to recognize.

The logarithmic transform of the display times was taken, and the median values for each criterion of familiarity and naming for each subject were found for all those observations left after following the procedures above. Thus the exclusion of unrecognized targets did not affect the total number of observations entering the analysis, while taking the logarithmic transform reduced the marked heterogeneity of variance seen in the un-transformed data. As a staircase starts from a set pair of extremes, the first few responses of each subject are established by the values chosen by the experimenter, not the response made. In order to give time for the subject to converge upon a stable value, only the second half of the data for each criterion were analysed. The mid-point of each half of the staircase was found and the data beyond it used.

The two types of response were analysed individually as it was felt that it was impossible to provide a useful mean. The means and standard errors of the conditions are provided in Figure 3. There was a significant effect of type of mask for the familiarity criterion, $F(3, 24) = 26.31$, $p < 0.0001$. A post-hoc Tukey HSD test showed that this could be attributed to a difference between the face mask and the other masks, which did not themselves differ significantly. There was also a significant effect of type of mask for the naming criterion, $F(3, 24) = 12.23$, $p = 0.0001$. A Tukey HSD showed that this reflected the same

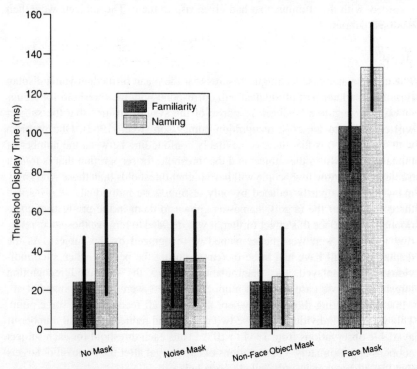

FIG. 3.   Mean thresholds (msec), with standard errors, found in Experiment 1.

pattern. A two-level within-subject ANOVA was performed between the two response criteria; this showed that there was a significant difference between the mean thresholds for familiarity and naming, $F(1, 27) = 5.63$, $p = 0.0250$.

The false-alarm rate was also considered—false alarms being scored on those occasions when the subject said "yes" or named an individual on a catch trial—and a percentage false-alarm rate was calculated for each subject and criterion. The error rates were in general very low. The mean false-alarm rates were 9.75% (SD 12.45%) for familiarity, and 1.88% (SD 5.00%) for naming. The absence of any false alarms from the naming criterion in the no-mask and noise mask conditions meant that there was a strong correlation between the group means and standard deviations, which could not be notably reduced by transformations. For this reason it was felt inappropriate to apply parametric statistics to these data. A Wilcoxon matched-pairs signed-ranks test between the familiarity and naming criteria (using average weights for ties) showed that there were more false alarms for the familiarity judgements than for naming, $T_+ = 47$, $n = 28$, $p = 0.0051$. Kruskal-Wallis non-parametric ANOVAs showed that there were no differences in the false alarm rates of different mask types for the familiarity judgements, $H(3) = 0.62$, $p = 0.8919$, nor were there differences for naming, $H(3) = 4.51$, $p = 0.2112$.

Discussion

This experiment suggests that although there is a significant effect of masking when faces are shown in close spatio-temporal contiguity, this is not a consequence of an energy-dependent visual masking process. Nor is it due to an interaction at an object-recognition level. If it were, a significant amount of masking would be expected from objects other than faces, and this was not found. However, our result gives no information as to whether the process producing the masking is located before or after this object-recognition level. The masking in the face condition could be due to specific overlaps between the target images and the contours of the masks. Alternatively, the interaction may occur within the face-processing system, owing to an interaction between complete faces. If the masking does operate within the face-processing system, it must do so before decisions of identity are made, as the pattern of masking was the same for the familiarity and naming criteria. The requirement for a consistently longer display time for naming than for recognition accords with the existence of independent, successive decision-making units, requiring different amounts of information, as well as with a single unit where the subject uses two different response criteria for the two responses. The masking must be operating before such a level is reached for there to be no interaction between type of mask and the type of response made.

The methodology used favours the suggestion that these results can be interpreted in terms of relatively natural dedicated face recognition processes. The subjects were not told the identity of the set of targets. Thus, to preserve optimal performance, they had to be prepared on any trial to recognize as known a face that they had not seen before in the experiment. Furthermore, the images used as masks and "false targets" in the catch trials were not repeated. Thus any strategy of determining identity by recognizing particular features of the targets would give sub-optimal performance, as it would lead to both false alarms and false rejections. A recognition strategy of such a critical feature type would also predict no difference between the thresholds for familiarity and naming. If anything, higher thresholds would be expected for familiarity; the unbalanced design means that subjects would tend to search for critical features to use on subsequent trials.

These two possible descriptions of the nature of this masking could be distinguished by considering the difference in the amount of masking between face masks and patterns. Although these patterns are not faces, they should have characteristics that make them very close to being faces. There are a number of different possible important relationships between the images, and these require different pattern masks to distinguish them. The masking effect may be due either to some general pattern masking, or to the characteristics of the process of finding features in the face. These twin possibilities can be contrasted by using a mask made of features of a face that have been jumbled so that they no longer form a face, although they still fill the same area and shape. This second outcome needs to be considered in combination with the possibility that the masking depends upon the extraction of configural information about the shape of the second face. This configural information is known to be disrupted by the use of inverted faces (Bruce, Doyle, Dench, & Burton, 1991; Rhodes, Brake, & Atkinson, 1993). A final outcome is that the different facial features may be of differential importance: it is possible either that masking depends upon the presence of a recognizable set of inner features (Ellis, Shepherd, & Davies, 1979) or that an outline or contour of the face is important (Fraser, Craig, & Parker, 1990). These two latter possibilities were tested by measuring the amount of masking obtained when the facial features were obscured but the outline of the face was intact.

Thus another experiment was performed with four different conditions: an intensity mask, a pattern mask formed by destroying the structure of the face, an inverted face, and a face with the internal features jumbled.

EXPERIMENT 2

Method

Subjects

A total of 28 subjects was used. All the subjects were undergraduate or postgraduate students at the University of Aberdeen. They were paid for their time.

Equipment

This was as in Experiment 1.

Stimuli

These were from the same source as those used in Experiment 1.

The target images were the same as those used in Experiment 1. The jumbled, inner-jumbled, and inverted images were formed from the same images used as masks in Experiment 1.

The jumbled images were formed by manipulating as 128×128 pixel images the FRAME distractors, using the HIPS image-processing package. For the jumbled images, the portion of the image including the face was cut into 28 squares, each of which measured 16×16 pixels, which were then randomly re-assembled differently for each face. The inverted and inner-jumbled images were also formed by manipulating the same images with the HIPS image-processing package. For the inner-jumbled images, the portion of the image including the central portion of the face was cut into 28 squares, each of which measured 8×8 pixels, which were then randomly re-assembled in different arrangements for each face. The intensity mask was set to the maximum value possible given the equipment. This was measured with an SEI photometer and found to be 1.6 *log foot-lamberts*, compared with 1.3 *log foot-lamberts* for the other masks and the targets. A set of examples of the masks used are provided in Figure 4.

Procedure

This was the same as in Experiment 1.

Results

The data points were transformed in the same way as those relating to Experiment 1. This reduced the total number of available observations from 1680 to 1225, and the means and standard deviations of the conditions are

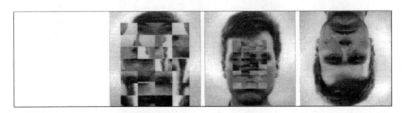

FIG. 4.   Examples of masks used in Experiment 2 (from left to right): Intensity Mask, Jumbled Face, Inner-Jumbled Face, and Inverted Face Mask.

provided in Figure 5. The data gathered from the "face" condition of Experiment 1 were also included in the analysis as a reference value. This was made possible by the completely between-subjects design. A one-way ANOVA showed that there was a significant effect of type of mask for the familiarity criterion, $F(4, 30) = 5.41$, $p = 0.0021$. A post-hoc Tukey HSD test showed that the conditions fell into two groups, which did not vary significantly within themselves. The face mask produced a significantly higher threshold than did the intensity mask, but the inner-jumbled, inverted face and the jumbled masks were not significantly different from either of these conditions.

There was also a significant effect of type of mask for the naming criterion, $F(4, 30) = 4.73$, $p = 0.0044$. A post-hoc Tukey HSD test showed that, once again, the data separated into two groups: the face mask had a significantly higher threshold than did the intensity and inverted face mask, but again the inner-jumbled and jumbled faces conditions were not significantly different from the other conditions. A two-item within-subjects ANOVA was performed

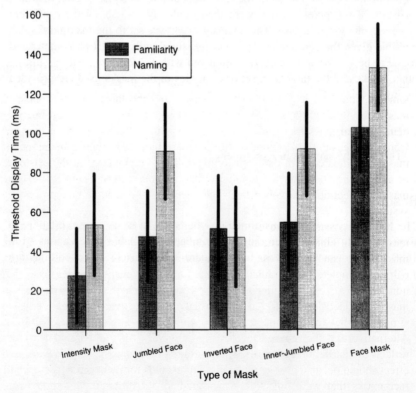

FIG. 5.   Mean thresholds (msec), with standard errors found in Experiment 2. This figure included the mean thresholds for the face mask condition from Experiment 1 for comparison.

on the means of the two criteria, and this showed that there was a higher threshold for naming than for familiarity judgements, $F(1, 34) = 12.35$, $p = 0.0013$.

Inspection of Figure 5 reveals that the inverted face mask has a negative familiarity-naming difference; for all the other masks, this difference was positive. Notwithstanding the reservations concerning the use of pooled measures with this design, a 2×5 ANOVA was performed upon the data. This showed that there was no significant Type of Mask $\times$ Response Criterion interaction, $F(4, 30) = 1.67$, $p = 0.1832$.

The false alarm rates were also analysed. The mean error rates were 12.99% for familiarity (SD 18.21%) and 3.78% for naming (SD 9.92%). These data were treated in the same way as those in Experiment 1 and subjected to non-parametric statistics. A Wilcoxon matched-pairs signed-ranks test showed that there was a significant difference in false-alarm rates between the familiarity and naming criteria, $T_+ = 71$, $n = 35$, $p = 0.0061$. Kruskal-Wallis non-parametric ANOVAs showed that there was no effect of the type of mask for familiarity judgements, $H(3) = 2.91$, $p = 0.5729$, nor was there an effect for naming, $H(3) = 5.89$, $p = 0.2073$.

Discussion

Although the data here are not as clear as in Experiment 1, they can be split into three groups: the first with the face mask alone, the second with the inner-jumbled, jumbled, and inverted face masks, and the third with the intensity mask. The inner-jumbled, jumbled, and inverted masks produced an intermediate level of masking, being neither significantly different from the face nor from the intensity mask, although the face mask induces a significant amount of masking compared with the intensity mask. This, combined with the existence of a difference between the familiarity and naming criteria, suggests that the masking effect noted largely reflects the operation of a specific face-processing system.

It is still possible, however, that the results could be the consequence of the inevitable differences in the physical resemblance between the target and the masks. This can be addressed by considering intra-class differences between pairs of complete faces, rather than inter-class differences between faces and non-faces or severely manipulated faces, as was done here. If the differences in masking reflect simple differences in visual similarity, then changing the visual similarity between complete faces should have comparable effects. Alternatively, if the reduced level of masking seen for the manipulated faces reflects the partial operation of a specific face-processing system, then no such effect should occur. Thus the recognition thresholds for faces in the presence of face-masks that were objectively measured to be similar or dissimilar were explored. As it is likely that such differences should be smaller than those seen when considering inter-class differences, a larger number of trials and smaller number of target images were used. This should allow the subjects to converge to a more stable threshold. Faces known to be familiar to the subjects (their lecturers) were used for the same reason. This would tend to reduce the noise introduced by faces that would not be recognizable with very long display times.

EXPERIMENT 3

Method

Subjects

A total of 16 subjects was used. All of the subjects were mathematics students at the University of Aberdeen, and they were paid for their time. One subject was dropped because she could not name any of the targets.

Equipment

This was the same as that used in Experiments 1 and 2.

Stimuli

These were from the same source as in Experiment 2.

Four targets were used here. All were familiar to the subjects, being lecturers in the Aberdeen Department of Mathematical Sciences. They were photographed taking every effort to produce the same conditions as had occurred in the original photographs, and they were digitized in exactly the same way. The target individuals were chosen to be the most recognizable and also to have been originally coded in the FRAME system (Shepherd, 1986). Each target face was coded by a trained FRAME operator on 14 facial attributes selected for salience in face recognition. For a list of these attributes see Appendix B.

The distractors—both the mask images and all those images used in the catch trials—were selected by automatically finding the 100 best matches between the ratings of the targets and the ratings of the FRAME faces using the FRAME search algorithm. Those images that were within the 100 closest matches of a target with 1000 faces formed the "similar" distractors category. The lists from each target face were filtered to remove duplications, so that each distractor face was used only once. Those images that were not in the best 100 matches to a target formed the "dissimilar" category. As there were a total of 594 unknown distractors and considerable overlap between the 100-strong lists from each target, this procedure formed approximately equal-sized categories.

Procedure

The procedure was exactly the same as that in Experiments 1 and 2, except that each target was seen eight times (four per half-staircase) per recognition criterion, and the subjects were told that they would be seeing members of the Department of Mathematical Sciences rather than universally well-known men. Thus each threshold involved the 64 judgements, with 32 target trials and 32 catch trials. The familiarity criterion was always measured before the naming criterion, and the presence of the "similar" or "dissimilar" distractors was a between-subjects factor.

Results

Data points were excluded on the same basis as operated in Experiments 1 and 2. This reduced the total number of observations from 1472 to 1191. The condition means are shown in Table 1. The logarithmic transformations of the data were then taken, and the median value for each criterion for each subject was found. The logarithmic transformations reduced the significant correlation between the means and standard deviations of the treatment groups to a non-significant value. The data were then subjected to a pair of one-way two condition ANOVAs, one for each criterion. This showed that there was no significant effect of the similarity between the targets and distractors for the familiarity criterion, nor was there one for naming, both $Fs \ll 1$. A one-way, two condition within-subject ANOVA between the two criteria showed that there was no significant difference in thresholds, $F < 1$.

The overall number of false alarms was extremely low, at 1.01%; the condition means are given in Table 2. As before, non-parametric statistics were applied. A Wilcoxon matched-pairs signed-ranks test showed that there were significantly more false alarms for the familiarity criterion than for the naming criterion, $T_+ = 17$, $n = 15$, $p = 0.0156$. A Wilcoxon rank-sum test showed that there was a marginally significant effect of mask similarity for the familiarity criterion, $W_s = 39.5$, $n_S = 7$, $n_L = 8$, $p = 0.0507$. However, there was

TABLE 1
Mean Thresholds Found in Experiment 3

| Mask Type | | Criterion | | |
		Familiarity	Naming	Mean
similar faces	mean	52.43	60.84	56.48
	SD	34.10	35.53	34.36
dissimilar faces	mean	54.04	58.59	56.27
	SD	29.74	30.59	29.75
mean	mean	53.18	59.78	56.38
	SD	31.63	32.74	32.04

Note: Thresholds given in msec.

TABLE 2
Mean False Alarm Rates Found in Experiment 3

Mask Type	Criterion		
	Familiarity	*Naming*	*Mean*
similar faces	5.41	1.23	2.77
dissimilar faces	0.31	0.05	0.15
mean	1.91	0.45	1.01

Note: False alarm rates given in percent.

no significant difference for the false alarms on the naming criterion, $W_s = 47.0$, $n_s = 7$, $n_L = 8$, $p = 0.2409$.

In an attempt to understand the data further, a post-hoc analysis on the basis of the similarity of the masks and targets was performed to see whether the null results concealed some non-significant trend. Because of the method used to select the similar images, it was not possible to find sub-groups within the dissimilar category. However, it was possible to rank the similar images on the basis of the FRAME algorithm's measure of their visual similarity to the targets (Shepherd, 1986). This was carried out, and all those masks with similarity ranks of 50 or more were discarded, leaving only the most similar masks. The masks thus identified as most similar were compared with the dissimilar ones. This left a total of 102 observations in the similar condition, as opposed to 233 in the dissimilar condition. The analysis was carried out in the same way as before, with one observation per subject per threshold, and thus the degrees of freedom were not affected. Even with this manipulation, there was no effect of mask similarity, and no familiarity-naming difference (all $Fs < 1$).

The catch trials were sorted so that those trials where the similarity rank of both the false targets and the mask was less than 71 were retained; 71 was chosen as $(50^2 + 50^2)^{1/2} = 70.71$, and this criterion should produce an approximately equal magnitude of effect from two independent variables that vary on a linear scale. This left 79 observations in the similar condition. These trials showed a significant difference for the error rates of the two response criteria, $T_+ = 10.5$, $n = 15$, $p = 0.0313$, and an effect of mask similarity for familiarity that was significant at the 0.1 level, $W_s = 41.5$, $n_s = 7$. There was no effect of mask similarity from naming, $W_s = 60.0$, $n_s = 7$, $n_L = 8$, $p = 0.3496$. $n_L = 8$, $p = 0.0789$.

Discussion

In this experiment, making the mask and catch images more like the targets had no effect upon the threshold for either recognition or naming, and for the false alarm rate for naming. There was, however, a slight effect of visual similarity upon the false alarm rate for familiarity judgements. This suggests that purely visual manipulations of the similarity of faces-masks does not affect the amount of masking achieved and implies that this type of masking cannot be purely visual in nature. The change in error rates suggests that the lack of effect is not due to a manipulation that is too weak to be detected by the experimental method. This conclusion is reinforced by the finding that increasing the strength of the manipulation by excluding the less similar images from the "similar" condition did not change the pattern of results. The slightly weaker effect of similarity for familiarity false alarms can be understood in terms of the loss of power involved in reducing the number of observations present.

The mean thresholds in this experiment were somewhat lower than those for complete faces in the previous experiments, and there was a rather smaller effect of moving from familiarity judgements to naming. There are two obvious explanations for this. One is that a priming effect operated with regard to the four target faces, reducing the thresholds to a level where no more information was required for naming than for familiarity. The second is that the greater familiarity of these faces, which were personally known to the subject, may lead to situation where partial or incomplete information is all that is required to allow recognition. However, if this interpretation of the lack of a familiarity-naming difference is correct, it undermines explanations of the results of Experiments 1 and 2 in terms of particular cues, and thus it is reasonable that differences in the amount of masking seen there reflect relatively high-level effects with the face recognition system.

GENERAL DISCUSSION AND CONCLUSIONS

These three experiments have shown that the time for which a face needs to be displayed for recognition to occur is significantly increased when the face is followed by another, unknown face that is displayed for an equal duration and with approximately equal contrast. This effect cannot be attributed solely to low-level, energy-based effects. It is also not attributable to an effect at the level of a general object-level recognition system. Noticeable masking effects were found with partial faces, whether or not these preserved the general shape of the face. However, no significant masking effect was found relative to the intensity mask when inverted faces were used as masks. Furthermore, varying the visual similarity between the targets and mask faces did not affect the amount of masking. These effects were consistent, regardless of the type of response that the subjects were asked to make.

These results allow us to suggest a localization of the reduction of recognition performance when faces are masked with other faces. The lack of any significant effect from the presence of non-object or non-face object masks suggests that the masking must be occurring at some higher level within the face-processing system. In addition, the consistent lack of an interaction between the type of response required and the type of mask suggests that this masking must occur before decisions on the familiarity of the face are made.

Within the Bruce and Young (1986) model, this would suggest that the two faces interact either at the Structural Encoding or FRU levels. It should be noted that the use of targets and masks of fixed contrast, with variable SOA and no temporal overlap (i.e. an ISI of zero), will tend to favour the discovery of relatively high-level effects. Under these circumstances, as only the pattern characteristics vary between conditions, those patterns that are the best masks will be found. The relatively long display times will tend to promote the perception of the mask as a separate object. An alternative strategy might have been to maintain fixed display times and vary the contrast of the two images. This might well have allowed a greater tendency towards rather low-level integration masking, with possibly the most masking from an intensity mask, as this would have the greatest biasing effect. This would be especially true if a relatively short SOA were used. In this respect, the results reported here are comparable with those of Calis et al. (1984) and Bachmann (1989), as well as pattern mask conditions used by Moscovitch et al. (1976), but not with those of Keenan et al. (1989).

It may be argued, however, that the difference between the non-face masks and the face, pattern, and partial face masks, all of which produce masking, is one of visual similarity; in the object mask condition there was a rather lower probability of the major contours of the face and the mask closely overlapping than in the other conditions. This may be supported by the distinction made by Potter (1976), Intraub (1984), and Loftus and Ginn (1984) between perceptual masking that occurs at SOAs of this order and conceptual masking, which occurs at longer times and relates to difficulties in memory consolidation. There are two problems with this explanation. The first problem arises from the results of Experiment 2. If pure visual similarity between the target and the mask were all that was important, then a significant amount of masking in the case of the inverted face would be expected, rather than from the pattern mask. The inverted faces have appropriate major contours and correctly arranged inner features, whereas the pattern mask has neither of these. However, it is not possible to reject the local-masking argument on these grounds alone, as the actual visual similarity between these and the targets is not clear.

The second problem with the visual similarity hypothesis stems from Experiment 3. If only visual overlap between the target and mask were important, then a higher threshold would be found for the similar masks than for the dissimilar ones. This was not found. An alternative explanation might be that the manipulation imposed in this experiment was too small to produce an effect that the experiment could detect. Although this explanation cannot be ruled out, it is made less likely by the observation that the subjects had a significantly greater tendency to claim that they had recognized faces on the similar-condition catch trials than on the dissimilar-condition ones. Assuming that the subjects were responding to the first image in the catch trials, then the change in false alarm-rate suggests that the manipulation was strong enough to be noticeable to the subjects. Alternatively, it is possible that the subjects may have been responding that the masks in the catch trials seemed familiar. This is unlikely, as the target images were only present in the first position. In this case, then, a proportion of the "yes" responses on the target trials needs to be discarded as really being false alarms, the threshold should in fact be higher, and some visual masking may have occurred. This latter explanation is made less likely by the maintenance of the same pattern when the data were sorted so that only trials with very similar masks were included in the analysis; equal and reciprocal masking and guessing effects would be required to maintain the overall lack of effect.

The local-masking option can be tested as it suggests how local and face masking may be distinguished. If non-local masking occurs within the face-recognition system, then psychologically meaningful manipulations of the nature of the mask and targets will change the ease of recognition of these faces. For example, variations in the typicality or memorability of faces should affect the amount of masking that they exhibit, and it should be possible to vary the relative typicality/distinctiveness of targets and masks independently of the specific similarity between individual targets and mask faces. Preliminary results suggest that when these factors are varied, a main effect of target typicality with less masking of distinctive faces is found. There is also an interaction with mask typicality, with the most masking when the targets were typical but the mask distinctive and target typicality having less effect for distinctive masks than for typical ones.

The results of Experiment 2 strongly suggest that the masking seen from whole faces can be attributed to the loss of configural information. The jumbled face mask, which we think of as a pattern mask, and the partial face mask both show significant amounts of masking, whereas the inverted face mask does not; and all show less masking than does a complete face. Inverted faces are very noticeably more difficult to identify than are upright ones (Yin, 1969, 1970). Bruce et al. (1991) suggest that this may reflect the loss of configural information. Configural processing usually implies the use of the spatial relationships between gross positions of large facial features (e.g. the eyes, nose, and mouth) (Rhodes, 1985b; Diamond & Carey, 1986), and its use is made possible by the relative similarity of faces; they all have the same major features in the same relative positions. This is supported by results that imply that although the formation of composite faces from the aligned top and bottom halves of the faces of known individuals gives rise to a strong sense of seeing a new face, this is lost when the composite is inverted (Young, Hellawell, & Hay, 1987). In addition, both jumbling the positions of features and also inverting faces causes the loss of an advantage in the identification of features that is present when they are learned within the correct orientation (Tanaka & Farah, 1993).

This explanation fails to account for the masking effect that the jumbled face and the partial face exert upon the face, but these can be covered if we allow that configural information can be extracted independently at a number of scales. Although the relationship between gross features is taken as the basic definition of configural information, Rhodes et al. (1993) suggest that variations within particular features (for example, whether the corners of a mouth turn up or down) may also be used to extract configuration. Thus a certain amount of the masking in the face-mask condition may occur because portions of the facial features are discovered on their own. In contrast, no large-scale configural information will be extracted from the jumbled face, as the orientation of the gross features is random. The relatively strong masking effect seen in the partial-face masks condition is also explicable in this way, as the major contour of the face is retained in this condition. That the masking is sensitive to this sort of manipulation and occurs with relatively short SOAs suggests that it probably occurs at a structural encoding processing level, and that this level codes the face in terms of visual distortions or features at a range of scales.

In summary, then, the results from our experiments are of interest in that they extend and replicate the results of Calis et al. (1984) and also of Bachmann (1989) in suggesting that it is possible to interrupt processing of a face at different stages within the face-processing system, and that interruption at these different levels will give varying amounts of masking. It seems that, with our methods at least, this masking does not occur at a low, physical masking level and can be placed up to and including the FRU level, with the most likely location at the structural encoding stage. In addition, the results from the jumbled face may suggest why medium- to high-frequency masks have the greatest effect (Tieger & Ganz, 1979; Moscovitch & Radzins, 1987; Keenan et al., 1989); they may well be occluding portions of features that would allow the extraction of configural information. Our results also suggest that this configural information should be thought of as occurring within features as well as between them. However, this interpretation—particularly the exclusion of masking from objects other than faces—is still open to the claim that it reflects only a low-level visual masking. Progress on resolving this ambiguity will await the non-visual manipulation of faces in terms both of the typicality of the faces and also of the priming state of the images.

REFERENCES

Bachmann, T. (1989). Microgenesis as traced by the transient paired-forms paradigm, *Acta Psychologica, 70,* 3–17.

Breitmeyer, B.G. (1984). *Visual masking: An integrative approach. Oxford Psychology Series.* Oxford: Oxford University Press.

Bruce, V., Doyle, A., Dench, N., & Burton, A.M. (1991). Remembering facial configurations. *Cognition, 38,* 109–144.

Bruce, V., & Valentine, T. (1985). Identity priming in the recognition of familiar faces. *British Journal of Psychology, 76,* 373–383.

Bruce, V., & Young, A.W. (1986). Understanding face recognition. *British Journal of Psychology, 77,* 305–327.

Brunas, J., Young, A.W., & Ellis, A.W. (1990). Repetition priming from incomplete faces: Evidence for part to whole completion. *British Journal of Psychology, 81,* 43–56.

Brunas-Wagstaff, J., Young, A.W., & Ellis, A.W. (1992). Repetition priming follows spontaneous but not prompted recognition of familiar faces. *Quarterly Journal of Experimental Psychology, 44A* (3), 423–454.

Bruyer, R. (1988). Some masked inconstancies about constancy. *Brain and Cognition, 7* (3), 374–376.

Burton, A.M., Bruce, V., & Johnston, R.A. (1990). Understanding face recognition with an interactive activation model. *British Journal of Psychology, 81,* 360–380.

Burton, A.M., & Bruce, V. (1992). I recognize your face but I can't remember your name: A simple explanation? *British Journal of Psychology, 83,* 45–60.

Calis, G., Sterenborg, J., & Maarse, F. (1984). Initial microgenetic steps in single-glance face recognition. *Acta Psychologica, 55,* 215–230.

Cornsweet, T.N. (1962). The staircase-method in psychophysics. *American Journal of Psychology, 75,* 485–491.

Diamond, R., & Carey, S (1986). Why faces are and are not special: An effect of expertise. *Journal of Experimental Psychology: General, 115,* 107–117.

Ellis, A.W. (1992). Cognitive mechanisms of face processing. In: V. Bruce, A. Cowey, A.W. Ellis, & D.I. Perrett (Eds.), *Processing the facial image* (pp.113–120). Oxford: Oxford University Press.

Ellis, A.W., Young, A.W., Flude, B.M., & Hay, D.C. (1987). Repetition priming of face recognition. *Quarterly Journal of Experimental Psychology, 39A,* 193–210.

Ellis, H.D. (1983). The role of the right hemisphere in face perception. In: A.W. Young (Ed.), *Functions of the right hemisphere.* London: Academic Press.

Ellis, H.D. (1986). Processes underlying face recognition. In: R. Bruyer (Ed.), *The neuropsychology of face recognition and facial expression.* Hillsdale, NJ: Lawrence Erlbaum Associates Inc.

Ellis, H.D., Shepherd, J.W., & Davies, G.M., (1979). Identification of familiar and unfamiliar faces from internal and external features: Some implications for theories of face recognition. *Perception, 8* (4), 431–439.

Ellis, H.D., Shepherd, J.W., Flin, R.H., Shepherd, J., & Davies, G.M. (1989). Identification from a computer-driven retrieval system compared with a traditional mug-shot album search: A new tool for police investigation. *Ergonomics, 32,* 167–177.

Fraser, I.H., Craig, G.L., & Parker, D.M. (1990). Reaction time measures of feature saliency in schematic faces. *Perception, 19,* 661–673.

Hay, D.C., & Young, A.W. (1982). The human face. In: A.W. Ellis (Ed.), *Normality and pathology in cognitive functions.* London: Academic Press.

Intraub, H. (1984). Conceptual masking: The effects of subsequent visual events on memory for pictures. *Journal of Experimental Psychology: Learning, Memory and Cognition, 10* (1), 115–125.

Keenan, P.A., Witman, R., & Pepe, J. (1989). Hemispheric asymmetry in the processing of high and low spatial frequencies: A facial recognition task. *Brain and Cognition, 11* (2), 229–237. [See also the erratum: P. Keenan, R. Witman, & J. Pepe. (1990). Hemispheric asymmetry in the processing of high and low spatial frequencies: A facial recognition task erratum. *Brain and Cognition, 13* (1), 130.]

Kolers, P.A. (1983). Perception and representation. *Annual Review of Psychology, 34,* 129–166.

Landy, M.S., Cohen, Y., & Sperling, G. (1984). HIPS: Image processing under Unix software and applications. *Behavior Research Methods, Instruments and Computers, 16,* 199–216.

Loftus, G.R., & Ginn, M. (1984). Perceptual and conceptual masking of pictures. *Journal of Experimental Psychology: Learning, Memory and Cognition, 10,* (3), 435–441.

Moscovitch, M. (1988). Further analyses of masking functions in laterality studies of face-perception. *Brain and Cognition, 7* (1), 377–380.

Moscovitch, M., & Radzins, M. (1987). Backward masking of lateralized faces by noise, pattern, and spatial frequency. *Brain and Cognition, 6* (1), 72–90.

Moscovitch, M., Scullion, D., & Christie, D. (1976). Early versus late stages of processing and their relation to functional hemispheric asymmetries in face recognition. *Journal of Experimental Psychology: Human Perception and Performance, 2* (3), 401–416.

Potter, M.C. (1976). Short-term conceptual memory for pictures. *Journal of Experimental Psychology: Human Learning and Memory, 2* (5), 509–522.

Rhodes, G. (1985a). Lateralised processes in face recognition. *British Journal of Psychology, 76,* 249–271.

Rhodes, G. (1985b). Perceptual asymmetries in face recognition. *Brain and Cognition, 4,* 197–218.

Rhodes, G., Brake, S., & Atkinson, A. (1993). What's lost in inverted faces? *Cognition, 47* (1), 25–57.

Rose, R., Teller, D.Y., & Rendleman, P. (1970). Statistical properties of staircase estimates. *Perception and Psychophysics, 8* (4), 199–204.

Shepherd, J.W. (1986). An interactive computer system for retrieving faces. In: H.D. Ellis, M.A. Jeeves, F. Newcombe, & A. Young (Eds.), *Aspects of Face Processing* (pp.398–409). Dordrecht: Martinus Nijhoff.

Tanaka, J.W., & Farah, M.J. (1993). Parts and wholes in face recognition. *Quarterly Journal of Experimental Psychology, 46A* (2), 225–245.

Tieger, T., & Ganz, L. (1979). Recognition of faces in the presence of two-dimensional sinusoidal masks. *Perception and Psychophysics, 26* (2), 163–167.

Yin, R.K. (1969). Looking at upside-down faces. *Journal of Experimental Psychology, 76,* 141–145.

Yin, R.K. (1970). Face recognition by brain-injured patients: A dissociable ability? *Neuropsychologica, 8,* 395–402.

Young, A.W., Hellawell, D., & Hay, D.C. (1987). Configural information in face perception. *Perception, 16,* 747-759.

Revised manuscript received 1 April 1994

APPENDIX

A. Names of Targets

Clive Anderson
Robbie Coltraine
Michael Elphick
John Thaw
Jeremy Paxman
Harrison Ford

B. FRAME factors

8   Hair length: range 1-5
10 Hair curls: range 1-5
13 Hair colour: range 1-5
17 Eyebrow width: range 1-5
25 Eye colour: range 1-5
34 Upper lip width: range 1-5
35 Lower lip width: range 1-5
39 No facial hair: binary characteristic
40 Moustache present: binary characteristic
41 Sideburns present: binary characteristic
42 Beard present: binary characteristic
46 Glasses present: binary characteristic
47 Earrings present: binary characteristic
48 Age: range 1-5

VISUAL COGNITION, 1994, *1* (2/3), 253–274

Are Faces Perceived as Configurations More By Adults than by Children?

Susan Carey and Rhea Diamond

Massachusetts Institute of Technology, Cambridge, Massachusetts, U.S.A.

Adult face recognition is severely hampered by stimulus inversion. Several investigators have attributed this vulnerability to the effect of orientation on encoding relational aspects of faces. Previous work has also demonstrated that children are less sensitive to orientation of faces than are adults. This has been interpreted as reflecting an increasing reliance on configural aspects of faces with increasing age and expertise.

Young, Hellawell, and Hay (1987) demonstrated that for adults the encoding of relations among facial parts is, indeed, sensitive to orientation. When chimeric faces are upright, the top half of one face fuses with the bottom half of the other, making the person depicted in the top half difficult to recognize. This effect (the composite effect) is not seen when the faces are inverted. The present study obtained the composite effect for 6-year-old and 10-year-old children, just as for adults. The composite effect was found to an equal degree at all ages tested and was seen both in tasks involving highly familiar faces and in those involving newly learned, previously unfamiliar faces. Thus, these data provided no support for the hypothesis of increasing reliance on configural aspects of faces with increasing age, at least in the sense tapped by this procedure.

However, the data did confirm an Age × Orientation interaction. In recognizing both familiar and previously unfamiliar faces, 6-year-olds were less affected by inversion than were 10-year-olds, who, in turn, were less affected than were adults. Increasing vulnerability to inversion of faces with age was independent of the composite effect. Apparently, there are two distinct sources to the large effect of inversion that characterizes adult face encoding: one seen throughout development and one acquired only with expertise.

Requests for reprints should be sent to S. Carey, Department of Brain & Cognitive Sciences, Massachusetts Institute of Technology, Cambridge, MA 02139, U.S.A.

This work was supported by grant R01-HD221666 from the National Institute of Health. We thank J. Hamilton and K. Nigam for technical assistance in these studies.

In spite of the impressive capacity for face encoding that infants display (Fagan, 1979; Johnson & Morton, 1991), young children are dramatically worse than adults at encoding and subsequently recognizing unfamiliar faces. Marked improvement between ages 2 and 10 is observed on simple recognition tasks in which a set of facial photographs is inspected, later to be picked out from distractors (Carey, 1981; Carey & Diamond, 1977; Carey, Diamond, & Woods, 1980; Flin, 1980.) Dramatic improvement with age is also apparent on tasks that place no demands on memory. For example, Benton and Van Allen required subjects to match a target photograph with photographs of the same person taken under different lighting or from a different point of view or with different facial expressions. On this simultaneous matching task, 6-year-olds performed at a level associated with right-hemisphere damage in adults (Benton & Van Allen, 1973; Carey et al., 1980). Other data also show that 6-year-olds are severely limited at recognizing whether or not two photographs (simultaneously presented) depict the same person if the photos differ in angle of view, expression, or clothing worn (Diamond & Carey, 1977; Ellis, 1992; Flin, 1980; Saltz & Sigel, 1967). Such data indicate that the child's problems are in the initial encoding of new faces, not just in memory or retrieval. Young children differ from adults, then, in the ability to encode a new face in terms of distinguishing features that ensure it is recognized and differentiated from other faces.

One indication that children are doing something *different* from adults, rather than just less of what adults do, is the evidence that children are less affected by the orientation of the face during encoding and recognition than are adults.

For adults, encoding individual faces is more affected by inversion than is encoding of individual members of almost any other class studied to date: houses, bridges, stick figures of men, buildings, landscapes, dog faces (Diamond & Carey, 1986; Scapinello & Yarmey, 1970; Yin, 1969, 1970). In these studies the stimuli are usually presented in the same orientation during both inspection and recognition; inverted stimuli are first seen upside down and are also presented for recognition upside down. Thus, the difficulty is in forming an adequate representation of an inverted face, not in coping with a mismatch in orientation between inspection and recognition. Typically, for faces there is a 20–30% decrement in recognition accuracy associated with the inverted condition, whereas there is only a 0–10% inversion decrement for stimuli from the other classes.

Two results emerge from studies of the developmental history of the inversion effect on face encoding. (1) As long as ceiling and floor effects are controlled for, face encoding is affected by orientation at every age, even in infancy (Carey, 1981; Fagan, 1979; Flin, 1983). At least by age 5 months, new faces are being encoded relative to specific knowledge of faces, knowledge better exploited from upright than from inverted stimuli. (2) There is often an Age × Orientation interaction, which, of course, is also sensitive to floor and ceiling effects. That is, the magnitude of the inversion effect increases with age

(Carey, 1981; Flin, 1983; Goldstein & Chance, 1964). Thus, if we understood the large inversion effect on face encoding, we might begin to understand what changes with development.

One approach to this problem is to probe more deeply the circumstances under which the large inversion effect obtains. As reviewed above, early studies showed face recognition to be more affected by inversion than was recognition of any other class of stimuli. However, Diamond and Carey (1986) showed that the large inversion effect is observed in at least one additional case: sporting dog experts are affected by inversion in encoding whole body profiles of such dogs as much as they (and other normal adults) are in encoding faces. Dog novices, in contrast, show the usual Stimulus Class × Orientation interaction, being affected by inversion in encoding faces far more than in encoding dog profiles. Thus, the Age × Orientation interaction for face encoding can be taken as an Expertise × Orientation interaction. It appears that such perceptual expertise requires about 10 years to develop, whether one is a child or an adult. It is at age 10 that children perform in the normal adult range on face encoding tasks. And the period of apprenticeship for becoming an American Kennel Club judge is 10 years!

What do expert face encoding and expert sporting dog encoding have in common? Faces share a configuration in a way that can be made precise: each face can be defined in terms of a fixed set of points, such that the average of a set of faces, so defined, is still recognizable as a face. This is not true of a randomly chosen set of bridges, houses, buildings, or landscapes. It is true, however, of a randomly chosen set of sporting-dog profiles. Furthermore, some of the features by which we individuate faces are distinctive variations of that basic configuration. This is seen by the recognizability of line drawings produced by connecting the same set of points defined on each face (see Rhodes, Brennan, & Carey, 1987). Diamond and Carey dubbed features that are distinctive variations of a shared configuration "second-order relational features" and hypothesized that the ability to encode individuals in terms of such features requires expertise and that it is particularly affected by inversion.

Diamond and Carey (1986) offered no direct evidence for this hypothesis, supporting it only with the finding that it accounts for the large inversion effect in both adult face encoding and expert dog encoding. Rhodes, Brake, and Atkinson (1993) directly manipulated the features by which faces differed (e.g. by adding a moustache or eye glasses, by changing a nose or eyes, by varying the internal spacing of parts) and explored whether detection of changes in these different types of features was differentially affected by inversion. They found, as hypothesized, that changes in internal spacing were among the transformations most affected by orientation, but so, too, were changes in single features (e.g. just the eyes). As Rhodes et al. pointed out, this latter finding is not inconsistent with the hypothesis that inversion affects encoding of second-order relational features, for when the eyes within a face are changed, so are the relations between points on the eyes and other features of the face.

There is ample additional evidence that adults use the spatial relations among the parts of a face as a basis for individuating and recognizing faces. For example, in a series of studies, Haig showed that manipulating the vertical spacing of parts of faces (e.g. raising the nose relative to the rest of the face) affected recognition rates (e.g. Haig, 1984).

There is also ample additional evidence that the encoding of the spatial relations among the parts of a face is sensitive to inversion. For instance, if the eyes and mouth are inverted within the face, the result is monstrous, but the grotesque appearance of such faces is perceived only if the face as a whole is upright (Thompson, 1980). In a related finding, Bartlett and Searcy (1993) showed that faces could be made to look grotesque by manipulating the spatial relations among their parts. Subjects judged such transformed faces less grotesque when inverted than when upright. Apparently, if the face is upside down, subjects cannot detect the subtle deviations from the normal configuration introduced by such transformations.

Tanaka and Farah (1993) and Farah, Tanaka, and Drain (in press) have offered an alternative analysis of why face recognition is so sensitive to inversion and, thus, what developmental changes in face representations underlie the orientation effect characteristic of adults. They distinguish between holistic and parts-based representations, arguing that faces are more likely to be encoded holistically than are other classes of stimuli. They further suggest that holistic encoding is more sensitive to inversion than is parts-based encoding.

In their papers, Tanaka and Farah (1993; Farah et al., in press) provide two distinct characterizations of holistic encoding. First, holistic representations are those in which the parts of the stimulus are not explicitly represented. In the case of faces, this would mean that a particular face would not be represented in terms of the identities of parts—such as the nose, eyebrows, mouth, for example—but, rather, in terms of a template-like representation of the whole. In such a representation, individual parts (e.g. Bob's nose) should be more difficult to recognize in isolation than in the context of the whole face, and, indeed, this is what Tanaka and Farah (1993) found. Evidence that holistic representations are sensitive to orientation was provided by the finding that the advantage for recognizing Bob's nose in the whole face disappeared when the stimuli were turned upside down.

This first characterization of holistic encoding raises the question of what is meant by "explicitly represented". One interpretation is that the parts are less accessible to analysis and report than is the whole, much in the same sense in which the syllable is more accessible than the phoneme in phoneme/syllable monitoring tasks (Fodor, Bever, & Garrett, 1975). Here "explicitly represented" means consciously accessible, or subject to attentional monitoring. A second interpretation is that the parts of a face, such as eyes, noses, and mouths, are not the atoms of face representations; that the face template is not built from these parts. These two interpretations are certainly different, for although phonemes are less accessible than syllables, nobody would deny that phonemes are the atoms of syllabic representations. The Tanaka and Farah demonstration actually supports the accessibility interpretation; subjects can, after all, recognize Bob's nose in isolation—but they do so more slowly than when it is in the context of the whole face.

In their second characterization of holistic encoding, Farah et al. (in press) state that in holistic representations, the spatial relations among the parts are more important in specifying an individual object than are the representations of the individual parts themselves. Note that this characterization is very different from the first, for in this second characterization there is no claim that the individual parts are not explicitly represented, in the sense of being the atoms of facial representations. Indeed, as Farah et al. admit, under this characterization, the distinction between holistic representations and configural representations becomes blurred to the point of disappearing.

In the remainder of this paper, we use "holistic encoding" when referring to the accessibility hypothesis—that representations of whole faces are more easily and quickly accessed than are representations of parts, and use "configural encoding" when referring to the hypothesis that the spatial relations *among* parts are especially important in face encoding.

Young et al. (1987) have provided a striking demonstration of one sense in which upright faces are encoded configurally, whereas inverted faces are not. They created composites of the top half of one person's face and the bottom half of another's (see Figure 1). In a typical experiment, the stimuli were photographs of famous faces, and the subject's task was to name the person depicted in the

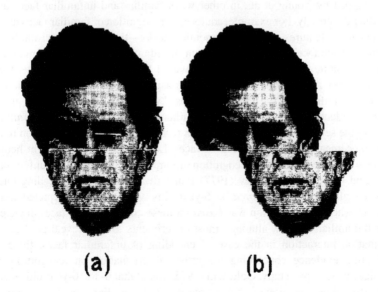

(a)   **(b)**

FIG. 1.   Sample stimuli.   1a. Composite Nixon/Prince Charles.   1b. Non-composite Nixon/Prince Charles.

top half, ignoring the bottom half. To control for possible interference from recognition of the bottom half, Young et al. also created non-composite faces (see Figure 1). They found that the reaction time (RT) to recognize the top half was slower for upright composites than for upright non-composites. Apparently, the two halves of the composites fused into a new face, making it much more difficult to identify the old top half, whereas the bottom half of the non-compesites could be ignored. Crucially, there was no difference between the composites and non-composites when the faces were inverted. Integration of the top and bottom halves so that it is difficult to disentangle them occurs only when the faces are upright. Young et al. also found this pattern of results when adults encoded unfamiliar faces—evidence that both unfamiliar and familiar faces are encoded configurally.

The Young et al. demonstration admits of interpretation in terms of both the hypothesis that inversion interferes with holistic encoding and that inversion interferes with configural encoding. With respect to the configural encoding hypothesis, note that many relational features are changed when the top half of one face is fused with the bottom half of the other. And as regards the holistic encoded hypothesis, note that the task requires accessing a part of a face (the top half) from within a whole face. The developmental course of the composite effect, then, will bear on evaluating the hypothesis that the Age × Orientation interaction in face encoding reflects increasing reliance on relational features and/or increasing reliance on holistic representations of faces.

Whereas adults encode both familiar and unfamiliar faces configurally in the sense tapped by Young et al., in other ways familiar and unfamiliar faces are encoding differently. For example, adults base recognition of familiar faces more on their inner features (eyes, nose, mouth, cheeks—those that reflect the bone structure of the face) whereas recognition of unfamiliar faces is based more on the outer features of the face (hair and overall face shape; Ellis, Shepherd, & Davies, 1979). Also, a more robust right-hemisphere advantage in recognition is found for familiar than for unfamiliar faces (Levine, 1981). Furthermore, there is some evidence that children encode familiar faces differently from unfamiliar faces, in the sense of relying on configural features of familiar faces but on relatively piecemeal features of unfamiliar faces. Levine (1981) found a right-hemisphere advantage at age 8 for recognition of familiar faces, but not for unfamiliar ones, and Diamond and Carey (1977) found that piecemeal, misleading cues (hats, eyeglasses), were *ignored* by 6-year-olds when the faces depicted were familiar, whereas recognition was *based* on these cues when the faces depicted were unfamiliar. Finally, although most experiments to date reveal an Age × Orientation interaction in the case of encoding of unfamiliar faces, there is conflicting evidence concerning the effect of orientation on recognition of familiar faces. In one study, Goldstein (1975) found that 6- to 10-year-olds were little affected by inversion of photographs of highly familiar peers (12% errors), and that the sensitivity to orientation increased markedly through the age range of 13–14 (19% errors), 17–18 (24% errors), and 19–20 (38% errors). However, in an earlier study, Brooks and Goldstein (1963) found that 6-year-olds made many errors (33%) in identifying inverted faces they could recognize upright, whereas error rates fell to 0 by age 10.

The present studies exploit the Young et al. paradigm to ask three questions: (1) In the sense tapped by this procedure, are there developmental changes in configural or holistic encoding of *familiar* faces? If children are less sensitive to the configuration of the face than are adults, they should show less difference between composites and non-composites in the upright condition. At all ages, we would expect no difference between composites and non-composites in inverted faces. Therefore, the development of sensitivity to facial configuration would be revealed by a three-way interaction between age, stimulus type (composite vs. non-composite), and orientation. (2) Are there developmental increases in configural encoding of *unfamiliar* faces? (3) What is the effect of orientation on children's encoding of familiar faces—is there or is there not an Age × Orientation interaction in the encoding of familiar faces? The answers to these questions will permit us to consider the relations between two phenomena: integration of the parts of an upright face into a unit (the Young et al. demonstration) and the developmental increase in the recognition advantage afforded the upright face.

EXPERIMENT 1

Configural Encoding of Familiar Faces

Method

Subjects.

Subjects were 20 first-graders (mean age 7;1), 20 fifth-graders (mean age 10;9) and 12 adults (mean age 28;3). At each grade, the 20 children were drawn from two separate classes (10 from each class). The adults were graduate students and research assistants in our department.

Stimuli.

Adults: Six males and six females from among the graduate students and staff of MIT's Department of Brain and Cognitive Science were photographed. The photographs were scanned into MacPaint files. Two stimulus sets were made by pairing the top half of each photograph with the bottom half of the photographs of all five other people of the same sex. Each pairing was made in two versions: Composite (with the two halves aligned) and non-composite (the two halves offset.) See Figure 1 for examples made from famous faces (Prince

Charles and Richard Nixon). Thus, there were 30 composite faces and 30 non-composite faces in each set. The 60 stimuli were randomized, subject to the constraint that runs of no more than 3 stimuli of the same type (composite or non-composite) were allowed, and runs of no more than 2 stimuli with the same person in the top half were allowed. A single random order of stimuli was used for the male and female sets.

Children: Six boys and six girls from each class were photographed, and stimulus sets for each class were constructed as for the adults. Thus, there were 2 male sets for each age and 2 female sets for each age, as there were two classes at each age.

Procedure

All children who served as subjects were photographed, and each was given a polaroid photograph of themselves, plus two printouts—one of their own face and one a composite with half of their own face and half of another child's face. These printouts served to motivate the children to participate in the study and to ensure they understood the construction of the stimuli. Subjects were tested on the two stimulus sets made from children in their own classes.

The task was run on a Macintosh Computer. Stimuli were presented until the subject responded with the name. A voice-key terminated the trial, and the experimenter recorded whether or not the response was correct. Each subject participated in two versions of the experiment—one upright and one inverted. Whether the male face set or the female face set was seen first, and whether upright or inverted faces were seen first was counterbalanced within each age group.

Subjects were instructed to respond loudly, as quickly as possible, avoiding errors. They were first presented with the whole faces (three runs through the set), which they were to name as quickly as possible. This gave them practice with the voice key. They were then shown the top halves of the faces upright and asked to name them as quickly as possible (one time each). Subjects at all ages found it very easy to name the top halves alone (see also Goldstein & Mackenburg, 1966; Chance, Goldstein, & Schict, 1967). The task proper was then explained to them. They were told to name the top half of the face (the part containing the eyes and forehead—the part they had just practised on) and to ignore the bottom halves. If they were in an inverted condition, they were first shown the relevant half faces alone upside down for one additional practice trial.

Results

Errors.

Error rates were around 10% at each age: First graders 8%; fifth graders, 8%; adults, 10%. Separate analyses of variance (ANOVA) on error rates at each age revealed that at all ages there was a main effect for stimulus type (more errors on composites than on non-composites) and that at no age was there a Stimulus Type × Orientation interaction. Fifth graders made more errors on inverted than on upright faces; this was the only main effect of orientation. Errors will not be discussed further.

Reaction Times.

Figure 2 shows the RT data for correct responses. An ANOVA was carried out, with age (6, 10, adult) as a between-subject variable and orientation (upright, inverted) and condition (composite, non-composite) as within-subject variables. There was a significant main effect for age, $F(2, 49) = 14.47$, $p < 0.001$. Six-year-olds were slower (1339 msec) than 10-year-olds (1023 msec), who, in turn, were slower than adults (980 msec). There was also a significant main effect for condition, $F(1, 49) = 37.71, p < 0.001$. RTs to composites were slower (1193 msec) than those to non-composites (1075 msec). Also, the Orientation × Condition interaction that constitutes Young et al.'s effect was significant, $F(1, 49) = 31.15, p < 0.001$. That is, RTs for upright composites (1222 msec) were slower than for upright non-composites (1024 msec), whereas RTs for inverted composites (1165 msec) did not differ from those for inverted non-composites (1126 msec). The two effects of theoretical significance for the issues addressed in this paper are: (1) there is no three-way Age × Condition × Orientation interaction—that is, the Young et al. effect is seen equally at each

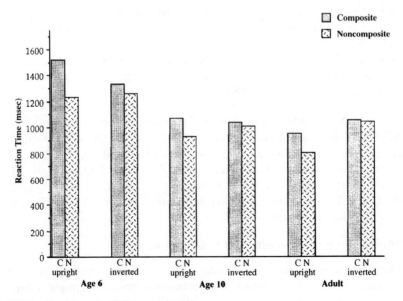

FIG. 2.   Experiment 1: RT for correct responses

age (see Figure 2). (2) The Age × Orientation interaction was significant, $F(2, 49) = 4.56, p < 0.025$. Let us examine these two effects in turn.

The major question asked here is whether children, like adults, would be more influenced by the mismatch between the top half and the bottom half of the face in upright composites than in upright non-composites, and would show no effect of stimulus type when the stimuli were inverted. The absence of a three-way-interaction indicates that there is no developmental change in these effects. As a check, we analysed each age group's data separately. The Orientation × Stimulus Type interaction was significant at the 0.05 level at every age, except for adults, for whom it approached that level: first-graders, $F(1, 18) = 25.1$, $p < 0.001$; fifth-graders, $F(1, 18) = 9.94, p < 0.006$; adults, $F(1, 11) = 4.42$, $p < 0.06$. Apparently, children fuse the halves of two different familiar upright faces into a new face, just as adults do. And, just as adults, children can ignore the interference from the bottom half of the face when the stimuli are inverted.

First-Graders. The subjects from each class showed the same pattern of results; there was no main effect of class and no interaction of class with any other variable. Neither was there any effect of sex of stimuli, nor of condition order (upright first or inverted first). The only significant effects were for stimulus type, $F(1, 18) = 25.66, p < 0.001$, composites RT = 1428 msec, non-composites RT = 1250 msec, and the interaction depicted in Figure 2. Notably, there was no main effect of orientation; the reaction time for upright faces was 1379 msec, and that for inverted faces was 1298 msec.

Fifth-Graders. As for the first-graders, there were no effects involving class, sex of stimuli, or condition order. The only significant effects were for stimulus type, $F(1, 18) = 14.48, p < 0.001$, composites RT = 1064 msec, non-composites RT = 982 msec, and the interaction depicted in Figure 2. Again, there was no main effect of orientation; the RT for upright faces was 1006 msec, and that for inverted faces was 1091 msec.

Adults. As for children, there were no effects of condition order or of sex of stimuli. Adult RTs yielded a main effect for orientation: $F(1, 11) = 7.6, p < 0.02$; RTs were faster for upright faces (892 msec) than for inverted faces (1067 msec). Also seen was a main effect for stimulus type, $F, 1, 11) = 5.83, p < 0.04$; RTs for composites were slower (1018 msec) than RTs for non-composites (941 msec). The interaction depicted in Figure 2 just missed significance, presumably due to the smaller sample of adults.

Age Changes in the Effect of Orientation.

As can be seen in Figure 2, inversion slows performance increasingly with age. Figure 3 shows the difference in RT between inverted and upright stimuli. For both composites and non-composites, this difference becomes greater with

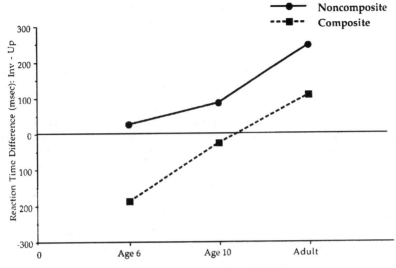

FIG. 3. Experiment 1: RT for inverted faces minus RT for upright faces.

increasing age, as confirmed by the Age × Orientation interaction reported above. Also evident from Figure 3 is the absence of a three-way Age × Orientation × Condition interaction. That is, the increased sensitivity to orientation with age was equally evident for composite and non-composite stimuli.

Averaged over composites and non-composites, first-graders are faster in the inverted condition, whereas adults are faster in the upright condition. However, all subjects are slowed by the mismatch of the bottom half of the composite face in the upright condition but not in the inverted condition, so RTs to composites do not give a pure indication of the effect of inversion. RTs to non-composites come closer to this, as in both orientations subjects are able to ignore the conflicting information and simply name the face whose top half is displayed. And as can be seen in Figure 3, 6-year-olds were equally fast on inverted (1263 msec) and upright (1237) non-composites, 10-year-olds were slower on inverted (1020 msec) than on upright (935 msec) non-composites, whereas adults were much slower on inverted (1063 msec) than on upright non-composites (818 msec).

Conclusions

The pattern of results reported by Young et al. is remarkably robust. Young et al.'s familiar faces were famous males; Experiment 1 extends their results to faces of familiar personal acquaintances of both sexes. In addition, the first- and fifth-grade groups each provided a complete replication of the pattern of data on two independent groups of subjects viewing different stimulus sets.

The data from Experiment 1 support two conclusions: (1) For familiar faces, there is no increase with age in configural or holistic encoding, at least in the sense tapped by the Young et al. procedure. That is, age had no effect on either the RT advantage for non-composites over composites, or on the restriction of this advantage to the upright condition. (2) The question of whether young children are as affected by the orientation of familiar faces as are adults receives an unequivocal answer: no. Older subjects were much more disrupted by stimulus inversion than were younger subjects. Indeed, first-graders were equally fast on the non-composite faces, whether they were right-side up or upside down. Adults, in contrast, were much slower when the faces were inverted, in spite of the fact that they had to differentiate only 6 highly familiar faces, each depicted in a single photograph seen many times in the experiment.

In sum, the important findings of Experiment 1 are that the Age × Orientation interaction typical of encoding unfamiliar faces is also seen here in the recognition of familiar faces, and that this effect is statistically independent of the orientation by composite effect that reveals configural or holistic encoding of faces.

As previously noted, there is reason to believe that children differ less from adults in their representations of highly familiar faces than in their capacity to encode unfamiliar faces (Diamond & Carey, 1977; see Carey, 1981, for a review). Thus, although there appear to be no changes between age 6 and adulthood in the degree to which familiar faces are encoded configurally or holistically, perhaps young children are less able to encode newly encountered faces in such a manner. In Experiment 2, we turn to the question of whether for unfamiliar faces there is evidence for increasing reliance on configural encoding with age.

EXPERIMENT 2

Configural Encoding of Unfamiliar Faces

Method

Subjects

The children who took part in Experiment 1 also took part in Experiment 2. Also, 18 young adults who had not taken part in Experiment 1 participated.

Materials

The two sets of faces (male and female) used with adults in Experiment 1 were used in Experiment 2. Neither the children nor the adults who served as subjects were familiar with these faces.

Procedure

Adults.   For each set of same-sex faces, subjects first learned the first name of each person, by cycling through the set of whole faces displayed on the Macintosh screen. Usually adults learned the set of six names after 2 or 3 runs through the whole set. Following this, the procedure of Experiment 1 was followed: three practice trials with whole faces to familiarize subjects with the voice key, then naming the top half faces alone, and finally naming the top half faces in the composite and non-composite photographs (the experiment proper). For the inverted condition, the names were learned on upright faces; only in the final experimental condition were the faces displayed upside down. As in Experiment 1, whether subjects learned male faces first or female faces first and whether the first set was seen upright or inverted was counterbalanced.

Children.   Pilot studies with 6-year-olds revealed that it was almost impossible for them to learn names for six faces under these conditions. Therefore, we modified the procedure as follows. Children began with two photographs, and learned the names of the two people depicted. Then a third photograph was added, and the set of three names practised until the children were fluent. This process was repeated until all six names were learned. At this point, additional practice was given with the stimuli presented on the Macintosh screen, until the children could produce all six names without hesitation. The procedure then continued as for adults. For first-graders, the initial learning process sometimes took two 20-minute sessions. Because of the extraordinary difficulty of learning to associate six names with six new faces, first-graders learned and were tested on only one set, presented in the upright orientation. Half the children learned the female set and half the male set. Fifth-graders learned both sets and were tested on one set upright and one inverted, counterbalanced as for the adults.

Results

Errors

Figure 4 shows the pattern of errors. The steep developmental function usually found on tasks involving the encoding of unfamiliar faces is reflected in these data. Both groups of children made substantial numbers of errors (first-graders, 21%, fifth-graders, 17%). These error rates were twice as high as those on familiar faces in Experiment 1 (8% at both ages). The adult error rate (10%) did not differ from that on familiar faces in Experiment 1 (10%).

The pattern of errors at all ages is consistent with configural encoding of unfamiliar faces. First-graders, who were tested only on upright faces, made twice as many errors on composites (28%) as on non-composites (14%), $F(1, 19) = 26.32$, $p < 0.001$. An ANOVA on the fifth-grade error data revealed a main effect for stimulus type, composites 21%, non-composites 14%, $F(1, 20) = 18.58$, $p < 0.001$, and a Stimulus Type × Orientation interaction (see Figure 4), $F(1, 20) = 10.45$, $p < 0.004$). An ANOVA on the adult error data revealed no effects of stimulus type or orientation, but the pattern was the same as that for the fifth-graders—more errors on composites than on non-composites upright, but no such difference for inverted faces (see Figure 4).

Reaction Times

An ANOVA on RT for correct responses was carried out at each age. Because of extremely long RTs (relative to other subjects of the same age) and high variability, two fifth-graders were removed from the analysis, leaving 18 of that age. As can be seen in Figure 5, subjects of each age were slower on upright composites than on upright non-composites. Adults and fifth-graders responded equally quickly to the two types when the stimuli were inverted. The Orientation × Stimulus Type interaction was significant for fifth-graders and approached this level for adults: fifth grade, $F(1, 17) = 5.58$, $p < 0.03$; adults, $F(1, 17) = 3.04$, $p < 0.09$.

First-Graders. Half of the youngest group of subjects learned the female faces and half the male faces. There was no effect of stimulus set. The difference between composites and non-composites (all upright) was significant, $F(1, 19) = 17.18$, $p < 0.001$).

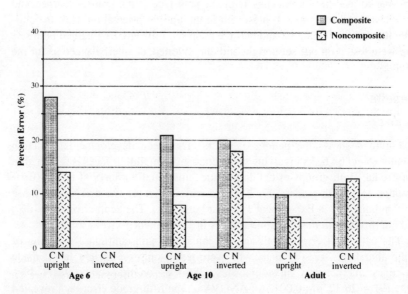

FIG. 4. Experiment 2: Error rates.

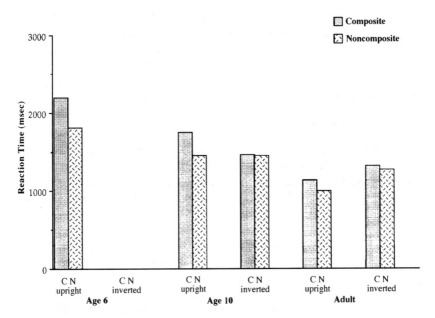

FIG. 5.   Experiment 2: RT for correct responses.

Fifth-Graders.   There were no effects of stimulus set or order (upright or inverted first). There was a main effect for stimulus type: $F(1, 17) = 10.93$, $p < 0.001$; RT for composites (1608 msec) was slower than for non-composites (1454 msec). The main effect for inversion approached significance, $p < 0.1$; RTs to upright faces (1602 msec) were *slower* than RTs to inverted faces (1460 msec). The only other significant effect was the Stimulus Type $\times$ Orientation interaction reported above (Figure 5).

Adults.   There were main effects both for orientation and stimulus type. RT to upright faces (1065 msec) was faster than to inverted faces (1303 msec), $F(1, 17) = 9.11$, $p < 0.008$. RT to composites (1231 msec) was slower than to non-composites (1137 msec), $F(1, 17) = 10.56$, $p < 0.005$. The stimulus type by orientation interaction is depicted in Figure 5, and as mentioned above, approached significance. There were no significant effects involving any other variable.

Age Changes in the Effect of Orientation

Just as with familiar faces, inversion interferes with performance increasingly with age. Figure 6 shows the difference between RTs to upright and inverted stimuli. For both composites and non-composites, this difference score is greater for adults than for fifth-graders. Averaged over both stimulus types, fifth-graders

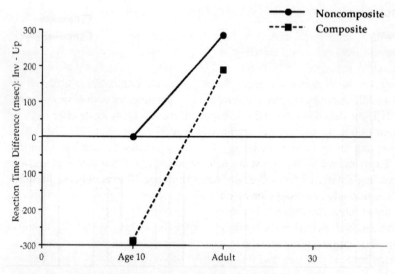

FIG. 6.   Experiment 2: RT for inverted faces minus RT for upright faces.

are actually slower in the upright condition, whereas adults are faster in the upright condition. The adult advantage for the upright holds for composites as well as non-composites. This result confirms the magnitude of the adult advantage in recognizing faces presented upright over those presented inverted; this effect is so robust that it overwhelms the difficulty associated with disentangling the top half of upright composites. Just as for the familiar faces in Experiment 1, the best estimate of the true inversion effect comes from the non-composites alone: adults responded much faster on upright (993 msec) than on inverted (1279 msec) non-composites, whereas the fifth-graders were equally fast on the two (upright non-composites, 1464 msec; inverted non-composites, 1455 msec).

An overall ANOVA including the data from both fifth-graders and adults revealed a main effect for age, $F(1, 34) = 11.829$, $p < 0.005$. Children (1531 msec) responded more slowly than did adults (1184 msec). There was also a main effect for stimulus type, $F(1, 34) = 20.499$, $p < 0.001$, with composites being responded to more slowly than non-composites, and a Stimulus Type × Orientation interaction, $F(1, 34) = 8.265$, $p < 0.01$. There was no main effect of orientation, $F(1, 34) = 0.703$, n.s. Most important is the Age × Orientation interaction, $F(1, 34) = 11.334$, $p < 0.005$, depicted in Figure 6, and the absence of a three-way Age × Stimulus Type × Orientation interaction, $F(1, 34) = 2.007$, n.s. Thus these results present exactly the same pattern as those from Experiment 1.

Conclusion

These data confirm and extend findings in the literature concerning the developmental function for face encoding. (1) Six-year-olds find it extremely difficult to encode new faces from still photographs, as shown by the fact that some six-year-olds took 40 minutes to learn the names of six unfamiliar adults, and as shown additionally by the steep developmental functions for both error rates and RT. (2) These data show that gains in expertise are still being made after age ten, ten-year-olds make more errors and have slower RTs than adults. (3) These data confirm that this gain in expertise is reflected in increased sensitivity to inversion. Experiment 2 is the first study to show an Age × Orientation interaction in encoding unfamiliar faces over the range from age 10 to adulthood, presumably because other investigations have looked only at error rates in identification, not at more sensitive RT measures.

These data also confirm the robustness of the Young et al. pattern of findings. Composite uprights were more difficult to identify than were non-composites, as reflected both in error rates and RT, and there was no difference between the two types of stimuli when they were inverted.

The new finding from Experiment 2 parallels that from Experiment 1. There is no hint of a developmental change in configural or holistic encoding of unfamiliar faces. Six-year-olds made twice as many errors naming the top half of upright composites as they did naming upright non-composites, and their correct RTs were over 25% slower. Ten-year-olds, like adults, showed the pattern typical of the subjects in Young et al.'s study—interference from the composites when the stimuli were upright but not when they were inverted.

GENERAL DISCUSSION

Young et al.'s composite effect certainly reflects holistic encoding of faces; when upright, the parts of a face are less accessible than are whole faces. Anecdotally, subjects who knew these people very well reported that composite faces, such as that of Nixon and Prince Charles in Figure 1, resembled both familiar people, and that sometimes it was difficult to access which half was whose. The data from Experiments 1 and 2 show that 6-year-old children, no less than 10-year-olds and adults, encode faces holistically. The composite effect is independent of age, even in the presence of the effect that reflects acquisition of expertise, that is, the increased effect of inversion on face recognition. What this means is that the expertise effects are not the result of an increased reliance on holistic encoding.

Tanaka and Farah's (1993) task implicates holistic encoding in the same sense tapped by the Young et al. procedure—the whole face is more accessible than its parts. If expertise is not necessary for holistic encoding, then we should predict no developmental change over the same ages probed in the present studies. Tanaka (personal communication) has carried out a study with 6-, 8-, and 10-

year-olds with just this result. When faces were upright, at all ages equally it was easier to identify Bob's nose in the context of Bob's face than alone. There was no interaction with age, and we would predict no three-way Age × Condition (whole face/part) × Orientation interaction either.

Why is holistic coding sensitive to orientation of the face? That is, why does the whole face interfere with access to the parts only when faces are upright? The first obvious response—that the whole face is represented in memory with respect to a frame of reference (i.e. is oriented)—is only part of an answer, for we *can* recognize faces upside down, however badly. The second response is that, in the upright condition, the relations among the parts of the face create emergent features used in recognition, and these are less accessible (and thus less interfering) when faces are inverted. That is, the second response draws on the hypothesis that upright faces are configurally encoded.

Besides tapping holistic encoding, in the access sense, the Young et al. procedure reflects configural encoding. When the top half of Prince Charles' face is joined to the bottom half of Nixon's face, new relational features among parts of the face are created. If expertise is required for configural encoding, should we not have expected the three-way Age × Stimulus Type (composite/non-composite) × Orientation interaction? Only if children have *no* configural features in their representations of faces. As long as they represent some features of that type, then the interference due to the access sense of holistic encoding should be seen at all three ages, as it was. Thus, these data rule out an encoding switch from complete reliance on piecemeal features of faces to greater reliance on configural features (as proposed in Carey & Diamond, 1977) between ages 6 and adulthood; configural features and clearly represented at all levels of expertise tapped in the present study.

Apparently, there are at least two sources of the inversion effect for faces. First there is holistic encoding, as tapped by the composite effect. This is present throughout the age/expertise range studied here. And then there is something else that is gained with expertise. The something else is the mystery factor.

What is the mystery factor? It is very likely that it is just what we always thought—greater reliance on relational features with expertise. Once the top half of the face has been accessed, it must still be recognized. Adult (expert) recognition is based more on features that can be extracted more easily from upright faces, just as expert dog recognition is based much more on features than can be extracted more easily from upright dogs. A minimal reliance on such features is all that is required for holistic encoding in the access sense; but expertise at face encoding (or dog encoding) requires greater reliance on such features.

Several important pieces of the puzzle still need to fall into place. Exactly how are these relational features represented? Are they simply represented as ratios of distances among various points on a face? Many have suggested another possibility—that the features of an individual face are encoded with reference to a norm (e.g. see Rhodes & Tremewan, this issue). Expertise is not required for norm-based coding; Rhodes and Tremewan showed caricature effects for inverted faces that were equal in magnitude to those for upright faces, even in the presence of large effects of orientation. Ellis (1992) showed that young children judged caricatures of Kylie Monogue to be her best likeness. Whatever features, including relational features, are used to individuate faces, they may be encoded relative to a norm.

Still, within the framework of norm-based coding, a possible way to think about the increased reliance on relational features with expertise is that the representation of the norm changes with expertise. At all levels of expertise, it crudely reflects the shared overall configuration of faces, but with increasing expertise it becomes more and more completely specified. A simple metaphor is that it becomes specified in terms of more and more points. Thus, with increasing expertise, norm-based coding will engage many more points, and many more spatial relations among points. At all levels of expertise, distinctive configural features are encoded relative to the norm, but these become more adequate to distinguishing among highly similar faces as the norm becomes more fleshed out. As inversion interferes with norm-based coding of relational distinguishing features, improvement with expertise at encoding upright faces will be greater than improvement at encoding inverted faces (the Expertise × Orientation interaction).

Several well-known phenomena are consistent with this picture. Valentine (1991) showed that inversion interferes more with adult (expert) encoding of typical faces than with atypical faces. On the assumption that typical faces are closer to the norm, and thus that more subtle relational features are required to distinguish among them, typical faces will place higher demands on the norm-based coding mechanism that inversion disrupts. This analysis also predicts a Race × Orientation interaction for subjects who are experts at distinguishing among faces of only one racial group. That is, subjects should show a larger inversion effect for faces at which they are expert than for those from other racial groups. Rhodes, Tan, Brake, & Taylor (1989) obtained this result.[1]

Recent developmental findings from Ellis (1992) bear on the hypothesis that acquisition of expertise involves a fuller specification of the norm—the shared configuration among faces. He found a Distinctiveness × Age interaction in a face recognition task; that is, 6- to 7-year-olds showed no recognition advantage for atypical faces, and over the age range from 6 to 14 developmental improve-

---

[1] Bruce and Valentine (1986) found the opposite interaction—greater inversion effect for other race faces—but they did not have a full crossover design, so that their finding may reflect differences in difficulty between the two sets of faces. Also, the faces within each race were not as homogeneous as those of Rhodes and Tremewan, as Bruce and Valentine included stimuli with beards, moustaches, and glasses. Finally, Bruce and Valentine equated performance on the upright by giving subjects less time to encode same-race faces, and this manipulation may have interfered with the encoding of just those subtle relational features that are more easily encoded from upright faces.

ment at encoding atypical faces was greater than that for encoding typical faces. Typicality was determined by adult (expert) ratings. These data show that the youngest children's norm is not adequate to distinguishing what adults judge as typical faces from those adults judge atypical. As the norm becomes more fully specified, distinguishing features from atypical faces are the first to become employable.

As previously noted, the results from these studies argue against the hypothesis that there is an encoding shift between ages 6 and 10 from complete reliance on relatively more piecemeal distinguishing features to greater reliance on relatively more cnfigural distinguishing features of faces (Carey & Diamond, 1977). At all ages, children encode faces in terms of configural distinguishing features. At all ages, children are sensitive to the orientation of the face; at least from age 6 they gain access to the whole upright face faster than to its parts, and at least from age 4 they show caricature effects when only the configuration of the face is manipulated. However, it is possible that the Age × Orientation interaction that marks increasing expertise at face encoding reflects a fuller specification of the shared configuration of the face, so that the young child's configural encoding involves many fewer features than does the 10-year-old's or the adult's. In this sense only, then, is it likely that expertise reflects increasing reliance on configural distinguishing features of the face.

REFERENCES

Bartlett, J.C., & Searcy, J. (1993). Inversion and configuration of faces. *Cognitive Psychology, 25* (3), 281–316.

Benson, P.J., & Perrett, D.I. (1991). Perception and recognition of photographic quality facial caricatures: Implications for the recognition of natural images. *European Journal of Cognitive Psychology, 3,* 105–135.

Benton, A.L., & van Allen, M.W. (1973). Test of facial recognition. *Neurosensory Center Publication No. 287.* Iowa City, IA: University Hospitals, Department of Neurology.

Blaney, R.L., & Winograd, E. (1978). Developmental differences in children's recognition memory for faces. *Developmental Psychology, 14,* 441–442.

Brennan, S.E. (1985). The caricature generator. *Leonardo, 18,* 170–178.

Brooks, R.M. & Goldstein, A.G. (1963). Recognition by children of inverted photographs of faces. *Child Development, 34,* 1033–1040.

Bruce & Valentine   (1986).

Carey, S.   (1981).   The development of face perception. In G. Davies, H. Ellis, & J. Shephard (Eds.), *Perceiving and remembering faces.* New York: Academic Press.

Carey, S. & Diamond, R. (1977). From piecemeal to configurational representation of faces. *Science, 195,* 312–314.

Carey, S., Diamond, R., & Woods, B. (1980). The development of face recognition—a maturational component? *Developmental Psychology, 16,* (4), 257–269.

Chance, J., Goldstein, A.G., & Schicht, W. (1967). Effects of acquaintance and friendship on children's recognition of classmates' faces. *Psychonomic Science, 7,* 223–224.

Diamond, R., & Carey, S. (1977). Developmental changes in the representation of faces. *Journal of Experimental Child Psychology, 23,* 1–22.

Diamond, R., & Carey, S. (1986). Why faces are and are not special: An effect of expertise. Journal of Experimental Psychology: *General, 115* (2), 107–117.

Ellis, H.D. (1992). The development of face processing skills. In V. Bruce, A. Cowey, A.W. Ellis, & D.I. Perrett (Eds.), *Processing the facial image* (pp. 105–111). Proceedings of a Royal Society Discussion Meeting, July 9–10, 1991. Oxford: Clarendon Press.

Ellis, H.D., Shepherd, J.W., & Davies, G.M. (1979). Identification of familiar and unfamiliar faces from internal and external features: Some implications for theories of face recognition. *Perception, 8,* 431–439.

Fagan, J.F. (1979). The origins of facial pattern recognition. In M.H. Bornstein & W. Kessen (Eds.), *Psychological development from infancy: Image to intention.* (pp. 83–113). Hillsdale, NJ: Lawrence Erlbaum Associates, Inc.

Farah, M.J., Tanaka, J.W. & Drain, H.M. (in press). What causes the face inversion effect? *Journal of Experimental Psychology: Human Perception and Performance.*

Flin, R. (1980). Age effects in children's memory for unfamiliar faces. *Developmental Psychology, 16,* 373–374.

Flin, R.H. (1983). *The development of face recognition.* Unpublished Ph.D. thesis, Aberdeen University.

Goldstein, A.G. (1975). Recognition of inverted photographs of faces by children and adults. *Journal of Genetic Psychology, 127,* 109–123.

Goldstein, A.G., & Chance, J.F. (1964). Recognition of children's faces. *Child Development, 35,* 129–136.

Goldstein, A.G., & Mackenberg, E.J. (1966). Recognition of human faces from isolated facial features: a developmental study. *Psychonomic Science, 6,* 149–150.

Haig, N.D. (1984). The effect of feature displacement on face recognition. *Perception, 13,* 505–512.

Johnson, M.H., & Morton, J. (1991). *Biology and Cognitive Development: The Case of Face Recognition.* Oxford: Basil Blackwell.

Levine, S.C. (1981). Developmental changes in right hemisphere involvement in face recognition. In C.T. Best (Ed.), *Developmental neuropsychology and education: Hemisphere specialization and integration,* (pp. 157–191). New York: Academic Press.

Posner, M.I., & Keele, S.W. (1968). On the genesis of abstract ideas. *Journal of Experimental Psychology, 77,* 353–363.

Rhodes, G., Brake, S., & Atkinson, A. (1993). What's lost in inverted faces? *Cognition, 47,* 25–57.

Rhodes, G., Brennan, S., & Carey, S. (1987). Identification and ratings of caricatures: implications for mental representations of faces. *Cognitive Psychology, 19* (4), 473–479.

Rhodes, G., Tan, S., Brake, S., & Taylor, K. (1989). Expertise and configural coding in face recognition. *British Journal of Psychology, 80,* 313–331.

Saltz, E., & Sigel, I.E. (1967). Concept overdiscrimination in children. *Journal of Experimental Psychology, 73,* 1–8.

Scapinello, K.F., & Yarmey, A.D. (1970). The role of familiarity and orientation in immediate and delayed recognition of pictorial stimuli. *Psychonomic Science, 21,* 329–330.

274 CAREY AND DIAMOND

Tanaka, J.W., & Farah, M.J. (1991). Second-order relational properties and the inversion effect: Testing a theory of face perception. *Perception and Psychophysics, 50,* 367–372.

Tanaka, J.W., & Farah, M.J. (1993). Parts and wholes in face recognition. *Quarterly Journal of Experimental Psychology, 46A,* 225–245.

Thompson, P. (1980). Margaret Thatcher: A new illusion. *Perception, 9,* 483–484.

Valentine, T. (1991). A unified account of the effects of distinctiveness, inversion, and race in face recognition. *The Quarterly Journal of Experimental Psychology, 43A* (2), 161–204.

Yin, R.K. (1969). Looking at upside-down faces. *Journal of Experimental Psychology, 81,* 141–145.

Yin, R.K. (1970). *Face recognition: A special process?* Ph.D. thesis, Massachusetts Institute of Technology.

Young, A.W., Hellawell, D., & Hay, D.C. (1987). Configural information in face perception. *Perception, 16,* 747–759.

Manuscript received 1 May 1994

VISUAL COGNITION, 1994, *1* (2/3), 275–311

Understanding Face Recognition: Caricature Effects, Inversion, and the Homogeneity Problem

Gillian Rhodes and Tanya Tremewan

University of Canterbury, Christchurch, New Zealand

Faces and other objects that share a configuration present a special problem to the visual system. Two components of the visual system's solution to this homogeneity problem have been identified. Inversion studies have identified the use of relational features (Diamond & Carey, 1986; Rhodes, Brake, & Atkinson, 1993), and caricature studies have identified norm-based coding (Carey, Rhodes, Diamond, & Hamilton, in preparation; Rhodes, Brennan, & Carey, 1987; Rhodes & McLean, 1990). Here we explore a possible link between these two components, asking whether caricature effects depend selectively on exaggeration of relational features. If so, then inversion, which makes relational features particularly difficult to code (compared with isolated features), should reduce caricature effects. In three experiments we found a caricature equivalence effect (caricatures identified as accurately as undistorted images and both better than anticaricatures) that was unaffected by orientation, suggesting that relational feature coding is not necessary for caricatures to be effective. Therefore, caricature and inversion effects reflect distinct components of face recognition. Caricature level and orientation also interacted differently with other factors, as would be expected if their effects depend

Requests for reprints should be sent to G. Rhodes, Department of Psychology, Canterbury University, Private Bag 4800, Christchurch, New Zealand. EMAIL: g.rhodes@psyc.canterbury.ac.nz

This research was supported by a grant from the New Zealand Foundation for Research, Science and Technology to the first author. Portions of the work were presented at the International Congress of Psychology, in Brussels, 1992, and at the meeting of the American Psychological Association, in Washington, DC, 1992. Special thanks are due to Ian McLean, who photographed all the classmates, and to Mark Tremewan for his excellent work creating the veridical images used by the caricature program. We also thank the students and staff of Hagley, Hillmorton, and Riccarton high schools for their generous participation in these studies, and Sue Allard, Douglas Harré, and Mark Tremewan for help recruiting subjects. Thanks also to Susan Carey and Rhea Diamond for many helpful discussions about this research.

upon different underlying processes. For one set of faces there was a caricature advantage in accuracy (Experiments 1 and 3). This superportrait effect occurred even for subjects who were unfamiliar with the faces prior to the experiment (Experiment 3), a result with important forensic implications. Furthermore, the effect was restricted to upright faces. Therefore, although caricatures can be recognized as well as undistorted images whatever features are exaggerated, exaggeration of relational features may be needed for a superportrait effect.

You're so exactly like other people ... the two eyes, so (marking their places in the air with his thumb) nose in the middle, mouth under. It's always the same. Now if you had the two eyes on the same side of the nose, for instance—or the mouth at the top—that would be *some* help.
[Humpty-Dumpty to Alice on the difficulty of recognizing her]

(Carroll, 1946)

Faces present a considerable challenge to the visual system, and meeting that challenge is a protracted process developmentally (for reviews see Carey, 1992; Ellis, 1992). Despite the fact that babies arrive with a special interest in faces (Goren, Sarty, & Wu, 1975; Johnson, Dziurawiec, Ellis, & Morton, 1991; Johnson & Morton, 1991; Morton & Johnson, 1991), it takes at least ten years for children to achieve adult levels of expertise (Carey & Diamond, this issue; Carey, Diamond, & Woods, 1980). Even then, performance is easily disrupted, with faces from unfamiliar races or in unfamiliar orientations creating difficulties (for reviews see Bothwell, Brigham, & Malpass, 1989; Diamond & Carey, 1986; Lindsay & Wells, 1983; Rhodes et al., 1993).

As Humpty-Dumpty pointed out, faces are difficult because they share a configuration, having the same basic parts in the same basic arrangement. They are unusually homogeneous. A few may have unique distinguishing features, like a scar or a handle-bar moustache, but such isolated features generally will not suffice for face recognition. Nor will the kind of part-based analysis used for basic-level recognition or primal access (Biederman, 1987; Marr, 1982), which can tell us that we're looking at a face, but not whose face it is (see Rhodes et al., 1993 for further discussion).

This *homogeneity problem* is most dramatically illustrated by faces, but it is not restricted to them. It is also important for many biologically significant discriminations, such as distinguishing between different kinds of animals and plants, as well as for more mundane discriminations between different cars or chairs. Isolated feature cues may suffice for some of these within-category discriminations (e.g. a zebra and a horse can be distinguished by the presence or absence of stripes), but to the extent that such cues are not available, the discrimination presents the same problem as face recognition. By understanding how faces are recognized, therefore, we may also extend our understanding of subordinate level and individual recognition more generally.

Any complete theory of recognition must give an account of how we solve the homogeneity problem. Yet most research has focused on the object constancy problem—i.e. how we recognize objects despite changes in their appearance due to changes in vantage point, lighting, and so on. Here we focus on the homogeneity problem. We begin by reviewing two separate lines of research, each of which has identified one component of the solution.

Using Transformations to Investigate the Homogeneity Problem

A fruitful approach to understanding how we solve the homogeneity problem has been to study the effects of stimulus transformations on recognition. Two kinds of transformations, *inversion* and *caricaturing*, have been especially revealing.

The Inversion Effect. Yin (1969, 1970) compared recognition of faces and other mono-oriented objects (all within-category discriminations) and found that faces were disproportionately affected by inversion. This disproportionate inversion effect can also be found for other homogeneous classes with which subjects have expertise. For example, Diamond and Carey (1986) found that dog experts, but not novices, showed inversion decrements for dog recognition that were as large as for face recognition. Therefore, inversion appears to disrupt the coding of information that experts normally use to solve the homogeneity problem. For ease of exposition we will normally refer to the *disproportionate* inversion effect simply as *the inversion effect*.

Caricature Effects. Caricaturing, in contrast, does not disrupt recognition of faces (e.g. Benson & Perrett, 1991, 1994; Carey, et al., in prep.; Mauro & Kubovy, 1992; Rhodes et al., 1987) or other homogeneous objects (Rhodes & McLean, 1990). On the contrary, caricatures,which exaggerate distinctive information in a face, are at least as recognizable as undistorted faces, and both are more recognizable than anticaricatures, which reduce distinctive information. This pattern has been obtained for identification of line drawings (Benson & Perrett, 1994; Carey et al., in prep., Rhodes et al., 1987) and photographic images of faces (Benson & Perrett, 1991) and for line drawings of birds (Rhodes & McLean, 1990). Using a different paradigm, old/new recognition of Identi-kit faces, Mauro and Kubovy also found that recognition memory (sensitivity to discriminate old from new items) was better for caricatures of studied faces than for the studied faces themselves. Only when cross-medium comparisons are made between line-drawn caricatures and undistorted photographs are caricatures less effective than undistorted images (e.g. Hagen & Perkins, 1983; Tversky & Baratz, 1985). Sometimes caricatures even function as "superportraits", with the paradoxical quality of being more recognizable than undistorted images (Benson & Perrett, 1994; Rhodes et al., 1987; Rhodes & McLean, 1990).

Terminology. Before considering how the inversion and caricature effects should be interpreted, let us introduce some terminology. We will talk about a *caricature advantage* or *superportrait effect* when caricatures are recognized better than veridical, undistorted images ($C > V$), and about a *caricature equivalence effect* when caricatures are recognized as well as veridical images and both better than anticaricatures ($C = V > A$). In caricature equivalence, the direction of exaggeration has a crucial effect on recognition of the image: distortion that exaggerates distinctive information relative to the norm—i.e. caricaturing— does not disrupt recognition, whereas an equal metric distortion in the opposite direction—i.e. a reduction of distinctiveness—does disrupt recognition. The stipulation that caricatures and veridicals should both be better than anticaricatures ensures that the equivalence of caricatures and veridicals is non-trivial (e.g. not due to their being perceptually indistinguishable). We will talk about *caricature effects* when we want to refer to both effects collectively ($C \geq V > A$).

Interpreting the Inversion and Caricature Effects

The Inversion Effect and Relational Features. Diamond and Carey (1986) have proposed that the features used to distinguish faces lie on a continuum from relatively isolated to relatively relational (many others have made a similar distinction between isolated features and relational or configural information— see Rhodes et al., 1993, for a review). Examples of isolated features would be colour and texture of hair and presence or absence of glasses or facial hair. Relational features are more complex than isolated features, in the sense that they cannot be specified without reference to several parts of the face at once. Examples would include the spacing of internal features, ratios of distances between parts of the face, and global shape. Diamond and Carey have argued that the (disproportionate) inversion effect for faces and other homogeneous classes with which we have expertise is the result of reliance on relational features, which are especially difficult to encode in inverted stimuli. Direct support for this view comes from a study by Rhodes et al. (1993), who showed that inverting faces disrupts detection of changes to relational features like spacing and orientation of internal features more than changes to simpler isolated features like the presence/absence of glasses or moustache.[1] Similarly, Bartlett and Searcy (1993; see also Bartlett, 1994) found that faces made to look grotesque by changing the spatial relations between parts no longer looked grotesque when inverted, whereas faces whose grotesqueness was associated

---

[1]Of course all the features are still present in the inverted images, in an objective sense, but something about the unfamiliar orientation seems to make relational features particularly difficult to encode. Perhaps the mismatch between the intrinsic and retinal/gravitational tops of inverted, but normally mono-oriented, objects (Rock, 1974) is especially disruptive to coding relational features, which already require reference to more than one part of the face.

with isolated feature changes (e.g. fangs added, eyes reddened) still looked grotesque when inverted. All these inversion studies strongly suggest that use of relational features is part of the visual system's solution to the homogeneity problem.

Caricature Effects and Norm-Based Coding. The effectiveness of caricatures has been interpreted as evidence for norm-based coding (Carey et al., in prep.; Rhodes et al., 1987; Rhodes & McLean, 1990). To see why, consider the nature of the caricature transformation. Under this transformation, all the points that describe a face move systematically with respect to the norm, exaggerating the differences between the face and the norm (for more details see the Method section of Experiment 1). Therefore, one can think of the norm as a frame of reference in which caricature transformations are systematic and simple. In any other co-ordinate system (e.g. the 2D picture plane or 3D space), all the points on the face move haphazardly. If, as seems reasonable, caricatures are effective because they exaggerate the very features we use to recognize faces, then those features seem to be norm-deviation features. Correspondingly, when these deviations from the mean are reduced in anticaricatures, then recognition suffers.

Alternatively, however, one might argue that caricature effects are simply distinctiveness effects, with no need to appeal to norm-based coding at all. A distinctive face activates fewer distractors in memory than does a typical face, making it easier to pick out the target activation from a background of distractor activation and so recognize the face (e.g. Bartlett, Hurry, & Thorley, 1984; Cohen & Carr, 1975; Going & Read, 1974; Light, Kayra-Stuart, & Hollander, 1979; Valentine, 1991; Winograd, 1981). Because caricatures are more distinctive than undistorted images, they will activate fewer distractors in "face-space", and this reduction might be sufficient to offset the mismatch between the caricature and the target. Anticaricatures would be especially ineffective because they both fail to match the target and are non-distinctive (thus activating many distractors). On this view faces would simply be stored as exemplars or points in a multidimensional space, and norm-deviation vectors would have no special psychological significance (e.g. Valentine, 1991).

However, a recent study by Carey et al. (in prep.; also briefly described in Carey, 1992) suggests that distinctiveness effects *alone* cannot account for caricature effects. If they could, then only an image's proximity to the target and its distinctiveness should determine its recognizability. Whether or not it lies on the norm-deviation vector would be irrelevant. Carey et al. set out to test this prediction by creating a new type of distortion, called a lateral caricature, in which the points on a face are moved in a direction orthogonal to the norm-deviation direction, rather than away from the norm as in a caricature, or towards the norm as in an anticaricature (see Figure 1). They created 50% caricatures, anticaricatures, and laterals, all equi-distant metrically from the veridical image but differing in distinctiveness (see Figure 2 for a sample set). Caricatures are most distinctive, anticaricatures are least distinctive, and laterals are intermediate. Therefore, if caricature effects are solely distinctiveness effects and do not depend on *how* an image deviates from the norm, then the laterals should be easier to recognize than the less distinctive anticaricatures. Of course, the caricatures should be easiest of all, because they are the most distinctive. As predicted, the laterals were significantly more difficult to recognize ($M = 0.13$) than the anicaricatures ($M = 0.22$), which, in turn, were significantly more difficult than the caricatures ($M = 0.45$). Caricatures and undistorted images ($M = 0.50$) were recognized equally well. These results show that caricature effects in face recognition cannot be explained *solely* as distinctiveness effects in an exemplar model. Rather, the way that a face deviates from a norm seems to provide crucial information for recognition.

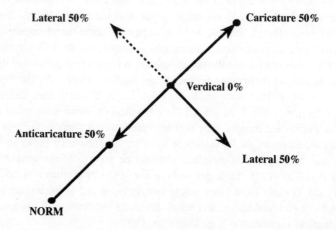

FIG. 1. Shows how a point on a face (Veridical 0%) moves in a caricature, anticaricature, and lateral caricature. The corresponding point on the norm (NORM) is found (e.g. the tip of the nose on the two faces would be corresponding points), and the point on the face is moved relative to that norm point. In a 50% caricature, the point on the face is moved 50% further away from the corresponding point on the norm, in the direction of the vector joining the two points. In a 50% anticaricature, the point is moved 50% back along that vector towards the corresponding point on the norm. In the lateral caricature, the point is moved orthogonally to the vector in one of the two possible directions shown. The choice of direction for the lateral move was constrained to reflect the bilateral symmetry of the face. All the points on the left side of the face moved the same way (either left or right, with respect to the norm-deviation direction), as did all points on the right side of the face. This resulted in four laterals for each face. The most face-like one was used in the recognition test. (Reproduced from Rhodes, 1994).

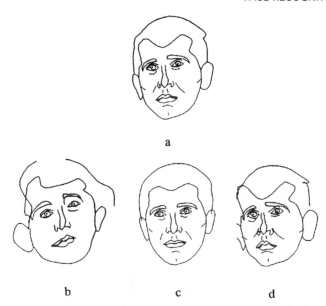

a

b   c   d

FIG. 2.   Images of Oliver North used by Carey et al. (in prep.): (a) undistorted 0%; (b) 50% lateral caricature; (c) –50% anticaricature; (d) 50% caricature. (Reproduced from Rhodes, 1994).

Do Relational Features Contribute to Caricature Effects?

The inversion and caricature studies have identified two components of the visual system's solution of the homogeneity problem. Relational features code spatial relations *within* a face, and norm-deviation features code differences *between* a face and a norm. However, the two may not be unrelated. Given that we use relational features to recognize faces, some of the norm-deviation features may code how these relational features deviate from the norm, and so caricature effects might depend on our ability to exploit relational features.

Alternatively, caricatures may exploit a more basic feature of recognition—namely, its reliance on distinctive features—with exaggeration of any kind of distinctive feature serving to capture or enhance a likeness. Support for this latter possibility comes from numerous discrimination learning studies with both humans and other animals, which have shown that the most effective way to signal category membership is often to exaggerate those features that distinguish the target category from distractor categories, even when those features are simple differences on a continuum such as wavelength (for recent reviews see Thomas, Mood, Morrison, & Wiertelak, 1991; Thomas, 1993). This caricature-like phenomenon, called "peak shift", has also been demonstrated in connectionist discrimination learning networks. For example, Enquist and Arak (1993) trained simple networks on a pattern recognition task and found enhanced responses to "caricatures" of the training stimuli when they tested generalization performance. Their results, together with the peak shift results in discrimination learning studies, suggest that caricature effects may be a very general feature of perceptual systems. (For further discussion see Rhodes, in preparation.)

THE EXPERIMENTS

In the experiments reported here, we investigated the role of relational feature coding in caricature effects. Specifically, we asked whether the exaggeration of relational features contributes selectively to caricature effects. If it does, then inversion, which disproportionately disrupts the coding of relational features (compared with isolated features), should reduce or eliminate caricature effects. If, instead, caricature effects are unmodified by inversion, then caricature effects must not depend particularly on the exaggeration of relational features. This is not to say that relational features are not being used to recognize the images—the overall inversion decrement might be quite large—only that the relative effectiveness of caricatures, undistorted images, and anticaricatures would not depend selectively on coding relational features. Rather, the exaggeration of other simpler features that can be encoded from inverted faces must be sufficient to generate caricature effects.

We also sought converging evidence on whether caricature and inversion effects reflect distinct components of face processing by examining how caricature level and orientation interacted with other factors. If the two effects are tapping distinct components of the visual system's solution to the homogeneity problem, then caricature level and orientation may well be modified in different ways by other factors. Alternatively, if they both reflect the use of relational feature coding, then similar patterns of interactions with other factors should be found.

The choice of other factors was guided by a desire to find out more about how caricatures effects operate. In contrast with inversion effects that have been studied for at least 25 years, caricature effects have only recently attracted the attention of cognitive psychologists. In an attempt to find out more about these effects, we selected additional factors that would allow us to address the following questions: Are caricatures only effective for impoverished stimuli, as some have suggested (Experiment 1)? Are they more effective for personally known than for famous faces (Experiments 1 and 2)? Are they only effective for highly familiar faces (Experiment 3)? These questions are discussed in greater detail in the introductions to the relevant experiments.

The logic of the experiments rests on two assumptions. The first—that inversion has greater impact on the coding of relational than isolated features—receives clear support from Rhodes et al.'s (1993) and Bartletts' studies described above. The second—that relational features are exaggerated in the caricatures we are using—needs some justification because the caricature generator (Brennan, 1982, 1985) does not *explicitly* code relational features. It simply codes deviations of landmark points on a face from corresponding points on the norm, and all these deviation vectors are increased in length by a specified

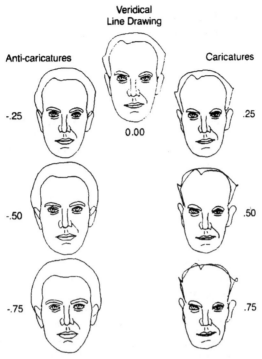

FIG. 3. A set of caricatures and anticaricatures for a face (exaggeration level's given as proportions). (Reproduced from Rhodes et al, 1987).

percentage to create a caricature. However, *distinctive relational features* are implicit in these representations, just as they are in an intensity array or a primal sketch, and are exaggerated[2] in the caricatures along with the more isolated features like the size of the eyes, nose, mouth, or ears. Take, for example, a face with an unusually high hairline (Figure 3). Points on this hairline will be higher than corresponding points on the norm's hairline and so will be shifted higher still in the caricature, thus exaggerating the distinctively high hairline. Had the hairline been unusually low, it would have become lower in the caricature. Figure 3 also shows that other distinctive relational figures are exaggerated. For example, the eyebrows are unusually close to the eyes and get even closer in the caricatures (decreasing to more normal proximity in the anticaricatures), and the distinctive asymmetry of the mouth increases. Therefore, although the caricature generator does not explicitly encode distinctive relational features, such features are implicit in the representations used, and at least some of them are exaggerated in the caricatures. This should not be surprising, because the landmark points were initially chosen to represent the spatial layout of the internal features

---

[2]Note that the exaggeration amplifies whatever tendency is present in the face: larger-than-average ears will get bigger in a caricature, and smaller-than-average eyes will get even smaller.

and face outline (Brennan, 1982, 1985), a layout that captures a face's relational features as well as the details of its isolated features.

EXPERIMENT 1

In Experiment 1, we asked whether orientation interacts with caricature level.[3] Additivity of these factors would suggest that caricature and inversion effects tap distinct aspects of face processing. We also sought converging evidence for the independence (or otherwise) of these two effects by examining whether caricature level and orientation interacted differently with other factors. These other factors were picture quality and type of face.

Picture quality was included to investigate whether caricature effects are an artefact of impoverished stimuli, as some have claimed (e.g. Benson & Perrett, 1991). It is certainly true that the more dramatic superportrait effects have been found with very simple line drawings (e.g. Benson & Perrett, 1994; Rhodes et al., 1987) and not with photographic caricatures (Benson & Perrett, 1991, although ceiling effects may have created problems with these images). Therefore, in Experiment 1, in addition to the plain drawings used previously, we included enhanced drawings to see whether caricatures are still effective with less impoverished images. Although less detailed than photographs, the enhanced drawings had the hair, irises, and brows filled in, and glasses, moustaches, earrings and any extra lines not available in the caricature program added where appropriate. Any impossible lines were also removed. Comparison of Figure 4 with Figures 2 and 3 shows the difference in quality of the plain and enhanced images. Varying stimulus quality also served as a manipulation check, ensuring that the size of the inversion decrement was sensitive to the use of relational features. The inversion decrement should be larger for plain than enhanced drawings, given that the former have fewer isolated feature cues than the latter (thus forcing reliance on relational features).

We also varied the type of face (personally known or famous). At the time the study was carried out it seemed that caricatures might be more effective for personally known faces than for famous faces. A caricature advantage in recognition had been reported for personally known faces (Rhodes et al., 1987), but not for famous faces (Benson & Perrett, 1991). Perhaps the greater familiarity we have with personally known faces increases the effectiveness of caricatures. We investigated this possibility by including both types of face in Experiment 1.[4]

---

[3]The predicted interaction between caricature level and orientation is not a cross-over interaction. Some might worry that such interactions are weak because they can be transformed away. Nevertheless, we believe that they can provide valuable information about underlying mechanisms. To see that this is so, one need only consider their role in the discovery that relational feature coding is used to solve the homogeneity problem (e.g. Yin, 1969, 1970; Diamond & Carey, 1986; Rhodes et al., 1993).

[4]Although type of face is probably largely a familiarity manipulation (although the type of experience also differs), it covers a relatively small range of familiarity, and we reserve the "familiarity" label for the more powerful familiarity manipulation in Experiment 3, where we compare personally known faces with faces that were completely unfamiliar to the subjects prior to the experiment.

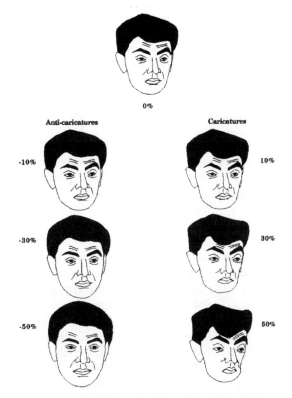

FIG. 4. A set of enhanced caricatures and anticaricatures of Rowan Atkinson used in Experiment 1 (exaggeration levels given as percentages). (Reproduced from Rhodes, 1994).

More recently, however, Benson and Perrett (1994) have reported a caricature advantage for speed and accuracy of recognizing famous faces, suggesting that type of face may not matter much.

Method

Subjects

Twenty-four senior students (12 females and 12 males) from Riccarton High School in Christchurch, New Zealand, were paid $10 each for participating in the experiment. Half of the subjects had participated in an earlier caricature experiment but had not yet been debriefed.

Stimuli and Apparatus

Thirty-three Riccarton high-school students (17 males and 16 females) were photographed full-face, with neutral expressions; 14 female and 14 male Riccarton faces were used as stimuli. Photographs of 15 famous females and 18 famous males[5] were also obtained, and 14 of each sex were used as stimuli. The famous faces varied more in angle of view (19 were not quite front-on, although none was as extreme as a three-quarter view) and facial expression (18 were smiling) than the high-school photographs. Sets of photographs were also obtained from two other schools and added to the Riccarton school faces to create the norms against which the faces were caricatured (see below). All photographs were digitized using a Scanman hand-held scanner and stored on a Macintosh LC computer.

A set of line-drawing caricatures was created for each face, using Brennan's caricature generator (Brennan, 1982, 1985; see Rhodes et al., 1987, for full details of the version used here). The drawings are created in three steps. (1) A photograph is digitized, and a fixed set of 169 points is found by eye and entered using the mouse. These points are joined automatically by the program, using spline curves, to make a line drawing representation of the face consisting of 37 line segments. (2) This line drawing is compared with a norm face, and corresponding points are found; and (3) all differences between corresponding pairs of points are exaggerated (caricatures) or reduced (anticaricatures) by a fixed percentage. Distinctive aspects are changed more than typical aspects of the face, because 50% of a 20-pixel difference is larger than 50% of a 2-pixel difference. Distinctive aspects of a face are exaggerated in the caricatures and reduced in the anticaricatures, and corresponding levels of caricature and anticaricature (e.g. 50% and −50%) are equal metric distortions from the undistorted drawing.

Seven caricature levels (−50%, −30%, −10%, 0%, 10%, 30%, 50%[6]) were created for each face, using separate male and female norms. Separate norms were also used for the personally known and famous faces, because the two groups had different age structures. The famous norms were produced by averaging all the same-sex famous faces, so that 15 faces went into the female norm and 18 went into the male norm. The classmate norms were produced by averaging the male and female Riccarton faces, respectively, together with the male and female faces from two other schools, so that a total of 48 and 44 faces went into the male and female classmate norms, respectively.

Both plain and enhanced versions of each drawing were created. The plain drawings were the simple line drawings produced by the caricature generator (like those shown in Figures 2 and 3). The "enhanced" drawings had the hair, brows, and irises filled in (using Superpaint), and glasses (for 1 famous and 1 Riccarton male), moustaches (for 4 famous males), earrings (for 6 famous and 11 Riccarton females), and additional facial lines not represented by the caricature program (e.g. double chin lines, dimples) were added ($M = 1$ extra line per

---

[5]Subjects from the high school were polled earlier on a large list of famous faces to see whom they would recognize. The selection of faces was based on these responses and on the availability of photographs.

[6]The 10% level was included because subjects had chosen 10% caricatures as the best likenesses for these faces in a pilot experiment.

face). No attempt was made to caricature the shape of these additional lines, and their position in the face was kept as constant as possible across the range of caricature levels. Impossible lines and features obscured by the hair were erased. A full set of enhanced drawings for a famous face is shown in Figure 4. The stimuli were presented on a Macintosh LC.

Procedure

Stimuli were blocked by picture quality (plain or enhanced), face type (classmate or famous), and orientation (upright or inverted). Eight different block orders were produced by varying quality order, type order, and orientation order. Three subjects received each of the eight orders. The order of trials within blocks was random. In each block four different faces (2 male, 2 female) were seen at each of the seven caricature levels (28 trials), so that each face was seen once in each block. The 28 faces were divided (randomly) into seven subsets of four faces (2 male and 2 female), and seven different assignments of subset to caricature level were generated (Sets 1, 2, 3, 4, 5, 6, 7 assigned to levels −50 to +50, respectively; Sets 2, 3, 4, 5, 6, 7, 1 assigned to levels −50 to +50, respectively; etc.). A different random selection to four of these assignments was used for each of the four Orientation × Face Type blocks, for each type of face.

At the beginning of each block, subjects were shown the names of the 28 faces that would appear in the block. They were instructed that on each trial a face would appear and that they should try to name it as accurately as they could. Speed was not emphasized. Subjects initiated each trial by pressing the space-bar. A drawing appeared immediately in the centre of the screen and remained on until the subject responded. The response, recorded manually by the experimenter, triggered a voice-activated relay and was timed by the computer. Subjects were asked not to say "umm" or anything else before the name. Subjects said if they did not recognize the face, and this was scored as an error. Each block was preceded by a practice set of 7 trials, one at each caricature level, and all at the orientation, quality, and face type of the upcoming block. Five faces were available for the practice trials, so that two were shown twice.

At the end of the session subjects rated all the photographs on a 7-point scale of familiarity, explained as follows: "Can you recognize the face instantly and put a name to it? Or is the face totally unknown to you? Or somewhere in-between?" The ends of the scale were labelled "1 = don't know it" and "7 = very familiar".

Results

Accuracy

Given that we were interested in how well people could identify (name) familiar faces from their caricatures, we excluded data from faces rated 1 or 2 on the 7-point familiarity scale ($M = 1.5$ famous faces, $M = 0.7$ Riccarton faces

TABLE 1
Proportion Correct as a Function of Caricature Level, Subject Experience, Orientation, Picture Quality, and Face Type in Experiment 1.

Orientation	Picture Quality	Face Type	Caricature Level (%)						
			−50	−30	−10	0	10	30	50
Naive subjects									
upright	enhanced	classmates	0.04 (0.06)	0.51 (0.09)	0.54 (0.08)	0.57 (0.05)	0.53 (0.08)	0.76 (0.07)	0.62 (0.06)
		famous	0.53 (0.06)	0.59 (0.08)	0.72 (0.06)	0.61 (0.08)	0.74 (0.03)	0.58 (0.09)	0.70 (0.08)
	plain	classmates	0.31 (0.10)	0.45 (0.10)	0.61 (0.07)	0.64 (0.05)	0.67 (0.06)	0.62 (0.06)	0.58 (0.06)
		famous	0.22 (0.05)	0.40 (0.08)	0.64 (0.07)	0.50 (0.07)	0.61 (0.09)	0.63 (0.09)	0.39 (0.08)
inverted	enhanced	classmates	0.19 (0.07)	0.19 (0.06)	0.38 (0.07)	0.32 (0.08)	0.25 (0.08)	0.26 (0.06)	0.37 (0.07)
		famous	0.27 (0.07)	0.37 (0.07)	0.56 (0.09)	0.52 (0.09)	0.39 (0.06)	0.54 (0.07)	0.54 (0.10)
	plain	classmates	0.15 (0.06)	0.23 (0.05)	0.19 (0.05)	0.27 (0.07)	0.33 (0.08)	0.32 (0.08)	0.27 (0.05)
		famous	0.15 (0.07)	0.12 (0.05)	0.27 (0.06)	0.31 (0.07)	0.24 (0.05)	0.36 (0.06)	0.32 (0.10)
Experienced subjects									
upright	enhanced	classmates	0.52 (0.06)	0.60 (0.08)	0.77 (0.06)	0.67 (0.09)	0.81 (0.06)	0.75 (0.07)	0.85 (0.06)
		famous	0.61 (0.06)	0.76 (0.05)	0.72 (0.09)	0.81 (0.07)	0.72 (0.07)	0.81 (0.06)	0.71 (0.06)
	plain	classmates	0.31 (0.08)	0.55 (0.08)	0.74 (0.08)	0.79 (0.07)	0.79 (0.06)	0.77 (0.07)	0.73 (0.08)
		famous	0.37 (0.08)	0.46 (0.08)	0.66 (0.08)	0.69 (0.08)	0.75 (0.08)	0.56 (0.08)	0.70 (0.05)
inverted	enhanced	classmates	0.42 (0.08)	0.31 (0.05)	0.36 (0.08)	0.51 (0.07)	0.52 (0.10)	0.57 (0.09)	0.51 (0.10)
		famous	0.30 (0.09)	0.52 (0.08)	0.63 (0.08)	0.61 (0.08)	0.54 (0.08)	0.56 (0.08)	0.60 (0.08)
	plain	classmates	0.15 (0.06)	0.30 (0.11)	0.35 (0.08)	0.42 (0.06)	0.48 (0.08)	0.38 (0.08)	0.40 (0.07)
		famous	0.24 (0.07)	0.40 (0.08)	0.32 (0.09)	0.45 (0.11)	0.39 (0.08)	0.38 (0.10)	0.26 (0.05)

Note: SEs in parentheses.

were excluded). A five-way ANOVA was carried out on the proportion of faces correctly identified, with subject experience as a between-subjects factor and caricature level, orientation, picture quality, and face type as within-subject factors. These data are shown in Table 1. Planned comparisons were carried out to test for a caricature equivalence effect and a caricature advantage. Recall that for caricature equivalence to be non-trivial, performance on caricatures must be better than on corresponding anticaricatures, as well as being as good as that on undistorted images. Therefore, caricature levels were compared with corresponding anticaricature levels as part of testing for caricature equivalence. Caricatures were compared with undistorted images to test for a caricature advantage.

There was a significant main effect of caricature level, $F(6, 132) = 36.99$, $p < 0.00001$. Planned comparisons showed that caricatures at all levels were recognized as accurately as were undistorted drawings, and that 30% and 50%— but not 10%—caricatures were recognized better than the corresponding anti-caricatures (all $ps < 0.01$, $Ms = 0.32, 0.42, 0.53, 0.54, 0.55, 0.55, 0.53$ for caricature levels -50%, -30%, -10%, 0%, 10%, 30%, 50%, respectively). Therefore, we obtained the equivalence effect ($C = V > A$). Caricature level did not interact with type of face, $F < 1$, or with face quality, $F(6, 132) = 1.55$, n.s.

There was a significant main effect of orientation, $F(1, 22) = 203.20$, $p < 0.00001$, with upright faces ($M = 0.62$) recognized better than inverted faces ($M = 0.37$). This difference of 25 percentage points matches the disproportionate inversion decrement normally found for faces (the inversion effect for other classes ranges from 2 to 10 percentage points—see Diamond & Carey, 1986, for

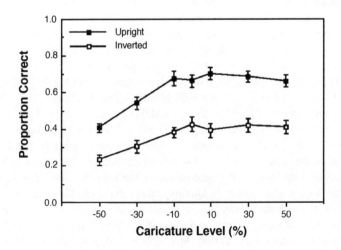

FIG. 5. Accuracy as a function of caricature level and orientation in Experiment 1. *SE* bars are shown.

a review). Although we obtained both a clear caricature effect and a clear inversion effect, there was no significant interaction between the two, $F(6, 132) = 1.76$, n.s. (Figure 5). The caricature effects were independent of orientation and so did not appear to depend selectively on the exaggeration of relational features.

Unsurprisingly, enhanced faces were identified more accurately ($M = 0.55$) than were plain drawings ($M = 0.44$), $F(1, 22) = 25.74$, $p < 0.00001$. Also as expected, there was a larger inversion decrement for plain faces ($M = 0.58$, upright; $M = 0.30$, inverted), which have fewer isolated feature cues, than for enhanced faces ($M = 0.66$, upright; $M = 0.43$, inverted), $F(1, 22) = 8.32$, $p < 0.009$. Two other interactions were found involving face type. Face type interacted with quality, $F(1, 22) = 33.10$, $p < 0.0001$, with famous faces benefiting more from enhancement ($M = 0.59$, enhanced; $M = 0.42$, plain) than classmates' faces ($M = 0.50$, enhanced; $M = 0.46$, plain). Face type also interacted with orientation, $F(1, 22) = 14.73$, $p < 0.0009$, with a larger inversion effect for classmates' faces ($M = 0.62$, upright, $M = 0.34$, inverted) than for famous faces ($M = 0.61$, upright; $M = 0.40$, inverted). The latter interaction might reflect greater use of relational features for the more familiar classmates' faces than for famous faces. There was a significant main effect of subject experience, $F(1, 22) = 6.85$, $p < 0.02$, with better recognition by experienced ($M = 0.55$) than inexperienced ($M = 0.43$) subjects. Experience also interacted with all four factors in a five-way interaction, $F(6, 132) = 2.20$, $p < 0.05$, which accounted for less than 1% of the variance and which we will not attempt to interpret.

A four-way ANOVA was carried out with stimuli as the random factor, to determine whether the results generalized across faces. Face type was a between-faces factor, and caricature level, orientation, and picture quality were within-face factors. The results matched those for the subjects-random ANOVA, with significant main effects of caricature level, $F(6, 324) = 25.48$, $p < 0.00001$ [$minF'(6, 427) = 15.09$, $p < 0.001$], orientation, $F(1, 54) = 227.68$, $p < 0.00001$ [$minF'(1,59) = 107.37$, $p < 0.001$], and picture quality, $F(1, 54) = 25.50$, $p < 0.00001$ [$minF'(1,63) = 12.81$, $p < 0.001$], and significant Quality × Orientation interactions, $F(1, 54) = 7.17$, $p < 0.01$ [$minF'(1, 66) = 3.85$, $p < 0.10$], Quality × Type interactions, $F(1, 54) = 9.59$, $p < 0.003$ [$min F'(1,74) = 7.44$, $p < 0.01$], and Orientation × Type interactions, $F(1,54) = 4.04$, $p < 0.05$ [$minF'(1, 74) = 3.17$, $p < 0.10$]. For all these effects the patterns of means exactly matched those obtained in the subjects analysis. Two additional interactions were significant in the analysis with faces as the random factor, but they did not generalize across subjects: a Caricature Level × Quality interaction, $F(6, 324) = 2.19$, $p < 0.05$ [$minF' < 1$], with the advantage for enhanced over plain drawings increasing with the level of exaggeration, and a significant three-way Caricature Level × Quality × Orientation interaction, $F(6, 324) = 2.14$, $p < 0.05$ [$minF'(6, 358) = 1.01$, n.s.], with the above-described pattern restricted to upright faces.

TABLE 2
Mean Correct Reaction Times (msec) as a Function of Caricature Level, Subject Experience, Orientation, Picture Quality, and Face Type in Experiment 1.

			Caricature Level (%)						
Orientation	Picture Quality	Face Type	−50	−30	−10	0	10	30	50
Naive subjects									
upright	enhanced	classmates	6644 (1623)	2777 (498)	2305 (376)	1773 (169)	2432 (318)	2472 (676)	2270 (275)
		famous	2276 (396)	3091 (501)	2019 (159)	2923 (647)	3542 (651)	2273 (305)	3633 (1010)
	plain	classmates	4538 (719)	4393 (816)	3069 (456)	2277 (309)	3189 (666)	4361 (1400)	2940 (486)
		famous	4859 (1222)	3770 (692)	4925 (1170)	4894 (1732)	4062 (554)	4177 (1082)	2797 (531)
inverted	enhanced	classmates	2798 (149)	4672 (852)	3515 (727)	2695 (271)	4639 (1268)	2458 (330)	4461 (1144)
		famous	3715 (914)	4257 (1061)	3714 (1270)	2871 (280)	2695 (401)	4201 (913)	4627 (869)
	plain	classmates	5010 (950)	3186 (480)	2592 (236)	6130 (1749)	3580 (740)	3441 (449)	4263 (894)
		famous	6908 (1075)	4545 (471)	4244 (599)	6834 (2449)	5770 (898)	5381 (2013)	4584 (425)
Experienced subjects									
upright	enhanced	classmates	3876 (816)	2157 (418)	1948 (276)	2324 (456)	1750 (229)	2056 (335)	2575 (510)
		famous	4068 (911)	2466 (413)	2562 (520)	2298 (340)	2221 (416)	2295 (309)	2335 (306)
	plain	classmates	4216 (430)	2519 (300)	2207 (313)	2368 (268)	2734 (352)	1844 (219)	1840 (160)
		famous	3044 (296)	2830 (392)	3180 (426)	3318 (656)	3177 (565)	2763 (559)	2511 (352)
inverted	enhanced	classmates	3098 (398)	3106 (393)	3650 (1281)	3125 (380)	2771 (385)	3046 (336)	3115 (304)
		famous	3547 (524)	3163 (347)	2044 (152)	3463 (448)	1738 (133)	2692 (555)	2806 (310)
	plain	classmates	4643 (725)	3822 (627)	4013 (766)	3101 (494)	2621 (279)	2999 (451)	2756 (300)
		famous	8538 (1875)	4139 (600)	3808 (621)	3398 (381)	3095 (310)	3747 (397)	3946 (350)

Note: SEs in parentheses.

291

Reaction Times (RTs)

Reaction times more than 2 standard deviations above each cell mean were omitted ($M = 1.8$ per subject). A five-way ANOVA was carried out on the mean correct RTs (see Table 2), with the same factors as the accuracy analysis. Because inverted and anticaricatured faces are difficult to recognize, many of the cells had very few RTs, making their means quite unstable. On average, 3.7 cells per subject had to be replaced by the group mean for the cell because they were empty (i.e. all responses incorrect), and the average number of RTs per cell was only 1.8 (the maximum possible was 4)[7]. The results of RT analysis are therefore included primarily for completeness and comparison with earlier studies.

There was a significant main effect of caricature level, $F(6, 132) = 10.20$, $p < 0.00001$. Planned comparisons were used to compare corresponding levels of caricature and anticaricature and to compare caricatures with undistorted drawings. Only the advantage for 50% caricatures ($M = 3216$ msec) over -50% anticaricatures ($M = 4486$ msec) was significant ($p < 0.01$). As in accuracy, caricature level did not interact with face type, $F < 1$. Thus the effect of caricature level did not differ for famous faces and classmates' faces, although classmates' faces ($M = 3199$ msec) were recognized significantly more quickly overall than were famous faces ($M = 3621$ msec), $F(1, 22) = 8.66$, $p < 0.008$.

As in the accuracy analysis, there was a significant main effect of orientation, $F(1, 22) = 29.69$, $p < 0.00001$, with faster RTs to name upright ($M = 3003$ msec) than inverted ($M = 3820$ msecs) faces. Again there was no interaction between caricature level and orientation, $F < 1$ (Figure 6). There were two significant three-way interactions: A Caricature Level $\times$ Orientation $\times$ Picture Quality interaction, $F(6, 132) = 3.46$, $p < 0.004$ and a Caricature Level $\times$ Orientation $\times$ Face Type interaction, $F(6, 132) = 4.11$, $p < 0.0008$. However, both interactions stemmed entirely from performance on the -50% anticaricatures (faster RTs to all upright than inverted faces except for enhanced anticaricatures, and faster RTs to all classmates' faces than to famous faces except for upright -50% anticaricatures). Given the large number of missing cells for the -50% anticaricatures, these interactions will not be interpreted.

There was a significant main effect of picture quality, $F(1, 22) = 12.47$, $p < 0.002$, with enhanced drawings recognized more quickly ($M = 3001$ msec) than plain drawings ($M = 3820$ msec). The Quality $\times$ Orientation interaction was marginal, $F(1, 22) = 3.77$, $p < 0.07$, with a larger inversion decrement for plain ($M = 3314$ msec, upright; $M = 4325$ msec, inverted; Diff = 1011 msec) than enhanced ($M = 2691$ msec, upright; $M = 3310$ msec, inverted; Diff = 619 msec) drawings, as expected if larger inversion decrements occur when subjects rely on relational features. There was no Quality $\times$ Caricature Level interaction, $F(6, 132) = 1.79$, n.s., but there was a Quality $\times$ Face Type interaction,

---

[7]Given the instability of these data, only the analysis with subjects as the random factor was carried out.

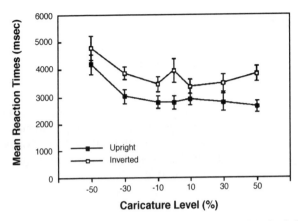

FIG. 6.   Mean reaction times (msec) as a function of caricature level and orientation in Experiment 1. *SE* bars are shown.

$F(1, 22) = 12.52$, $p < 0.002$. As in the accuracy analysis, enhancement improved recognition (over plain faces) more for famous faces ($M = 2983$ msec, enhanced; $M = 4259$ msec, plain; Diff = 1276 msec) than for classmates' faces ($M = 3018$ msec, enhanced; $M = 3380$ msec, plain; Diff = 362 msec). There were no other significant main effects or interactions.

Familiarity

Classmates' faces were rated as significantly more familiar ($M = 5.3$) than were the famous faces ($M = 5.0$), $F(1, 23) = 6.70$, $p < 0.02$.

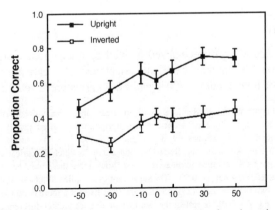

FIG. 7.   Accuracy as a function of caricature level and orientation for enhanced classmates' faces in Experiment 1. *SE* bars are shown.

Postscript

Although no caricature advantage was found in the above analyses, we decided to examine the four sets of upright faces separately to see whether there was any hint of a superportrait effect. Caricatures appeared to be identified more accurately than undistorted images for the enhanced classmates set (see Figure 7). A separate two-way ANOVA was carried out on these data, with orientation and caricature level as within subject factors. There was a significant main effect of caricature level, $F(6, 138) = 6.36$, $p < 0.00001$, and the advantage for upright 30% and 50% caricatures over undistorted drawings was significant by planned comparisons, $t(138) = 1.85$, $p < 0.05$ (1-tailed) and $t(138) = 1.71$, $p < 0.05$ (1-tailed), respectively. One might challenge the use of such planned comparisons on a subset of the data. However, a failure to find a predicted effect across the board does not make a test of the effect post hoc for the subset of data where the effect occurs. Our strategy therefore is to use planned tests, but to try to ensure reliability by replication (Experiments 2 and 3). There was a significant main effect of orientation, $F(1, 23) = 125.11$, $p < 0.00001$. There was no significant Orientation $\times$ Caricature Level interaction, $F < 1$, although the inverted faces showed no sign of the caricature advantage found for upright faces.[8]

A two-way ANOVA was carried out on the RT data for these faces, with the same factors as above. There was a significant main effect of caricature level, $F(6, 138) = 5.41$, $p < 0.01$. Only the -50% anticaricatures differed from the other caricature levels (all ps < 0.01 on planned comparisons), so that the caricature advantage in accuracy does not appear to be due to a speed-accuracy trade-off. There was a significant main effect of orientation, $F(1, 23) = 6.41$, $p < 0.02$ ($M = 2668$ msec, upright; $M = 3368$ msec, inverted) and a significant Caricature Level $\times$ Orientation interaction, $F(6, 138) = 5.41$, $p < 0.00001$, which resulted entirely from performance on -50% anticaricatures, for which very few RTs were available.

Discussion

Overall, caricatures were recognized as well as undistorted images, and both were recognized better than were anticaricatures. This caricature equivalence effect held for both accuracy (30% and 50% caricature levels) and RTs (50%

---

[8]We also used contrasts to test whether the caricature advantage was, indeed, restricted to upright faces. Each subject's means for the 0% upright, 30% upright, 0% inverted, and 30% inverted drawings were multiplied by the contrasts $-1, 3, -1$, and -1 respectively. The resulting numbers were added together to give a single number that reflects the extent to which the caricature advantage was restricted to upright faces. A repeated measures t-test showed that these numbers were significantly greater than zero, $t(23) = 4.82$, $p < 0.001$. The same contrasts applied to the 0% and 50% levels also yielded a highly significant effect, $t(23) = 5.15$, $p < 0.001$. Even if a more conservative significance level is adopted (e.g. $p < 0.01$) to reflect the fact that we did not predict different caricature effects for upright and inverted faces, the results corroborate the observation that the caricature advantage was restricted to upright faces.

level). Upright faces were recognized better than inverted ones, and the size of the inversion decrement (about 25 percentage points) was consistent with the use of relational features for these stimuli. So, too, was the interaction between orientation and picture quality, which showed a larger inversion decrement for plain faces, where subjects must rely more heavily on relational features, than for enhanced faces with more isolated feature cues.

Our main question was whether the use of relational features contributes to the caricature effects. The answer appears to be no, because caricature level and orientation did not interact for either accuracy or RT. Thus differences in performance between the caricature levels do not appear to be due to differences in the availability or use of relational features. Rather, differences in isolated features (and possibly some very simple relational features that might still be encodable from inverted faces) seem sufficient to make caricatures as recognizable as veridicals and to make anticaricatures less recognizable than either. Converging evidence that caricature effects and inversion effects reflect different aspects of face processing came from the finding that caricature level and orientation interacted differently with other factors, orientation interacting with picture quality and face type, but caricature level interacting with neither.

We were also interested in whether caricature effects are an artefact of impoverished stimuli and whether the type of face (famous or personally known) matters. In both cases the answer appears to be no, given that caricature level did not interact with either picture quality or face type. Of course both plain and enhanced drawings are impoverished compared with photographs, and we cannot rule out the possibility that caricature effects would be modified by a more powerful manipulation of quality.

For one group of faces—upright, enhanced classmates—there was some suggestion of a caricature advantage, with 30% and 50% caricatures recognized more accurately than undistorted images. However, this superportrait effect was only significant on a one-tailed planned comparison, so we will postpone discussion of it until we see whether it replicates.

EXPERIMENT 2

In Experiment 2 we aimed to replicate the independence of caricature level and orientation. We also wanted to see whether the caricature advantage found for enhanced classmates' faces would replicate using a new set of classmates' faces. We used fewer caricature levels (−30%, 0%, 30%) with more faces at each level in an attempt to get more reliable RTs. We included famous faces as well as classmates, but only enhanced drawings were used.

Method

Subjects

Twenty-four senior students (11 females, 13 males) from a different high school (Hagley) were paid $10 each for participating.

Stimuli

Caricatures were made from photographs of 24 classmates from this new population using the classmate norms from Experiment 1. Caricatures of the 24 famous faces from Experiment 1 were also used. Only −30%, 0%, and 30% caricature levels were used, and all the drawings were enhanced.

Procedure

The procedure was the same as for Experiment 1, with trials blocked by caricature level, orientation, and face type. The 24 faces of each type were divided into 3 sets of 8 (4 male, 4 female), and each set was assigned to a different caricature level. Three different assignments were used (Sets 1, 2, & 3 to −30, 0, & 30, respectively; Sets 2, 3, & 1 to −30, 0, & 30; Sets 3, 1, & 2 to −30, 0, 30), and these three assignments were crossed with the order of orientation and type to give 12 different order/assignment conditions, with two subjects assigned to each condition. Otherwise the procedure was the same as in Experiment 1.

Results

Accuracy

Faces rated 1 or 2 on the 7-point familiarity scale were excluded ($M = 1.3$ famous faces, $M = 2.5$, Hagley faces were excluded). A three-way ANOVA was carried out on the mean proportion correct, with caricature level (-30%, 0%, 30%), orientation (upright or inverted), and face type (classmate or famous) as within-subject factors (see Table 3).

There was a significant main effect of caricature level, $F(2, 46) = 12.41, p < 0.00001$, and planned comparisons showed that both the caricatures ($M = 0.41$) and undistorted drawings ($M = 0.41$) were recognized significantly more accurately than were the anticaricatures ($M = 0.32$) (both $ps < 0.01$), but did not differ from one another. Thus we obtained the equivalence effect. However, there was no caricature advantage for upright classmates' faces ($M = 0.40$ for both caricatures and undistorted images, which was considerably lower than the means in Experiment 1) or any other set of faces.

We also obtained the inversion effect. There was a significant main effect of orientation, $F(1, 23) = 53.21, p < 0.00001$. Upright faces ($M = 0.47$) were recognized 18 percentage points better than inverted faces ($M = 0.29$), a difference that is within the usual range of disproportionate inversion effects for faces. As

TABLE 3
Proportion Correct as a Function of Caricature Level, Orientation,
and Face Type in Experiment 2.

Orientation	Face Type	Caricature Level (%)		
		-30	0	30
upright	classmates	0.31 (0.04)	0.40 (0.06)	0.40 (0.05)
	famous	0.51 (0.05)	0.62 (0.04)	0.59 (0.03)
inverted	classmates	0.16 (0.03)	0.21 (0.04)	0.18 (0.04)
	famous	0.30 (0.04)	0.42 (0.04)	0.45 (0.04)

Note: SEs in parentheses.

in Experiment 1, caricature level and orientation did not interact, $F < 1$ (Figure 8). Famous faces ($M = 0.48$) were recognized significantly better than classmates' faces ($M = 0.28$), $F(1, 23) = 65.27$, $p < 0.00001$, but no other effects were significant, all F's < 1.13 n.s.

A three-way ANOVA with stimuli as the random factor, face type as a between-faces factor, and caricature level and orientation as within-face factors showed that these results generalized across faces as well as subjects. There were significant main effects of caricature level, $F(2, 92) = 6.00$, $p < 0.004$ [$\min F'(2, 138) = 4.04$, $p < 0.05$], orientation, $F(1, 46) = 61.88$, $p < 0.00001$ [$\min F'(1, 58) = 28.61$, $p < 0.001$], and face type, $F(1, 46) = 10.93$, $p < 0.002$ [$\min F'(1, 59) = 9.36$, $p < 0.01$], and in all cases the patterns of means matched those found in the subjects analysis.

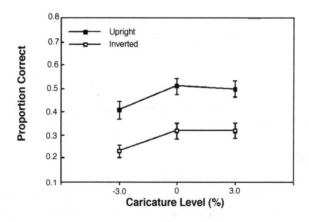

FIG. 8.   Accuracy as a function of caricature level and orientation in Experiment 2. SE bars are shown.

TABLE 4
Mean Correct Reaction Times (msec) as a Function of Caricature Level,
Orientation, and Face Type in Experiment 2

Orientation	Face Type	Caricature Level (%)		
		-30	0	30
upright	classmates	5997 (1180)	3598 (476)	5042 (676)
	famous	3307 (279)	3200 (464)	2721 (249)
inverted	classmates	5351 (676)	4661 (469)	4611 (474)
	famous	3299 (249)	5093 (863)	3200 (373)

Note: SEs in parentheses.

Reaction Times

A three-way ANOVA was carried out on the mean RTs for correct responses, with the same factors as in the accuracy analysis (see Table 4). Reaction times more than 2 standard deviations above each cell mean were dropped ($M = 0.3$ per subject). There were an average of 2.7 RTs per cell mean (maximum possible $= 8$), better than in Experiment 1, but still very few.[9] On average, 3.1 empty cells per subject were replaced by the group mean for that cell.

There was no significant main effect of caricature level, $F(2, 46) = 1.24$, n.s. ($Ms = 4507, 4232, 3964$ msec, respectively, for $-30\%, 0\%, 30\%$ drawings) and only a marginal effect of orientation, $F(1, 23) = 3.22$, $p < 0.09$ ($M = 3870$ msec, upright faces; $M = 4598$ msec, inverted faces). There was a significant Orientation $\times$ Caricature Level interaction, $F(2, 46) = 3.93$, $p < 0.03$ (for the $-30\%, 0\%,$ and 30% levels, respectively: Upright $Ms = 4412$ msec, 3354 msec, 3846 msec; Inverted $Ms = 4601$ msec, 5110 msec, 4083 msec). However, given that the basic caricature and inversion effects were not present, this interaction does not seem interpretable in terms of relational features. There was no evidence for a speed-accuracy trade-off. Famous faces ($M = 3474$ msec) were recognized significantly faster than classmates' faces ($M = 4994$ msec), $F(1, 23)$ $= 25.04$, $p < 0.00001$.

Familiarity

There was no difference in the familiarity of classmates' faces ($M = 5.3$) and famous faces ($M = 5.3$), $F < 1$.

Discussion

The accuracy results replicated those obtained in Experiment 1, with significant main effects of caricature level and orientation and no interaction, again suggesting that caricature and inversion effects reflect distinct components of

---

[9]As in Experiment 1, only the analysis with subjects as the random factor was carried out, and the results are reported primarily for comparative purposes.

face processing. However, this conclusion was not as strongly supported as in Experiment 1. There was no converging evidence from the pattern of interactions (neither orientation nor caricature level interacted with face type), and the RT data were difficult to interpret (no caricature effect and a bizarre interaction between caricature level and orientation). Of course, given the problems of missing RT data, the accuracy data carry greater weight.

The caricature advantage found for enhanced classmates' faces in Experiment 1 did not generalize to the new set of classmates' faces used here. Instead, we found caricature equivalence for the new set of classmates' faces as well as for the famous faces.

EXPERIMENT 3

The caricature advantage found for enhanced classmates' faces in Experiment 1 did not generalize to a new set of classmates' faces in Experiment 2. One possibility is that a caricature advantage only occurs for certain sets of faces (depending perhaps on factors like distinctiveness or familiarity). Alternatively, the caricature advantage found in Experiment 1 may simply have been an unreliable result. In Experiment 3, we attempt to distinguish between these two possibilities by trying to replicate the caricature advantage for the original Riccarton classmates' faces. Once again, we examined the effect of orientation.

We were also interested in whether familiarity is needed for caricatures to be effective—a question with important practical implications. For example, if familiarity turns out *not* to be necessary, then caricature effects could be studied more easily (using unfamiliar faces) and could be exploited in forensic settings. Contrary to initial suggestions that familiarity might be needed for caricatures to be effective (e.g. Rhodes et al., 1987; Rhodes & Moody, 1990), recent evidence by Mauro and Kubovy (1992) suggests that it might not be. They found that sensitivity to discriminate between old items and new ones was better for caricatures of studied Identi-kit faces than for the studied faces themselves. However, this measure reflects the ability to reject new faces correctly as well as to detect old faces, and more distinctive new faces (e.g. caricatures) are certainly easier to reject than are less distinctive ones (e.g. undistorted faces) (e.g. Light et al., 1979), and so the sensitivity result may not mean that caricatures facilitate recognition of previously seen faces. Therefore in Experiment 3 we examined whether caricatures of initially unfamiliar faces are effective in a simple identification task. Familiarity was manipulated by comparing recognition of the subjects' own classmates with their recognition of classmates from a different school who were unknown prior to the experiment.

We used the Riccarton faces that gave a caricature advantage in Experiment 1, together with a new set of classmates' faces from a different school (Hillmorton), and tested subjects from both schools, so that each set of faces was familiar to one group of subjects and (initially) unfamiliar to the other. The procedure was similar to that of Experiment 2, except that prior to each recognition block, subjects learned to name photographs of the faces they would see in the recognition test. The same procedure was followed for both familiar and unfamiliar faces, even though subjects already knew their own classmates' names, to ensure that the conditions differed only in familiarity.

Method

Subjects

Twenty-four subjects from each of two schools, Riccarton and Hillmorton, participated in the study ($N = 48$). All but one of the Riccarton subjects had been in at least one previous study using the Riccarton faces (Experiment 1 and/or an unpublished likeness rating study); all the Hillmorton subjects were naive.

Stimuli

Twenty-four faces from each school were used as stimuli. Most of these would be familiar to the subjects from that school and unfamiliar to the subjects from the other school. Three caricature levels were used, -30%, 0%, and 30%, and all the drawings were enhanced. Different photographs (smiling) from those used to created the drawings (neutral expressions) were used in the training phase.

Procedure

Training. Subjects learned names for the (smiling) photographs. Familiar faces were presented in sets of twelve and unfamiliar faces in sets of six. Training began by showing all the faces in the set with their correct names, one after the other. This cycle was repeated. Then the faces were presented without names, and the subject attempted to name each one, with the experimenter supplying the name if necessary. The cycle was repeated until all the faces were correctly named twice in a row. Obviously this training was not needed for the familiar faces, but we kept the procedure comparable for both types of face. Each set was learned twice, once upright and once inverted, making a total of twelve training blocks, each followed by the appropriate test block. The order of orientations and face types was counterbalanced across subjects.

Recognition Test. Immediately after each set was learned, recognition of the drawings for that set was tested. The drawings were in the same orientation as the training set. Subjects initiated each trial by pressing the space-bar. Then a drawing appeared and remained on until they responded with the name. Subjects were asked to respond as quickly and accurately as they could. No feedback was given. One third of the faces were shown at each caricature level in each test block. Four of the faces (randomly chosen) were shown again at the end of the block, two as 10% and two as 50% caricatures, so that subjects could not predict how many times each face would appear. There were three different assignments of faces to caricature level for each sextet (2 at each caricature level) and set of 12 faces (4 at each caricature level), and a different one (chosen randomly) was used for the upright and inverted presentations of each set. Familiarity ratings were obtained as in the previous experiments, with subjects from each school rating their own classmates' faces.

Results

Accuracy

Data from unfamiliar faces in the "familiar" set (rated 1 or 2 on the familiarity scale) were excluded from the analysis ($M = 0.6$, Riccarton subjects; $M = 1.0$, Hillmorton subjects), as were data from faces in the "unfamiliar" set that subjects claimed to recognize ($M = 0.5$, Riccarton subjects; $M = 0.6$, Hillmorton subjects). A four-way ANOVA was carried out on the mean proportions correct, with school as a between-subjects factor and caricature level, familiarity, and orientation as within-subject factors (see Table 5). The average number of blocks needed to learn the names ranged from 2.0 to 4.8.

There was a significant main effect of school, $F(1, 46) = 7.85, p < 0.008$, with the more experienced Riccarton subjects performing better ($M = 0.68$) than the naive Hillmorton subjects ($M = 0.61$), and a significant main effect of familiarity, $F(1, 46) = 44.72, p < 0.00001$, with all subjects recognizing familiar faces ($M = 0.70$) better than unfamiliar faces ($M = 0.58$). There was also a significant main effect of orientation, $F(1, 46) = 144.24, p < 0.00001$ ($M = 0.74$, upright; $M = 0.55$, inverted). Accuracy was quite low, considering that the subjects had just learned these faces, but remember that they were trained on photographs and tested on drawings, and that the drawings were based on different photographs from those used in training.

TABLE 5
Proportion Correct as a Function of Caricature Level, School,
Orientation, and Familiarity in Experiment 3

School	Orientation	Familiarity	Caricature Level (%)		
			−30	0	30
Riccarton	upright	familiar	0.88 (0.03)	0.94 (0.02)	0.95 (0.01)
		unfamiliar	0.55 (0.04)	0.59 (0.04)	0.66 (0.05)
	inverted	familiar	0.54 (0.05)	0.65 (0.04)	0.68 (0.04)
		unfamiliar	0.54 (0.04)	0.61 (0.04)	0.59 (0.05)
Hillmorton	upright	familiar	0.75 (0.04)	0.86 (0.03)	0.84 (0.04)
		unfamiliar	0.53 (0.04)	0.63 (0.04)	0.74 (0.04)
	inverted	familiar	0.44 (0.04)	0.46 (0.04)	0.47 (0.04)
		unfamiliar	0.48 (0.04)	0.53 (0.03)	0.56 (0.05)

Note: SEs in parentheses.

The caricature equivalence effect was obtained. There was a significant main effect of caricature level, $F(2, 92) = 18.10$, $p < 0.00001$, with 30% caricatures ($M = 0.69$) and 0% undistorted drawings ($M = 0.66$) both recognized significantly more accurately than -30% anticaricatures ($M = 0.57$) (both $ps < 0.01$). The 30% caricatures were recognized as accurately as were the 0% drawings. Familiarity did not interact with caricature level, $F < 1$. As in Experiments 1 and 2, the effects of caricature level and orientation were additive, $F(2, 92) = 1.28$, n.s. (Figure 9).

We also examined the performance of both groups of subjects on the upright Riccarton faces, which had yielded a caricature advantage in Experiment 1 (Figure 10). Planned comparisons were carried out to see whether either group showed a significant caricature advantage on these faces. There was a significant caricature advantage for the Hillmorton subjects, $t(92) = 2.26$, $p < 0.025$, 1-tailed, but not for the Riccarton subjects, $t < 1$. However, all but one of the Riccarton subjects were already familiar with these stimuli, and ceiling effects appear to have contaminated their data (Figure 10). Neither group showed a significant caricature advantage for inverted faces (Hillmorton Ss: $M = 0.56$, caricatures, $M = 0.53$, undistorted faces; Riccarton Ss: $M = 0.68$, caricatures, $M = 0.65$, undistorted faces; both $ts < 1$). As in Experiment 1, we applied the contrasts -1, $+3$, -1, -1 to the 0% upright, 30% upright, 0% inverted, and 30% inverted means, respectively, to test whether the caricature advantage was indeed restricted to upright faces. The effect was highly significant, $t(23) = 4.24$, $p < 0.001$.

The only other significant effects were an Orientation × Familiarity interaction, $F(1, 46) = 68.73$, $p < 0.00001$, with a much larger inversion decrement for familiar ($M = 0.87$, upright; $M = 0.54$, inverted) than for unfamiliar ($M = 0.61$,

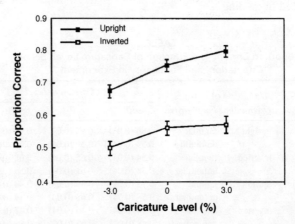

FIG. 9.   Accuracy as a function of caricature level and orientation in Experiment 3. *SE* bars are shown.

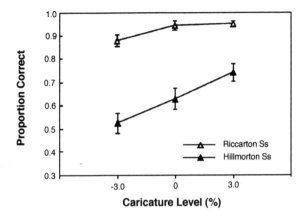

FIG. 10. Accuracy as a function of caricature level for upright, Riccarton faces, for Riccarton and Hillmorton subjects in Experiment 3. *SE* bars are shown.

upright; $M = 0.55$, inverted) faces and an Orientation $\times$ School interaction, $F(1, 46) = 5.54$, $p < 0.03$, with orientation having a larger effect for the naive Hillmorton subjects ($M = 0.74$, upright; $M = 0.49$, inverted) than for the experienced Riccarton subjects ($M = 0.76$, upright; $M = 0.60$, inverted). Caricature level did not interact with either of these factors, so that once again the different pattern of interactions for caricature level and orientation provide converging evidence that they are tapping distinct aspects of face processing.

A four-way ANOVA was carried out with stimuli as the random factor, to determine whether the results generalized across faces. School of face was a between-faces factor and caricature level, orientation, and familiarity were within-face factors. As in the subjects-random analysis, there were significant main effects of caricature level, $F(2, 92) = 12.79$, $p < 0.00001$ [min$F'(2, 179) = 7.49$, $p < 0.001$], orientation, $F(1, 46) = 156.69$, $p < 0.00001$ [min$F'(1, 92) = 75.10$, $p < 0.001$], and familiarity, $F(1, 46) = 20.35$, $p < 0.00001$ [min$F'(1, 81) = 13.99$, $p < 0.001$]. There were also significant School $\times$ Familiarity, $F(1, 46) = 6.46$, $p < 0.02$ [min$F'(1,86) = 4.06$, $p < 0.05$][10], and Familiarity $\times$ Orientation, $F(1, 46) = 99.29$, $p < 0.00001$ [min$F'(1, 89) = 40.62$, $p < 0.001$] interactions, as in the subjects analysis. The patterns of means for all these effects matched those obtained in the subjects analysis. The only other significant effect was a three-way School $\times$ Familiarity $\times$ Orientation interaction, $F(1, 46) = 8.52$, $p < 0.005$ [min$F' < 1$], with the difference in inversion decrement between familiar and unfamiliar faces (larger for familiar faces) greater for Hillmorton than for Riccarton faces.

---

[10]Given that "school" refers to school of subject in the subjects analysis and school of face in the faces analysis, the minF' is not really interpretable.

Reaction Times

RTs more than two standard deviations above each cell mean were excluded from the analysis (M = 2.3 excluded per subject). The mean number of RTs per cell was 4.8 (SD = 1.2). Mean RTs were subjected to the same four-way ANOVA as accuracy (see Table 6). There was a significant main effect of orientation, $F(1, 46)$ = 18.92, $p < 0.0001$ (M = 2401 msec, upright; M = 3116 msec, inverted), and a significant main effect of familiarity, $F(1, 46)$ = 75.11, $p < 0.00001$, with faster RTs for familiar (M = 1985 msec) than for unfamiliar (M = 3532 msec) faces. As for accuracy, there was a significant Familiarity × Orientation interaction, $F(1, 46)$ = 5.52, $p < 0.03$, with a larger effect of orientation for familiar (M = 1486 msec, upright; M = 2483 msec, inverted; Diff = 997 msec) than for unfamiliar (M = 3316 msec, upright; M = 3748 msec, inverted; Diff = 432 msec) faces. There was also a significant School × Familiarity interaction, $F(1, 46)$ = 8.93, $p < 0.00001$, with Riccarton subjects showing a larger familiarity advantage (M = 1594 msec, familiar; M = 3675 msec, unfamiliar) than Hillmorton subjects (M = 2375 msec familiar; M = 3389 msec, unfamiliar). No other effects were significant. In particular, there was no main effect of caricature level, $F < 1$, (Ms = 2806 msec, 2756 msec, 2712 msec, for −30%, 0%, 30%, respectively) and no Caricature Level × Orientation interaction, ($F(2, 92)$ = 1.08, n.s., or Caricature Level × Familiarity interaction, $F(2, 92)$ = 1.57, n.s.

Familiarity Ratings

The Hillmorton faces were rated as significantly more familiar (M = 5.8) than the Riccarton faces (M = 5.3), $F(1, 46)$ = 14.57, $p < 0.0004$.

TABLE 6

Mean Correct Reaction Times as a Function of Caricature Level, School, Orientation, and Familiarity in Experiment 3.

School	Orientation	Familiarity	Caricature Level (%)		
			−30	0	30
Riccarton	upright	familiar	1365 (93)	1175 (56)	1123 (56)
		unfamiliar	3938 (426)	3136 (315)	3559 (301)
	inverted	familiar	1969 (182)	1899 (172)	2034 (204)
		unfamiliar	3628 (470)	4112 (700)	3674 (471)
Hillmorton	upright	familiar	1845 (157)	1768 (144)	1640 (143)
		unfamiliar	3097 (377)	3195 (334)	2968 (229)
	inverted	familiar	3342 (342)	3162 (421)	2943 (210)
		unfamiliar	3267 (283)	3601 (589)	4206 (488)

Note: SEs in parentheses.

Discussion

Once again we replicated the independence of caricature and inversion effects. Not only was there no interaction between caricature level and orientation, but the two factors also interacted differently with other factors. Therefore, all three experiments consistently show that caricature and inversion effects reflect distinct components of face processing.

Caricatures were recognized at least as well as undistorted drawings, for both familiar and unfamiliar faces. The caricature advantage for Riccarton faces, found in Experiment 1 for subjects familiar with those faces, was also found here for subjects who were unfamiliar with these faces prior to the experiment. Therefore, although a superportrait effect did not generalize to other sets of classmates' faces here and in Experiment 2, it seems to be reliable for this one set of faces. The conclusion would be stronger if the Riccarton subjects in Experiment 3 had also shown a caricature advantage for these faces, but these subjects were experienced and performed close to ceiling on the upright faces, making it difficult for any caricature advantage to show up. Therefore, given the superportrait effect for the Hillmorton subjects and the ceiling effect for Riccarton subjects, it seems reasonable to conclude that a caricature advantage is reliable for Riccarton faces. Taken together with other recent reports of a superportrait effect in recognition accuracy (Benson & Perrett, 1994; Mauro & Kubovy, 1992), our results suggest that caricatures can genuinely enhance recognition accuracy, at least for some faces.

GENERAL DISCUSSION

Relational Features and Caricature Effects

We began by suggesting that a complete theory of object recognition requires an account of how the visual system deals with the homogeneity problem. Studies of inversion and caricature transformations have identified two components of the solution, the use of relational features (e.g. Diamond & Carey, 1986; Rhodes et al., 1993) and norm-based coding (e.g. Carey et al., in prep.; Rhodes, et al., 1987), respectively. Here we asked whether these components are genuinely distinct, or whether caricature effects might themselves depend on relational feature coding.

The answer appears to be that caricature and inversion effects reflect distinct aspects of the visual system's solution to the homogeneity problem. In three experiments we obtained a caricature equivalence effect and a large inversion effect, with no interaction between caricature level and orientation. Exaggeration of relational features did not therefore appear to contribute to the caricature equivalence effect, even though the large inversion decrement for images at all caricature levels suggests that relational features were used to recognize these faces. Furthermore, orientation and caricature level interacted differently with other factors (familiarity, picture quality, and face type), contrary to what would be expected if they depended on the same mechanism.

Whereas caricature equivalence does not depend selectively on relational feature coding, a superportrait effect might. Although there was no significant interaction between caricature level and orientation for the faces showing a superportrait effect, the effect was consistently restricted to upright faces, for which relational features can be used. Restriction of a superportrait effect to upright faces also suggests that it might require expertise, as we have expertise with upright but not with inverted faces. In contrast, caricature equivalence, which occurs with inverted as well as upright faces, clearly does not require expertise. Rhodes and McLean's (1990) report of a superportrait effect for experts and caricature equivalence for non-experts in their bird recognition study is consistent with this speculation.[11] Interestingly, it may be no coincidence that exaggeration of relational features and expertise are both implicated in super-portrait effects, because expertise is needed to use relational features (Diamond & Carey, 1986; Rhodes, Tan, Brake, & Taylor, 1989).

Initially we distinguished between two forms of caricature effect, a caricature advantage $(C > V > A)$, and a caricature equivalence effect $(C = V > A)$, simply to provide a vocabulary for describing our results. However, the two effects behaved differently in our experiments, the caricature equivalence effect requiring neither relational feature coding nor expertise and the superportrait effect seeming to require both. This pattern is analogous to that found for inversion effects. A *disproportionate* inversion effect requires expertise and reliance on relational features and requires expertise (e.g. Diamond & Carey, 1986), whereas more modest inversion decrements are ubiquitous and require neither. If we think of a caricature advantage as a *disproportionate caricature effect*, then a similar pattern holds, with the caricature advantage, but not the more modest equivalence effect, requiring exaggerated relational features and expertise.

---

[11]Recent developmental data, however, show that the issue is far from settled. Ellis (1992; see Ellis, 1991, for more methodological details) asked children to choose the best likeness from a range of caricatures and anticaricatures (-48%, -32%, -16%, 0%, 16%, 32%, & 48%) of the very familiar Kylie Minogue. He predicted that a preference for caricatures should increase with age, given the apparent role of expertise in producing a caricature advantage. However, to his surprise and ours, he found precisely the opposite. The youngest subjects (4-6 year olds) showed the most extreme preference for caricatures, with a mean caricature level of the most preferred image of 15%, and by age 10 the preference was for an anticaricature ($M = -10\%$). Unfortunately, it is not reported whether any of these preferences were significantly different from an undistorted image. Similar results were obtained for a second familiar face (Jason Donovan), but the age effect was not significant. One probably should not make too much of these exploratory data, especially as there was no caricature advantage for the adult subjects. However, they are provocative and highlight the need for developmental studies that track the time course of caricature effects and their relationship to distinctiveness and other expertise effects (e.g. inversion and other-race effects) in face recognition.

However, these speculations should not be accepted uncritically, because Carey and Diamond (this issue) have shown that orientation-specific face effects can occur in the absence of expertise and reliance on relational features. They found that young children, who are not face experts and who do not code relational features to the same extent as adults, nevertheless have as much difficulty as adults identifying two component faces when the top half of one and the bottom half of the other are juxtaposed to create a new face. This difficulty is orientation-specific (Young, Hellawell, & Hay, 1987), yet it does not require expertise. Carey and Diamond speculate that the composite face task reflects the primacy of the holistic facial configuration, an effect that is lost with inversion, but that does not require expertise.

Familiarity and Caricature Effects

Contrary to previous suggestions (Benson & Perrett, 1991; Rhodes et al., 1987), familiarity was not needed for caricature effects. Both caricature equivalence and a superportrait effect were obtained for unfamiliar as well as for familiar faces. The fact that caricatures can enhance recognition of unfamiliar faces has obvious forensic implications. Of course, even our enhanced line drawings are more difficult to recognize than are photographs, and it would be very interesting to see whether similar results are obtained with photographic-quality caricatures. However, even a caricature advantage limited to enhanced drawings could be exploited to aid face recall when, as must often be the case, photographs of the target face are not available.

Distinctiveness and Caricature Effects

There is considerable variability in the form of caricature effect found both here and elsewhere. Some studies have found caricature equivalence, and others have found superportrait effects (see Rhodes, in preparation, for a review). This variability suggests that caricatures may only facilitate recognition for some faces. If so, then knowing which faces benefit from caricaturing would help us both to design better caricature studies and to assess the forensic potential of caricatures.

Rhodes and McLean (1990) have suggested that distinctiveness might be important, because their bird experts showed a larger caricature advantage for less distinctive passerine birds than for more distinctive ones. Mauro and Kubovy's (1992) caricature advantage for unfamiliar Identi-kit faces is also consistent with this view, as each of those faces had only a single distinctive feature (relative to population norms) and so would be low in overall distinctiveness. So, too, is Benson and Perrett's (1994) finding that more extreme caricatures are chosen as the best likeness for less distinctive faces. In contrast, Rhodes et al. (1987) failed to find an effect of distinctiveness on the size of their caricature advantage, and Rhodes et al. (in prep.) failed to find any consistent effect of distinctiveness on likeness judgements.[12]

Nevertheless, the distinctiveness idea remains an appealing hypothesis, for two reasons: (1) Distinctiveness is related to the density of distractors in memory, and so it *ought* to matter if distinctiveness plays any role at all in the effectiveness of caricatures.[13] In particular, distinctive faces already have few neighbours (similar faces) in face-space, so there would be little to gain from caricaturing them. (2) If a caricature advantage requires exaggeration of relational features, as we have suggested, then it might well be confined to less distinctive faces, which have few distinctive isolated features and for which relational features would therefore be more crucial than for more distinctive faces. Therefore, further studies of distinctiveness effects seem desirable, including modelling studies of how target distinctiveness affects caricature recognition and developmental studies relating the ontogeny of a caricature advantage to that of other distinctiveness effects and to the ability to use relational features.

Use of Line Drawing Caricatures

Psychology has a long tradition of using simplified or artificial stimuli to address questions about perception and mental representation (e.g. Shepard, 1984, 1990), and our use of line-drawing images is in that tradition. Although they are certainly more difficult to recognize than either photographs of faces or real faces, there is no evidence that these line drawings are treated differently from more realistic representations of faces in any theoretically interesting way. For example, the same disproportionate inversion decrement is found as when photographs of faces are used, suggesting that relational features are being used. Nor is there any reason to believe that the power of caricatures is an artefact of impoverished stimuli. Caricatures were just as effective for enhanced as for plain drawings, and the most effective caricatures, those that generated a superportrait effect, were enhanced drawings. Photographic-quality caricatures are also effective, although they have not yet been shown to generate a superportrait effect (Benson & Perrett, 1991). It would certainly be interesting if they did, although perhaps more for the forensic reasons discussed above than for theoretical ones.

---

[12]Actually, distinctiveness may have little effect on likeness judgements given that distinctiveness affects the ease with which target activity can be detected against a background of distractor activation. In a likeness task the subject is told whom the image depicts, and so the target is already activated and need not be picked out against distractor activation. If this is correct, then distinctiveness effects would be more likely to show up in recognition studies than in studies of likeness judgements.

[13]Carey, et al.'s (in prep.) laterals result (see Introduction) shows that distinctiveness cannot be the sole source of caricature effects, but there is no suggestion that it makes no contribution at all.

Face and Objects

The present experiments examined face recognition. However, by focusing on faces, we do not mean to imply that faces present a unique computational problem to the visual system. On the contrary, our research is guided by the view that faces exemplify the much broader problem of distinguishing between homogeneous objects. Because such objects share a configuration, having the same basic parts in the same basic arrangement, neither part-based schemes (e.g. Biederman, 1987; Marr, 1982) nor schemes emphasizing the overall arrangement of parts (e.g. Cave & Kosslyn, 1993) offer a solution. Instead, the visual system seems to use relational features and norm-based coding to solve homogeneity problems, and neither is restricted to face recognition.

Of course faces may be special in other ways. For example, babies come predisposed to look more at faces than at other objects (Johnson & Morton, 1991). More generally, the evolutionary importance of face recognition may have provided the selection pressure needed to develop a solution to the homogeneity problem in the first place. Nevertheless, from a computational perspective, there is no evidence that these skills are used only for faces.

An important question for future research is how norm-based coding (and relational feature coding) and the part-based analysis used for basic level recognition fit together in the overall architecture of recognition. Are they distinct systems operating in parallel, as some have suggested (Corballis, 1991; Farah, 1992), or are they organized hierarchically, with relational features and norm-deviations made explicit only after a more basic part-description has been derived (Rhodes et al., 1993)?

REFERENCES

Bartlett, J.C. (1994). Inversion and configuration of faces. In J. Bartlett (Chair), *Face recognition by computers and people*. Symposium conducted at the meeting of the American Academy for the Advancement of Science, San Francisco (February).

Bartlett, J.C., Hurry, S., & Thorley, W. (1984). Typicality and familiarity of faces. *Memory & Cognition, 12,* 219–228.

Bartlett, J.C., & Searcy, J. (1993). Inversion and configuration of faces. *Cognitive Psychology, 25,* 281–316.

Benson, P.J., & Perrett, D.I. (1991). Perception and recognition of photographic quality facial caricatures: Implications for the recognition of natural images. *European Journal of Cognitive Psychology, 3,* 105–135.

Benson, P.J., & Perrett, D.I. (1994). Visual processing of facial distinctiveness. *Perception, 23,* 75–93.

Biederman, I. (1987). Recognition-by-components: A theory of human image understanding. *Psychological Review, 94,* 115–147.

Bothwell, R.K., Brigham, J.C., & Malpass, R.S. (1989). Cross-racial identification. *Personality and Social Psychology Bulletin, 15,* 19–25.

Brennan, S.E. (1982). *Caricature generator.* Unpublished Master's thesis. MIT, Cambridge, MA.

Brennan, S.E. (1985). The caricature generator. *Leonardo, 18,* 170–178.

Carey, S. (1992). Becoming a face expert. *Philosophical Transactions of the Royal Society of London, Series B, 335,* 95–103.

Carey, S., Diamond, R., & Woods, B. (1980). The development of face recognition: a maturational component? *Developmental Psychology, 16,* 257–269.

Carey, S., & Diamond, R. (1994, this issue). Are faces perceived as configurations more by adults than by children? *Visual Cognition.*

Carey, S., Rhodes, G., Diamond, R., & Hamilton, J. (in prep.). *Norm-based coding of faces: Evidence from studies of caricatures.*

Carroll, L. (1946). *Through the looking glass and what Alice found there.* New York: Random House.

Cave, C.B., & Kosslyn, S.M. (1993). The role of parts and spatial relations in object identification. *Perception, 22,* 229–248.

Cohen, M.E., & Carr, W.J. (1975). Facial recognition and the von Restorff effect. *Bulletin of the Psychonomic Society, 6,* 383–384.

Corballis, M.C. (1991). *The lopsided ape: The evolution of the generative mind.* New York: Oxford University Press.

Diamond, R., & Carey, S. (1986). Why faces are and are not special: An effect of expertise. *Journal of Experimental Psychology: General, 115,* 107–117.

Ellis, H. (1991). *The development of face processing skills.* Final report to ESRC on grant XC15250003.

Ellis, H. (1992). The development of face processing skills. *Philosophical Transactions of the Royal Society of London, Series B, 335,* 105–111.

Enquist, M., & Arak, A. (1993). Selection of exaggerated male traits by female aesthetic senses. *Nature, 361,* 446–448.

Farah, M.J. (1992). Is an object an object an object? Cognitive and neuropsychological investigations of domain specificity in visual object recognition. *Current Directions in Psychological Science, 1,* 164–169.

Going, M., & Read, J.D. (1974). Effects of uniqueness, sex of subject, and sex of photograph on facial recognition. *Perceptual & Motor Skills, 39,* 109–110.

Goren, C.C., Sarty, M., & Wu, P.Y.K. (1975). Visual following and pattern discrimination of face-like stimuli by newborn infants. *Pediatrics, 56,* 544–549.

Hagen, M.A., & Perkins, D. (1983). A refutation of the superfidelity of caricatures relative to photographs. *Perception, 12,* 55–61.

Johnson, M.H., Dziurawiec, S., Ellis, H.D., & Morton, J. (1991). Newborns' preferential tracking of faces and its subsequent decline. *Cognition, 38,* 1–23.

Johnson, M.H., & Morton, J. (1991). *Biology and cognitive development: The case of face recognition.* Oxford: Blackwell.

Light, L.L., Kayra-Stuart, F., & Hollander, S. (1979). Recognition memory for typical and unusual faces. *Journal of Experimental Psychology: Human Learning & Memory, 5,* 212–228.

Lindsay, R.C.L., & Wells, G.L. (1983). What do we really know about cross-ethnicity eyewitness identification? In S. Lloyd-Bostock & B.R. Clifford (Eds.), *Evaluating eyewitness evidence: Recent psychological research and new perspectives.* Chichester: Wiley.

Marr, D. (1982). *Vision.* San Francisco, CA: Freeman.

Mauro, R., & Kubovy, M. (1992). Caricature and face recognition. *Memory & Cognition, 20,* 433–440.

Morton, J., & Johnson, M.H. (1991). CONSPEC and CONLERN: A two-process theory of infant face recognition. *Psychological Review, 98,* 164–181.

Rhodes, G. (in prep.). *Superportraits: Caricatures and recognition.* Hove: Lawrence Erlbaum Associates Ltd.

Rhodes, G. (1994). Secrets of the face. *New Zealand Journal of Psychology, 23.* 3–17.

Rhodes, G., Brake, S., & Atkinson, A.P. (1993). What's lost in inverted faces? *Cognition, 47,* 25–57.

Rhodes, G., Brennan, S., & Carey, S. (1987). Identification and ratings of caricatures: Implications for mental representations of faces. *Cognitive Psychology, 19,* 473497.

Rhodes, G., Carey, S., Diamond, R., & Tremewan, T. (submitted). *Are caricature effects simply distinctiveness effects?*

Rhodes, G., & McLean, I.G. (1990). Distinctiveness and expertise effects with homogeneous stimuli: Towards a model of configural coding. *Perception, 19,* 773–794.

Rhodes, G., & Moody, J. (1990). Memory representations of unfamiliar faces: Coding of distinctive information. *New Zealand Journal of Psychology, 19,* 70–78.

Rhodes, G., Tan, S., Brake, S., & Taylor, K. (1989). Expertise and configural coding in face recognition. *British Journal of Psychology, 80,* 313–331.

Rock, I. (1974). The perception of disoriented figures. *Scientific American, 230,* 78–85.

Shepard, R.N. (1984). Ecological constraints on internal representation: Resonant kinematics of perceiving, imagining, thinking, and dreaming. *Psychological Review, 91,* 417–447.

Shepard, R.N. (1990). *Mind sights.* New York: W.H. Freeman.

Shepherd, J. (1981). Social factors in face recognition. In G. Davies, H. Ellis, & J. Shepherd (Eds.), *Perceiving and remembering faces.* (pp. 55–80). New York: Academic Press.

Thomas, D.R. (1993). A model for adaptation–level effects on stimulus generalization. *Pyschological Review, 100,* 658–673.

Thomas, D.R., Mood, K., Morrison, S., & Wiertelak, E. (1991). Peak shift revisited: A test of alternative interpretations. *Journal of Experimental Psychology: Animal Behaviour Processes, 17,* 130–140.

Tversky, B., & Baratz, D. (1985). Memory for faces: Are caricatures better than photographs? *Memory & Cognition, 13,* 45–49.

Valentine, T. (1991). A unified account of the effects of distinctiveness, inversion, and race in face recognition. *Quarterly Journal of Experimental Psychology, 43A,* 161–204.

Winograd, E. (1981). Elaboration and distinctiveness in memory for faces. *Journal of Experimental Psychology: Human Learning & Memory, 7,* 181–190.

Yin, R.K. (1969). Looking at upside–down faces. *Journal of Experimental Psychology, 81,* 141–145.

Yin, R.K. (1970). Face recognition. A dissociable ability? *Neuropsychologia, 8,* 395–402.

Young, A.W., Hellawell, D., & Hay, D.C. (1987). Configural information in face perception. *Perception, 16,* 747–759.

Revised manuscript received 1 April 1994

VISUAL COGNITION, 1994, *1* (2/3), 313–348

Learning New Faces
in an Interactive Activation
and Competition Model

A. Mike Burton

University of Stirling, Stirling, UK

Certain contemporary accounts of object and face recognition use connectionist networks with local representations. This paper describes and extends one such account: an interactive activation and competition (IAC) model of face recognition. In contrast to many networks with distributed representations, IAC models do not incorporate a learning mechanism. This limits their use in psychological modelling. This paper describes how a learning mechanism can be built into an IAC model. The mechanism automatically learns new representations and appears to have many of the desirable properties traditionally associated with distributed networks. Some simulations that produce results consistent with our knowledge of human face learning are reported. Finally, the relation between this work and current theories of visual object recognition is discussed.

The current interest in connectionist architectures has had a dramatic effect on theorizing in cognition. These new techniques appear to offer hope in understanding problems that have proved difficult for cognitive psychology. In particular, it is now possible to demonstrate, using computer simulation, that combinations of very simple processing units can combine to produce complex patterns of behaviour.

In this paper I describe an existing model of face recognition based on one of the simplest types of connectionist architecture: interactive activation and competition, or IAC (McClelland, 1981). An IAC model has been used to provide accounts of several phenomena from face recognition (Burton, Bruce, & Johnston, 1990; Bruce, Burton, & Craw, 1992). In contrast to some connectionist

Requests for reprints should be sent to Mike Burton, Department of Psychology, Glasgow University, Glasgow, Scotland, G12 8QQ.

This research was supported by a grant from ESRC to Mike Burton and Vicki Bruce (R000 23 2898). I would like to thank Vicki Bruce, Glyn Humphreys, and two anonymous referees for helpful comments on an earlier version of this paper.

techniques, the model uses a localist representations scheme, i.e. individual units have particular referents.

Connectionist models using local representations have proved popular in a number of fields. For example, Hummel and Biederman (1992) propose a very detailed model of object recognition using this type of network. In a different area of research, Burgess and Hitch (1992) propose a localist network model of the articulatory loop. Although this type of architecture is attractive to researchers, it apparently has some drawbacks when compared to connectionist networks using distributed representations. In particular, it is difficult to build certain types of learning into these networks.

In the remainder of this paper I describe how it is possible to build learning directly into an IAC model of face recognition. The aim is to demonstrate that simple modifications to the architecture allow the formation of new representations. So, the existing IAC model will be extended to allow learning of new faces. In the following section I briefly describe previous work with the model. I then go on to describe the learning extension and provide example simulations. The eventual utility of this scheme will depend on progress from general research in vision and object recognition. Therefore, the final section of the paper describes the relation between the work presented here and current theoretical developments in general object recognition.

The IAC Model of Person Recognition

Figure 1 shows the central aspects of Burton et al.'s (1990) IAC model of face recognition. The architecture is a simple interactive activation and competition network (McClelland, 1981; McClelland & Rumelhart, 1981). There are a number of pools of units. Within each pool, every unit is connected to every other unit with an inhibitory link (not shown in the figure). There are also excitatory links between the pools, connecting particular units. These are the links shown in the figure.

This model is an implementation and development of Bruce and Young's (1986) functional account of face recognition. (A review of the status of that model, together with accounts of empirical testing, can be found in Young & Bruce, 1991.) Following Bruce and Young (1986), there are pools of units containing face recognition units, person identity nodes, and semantic information units. Face recognition units (FRUs) represent view-independent units that become active after presentation of any (recognizable) view of a familiar face. This activation is passed by the appropriate excitatory link to the person identity node (PIN). These units are domain- and modality-free gateways into semantic information. So, although not shown in Figure 1, there will also be links into the PIN pool from systems that process names, voices, and so forth. The PINs are also linked to semantic information units (SIUs). As a PIN gains in activation, connected SIUs are excited, allowing retrieval of facts known about the recog-

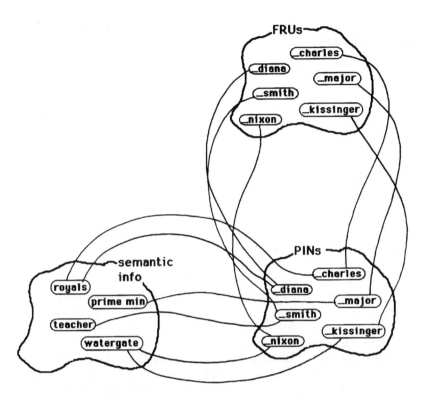

FIG. 1.   Central architecture of the IAC model of face recognition. Face Recognition Units (FRUs) represent classification at the level of the face. Person Identity Nodes (PINS) represent classification at the level of the person. Semantic Information Units (SIUs) represent items of information (e.g. occupation, nationality, etc.) Within each pool, all units are connected with bi-directional inhibitory links. The links shown are bi-directional excitatory connections between particular units.

nized person. Activation at a PIN is taken to signal familiarity, whereas activation at an SIU allows retrieval of particular information about the person.

The model briefly described here has been used to provide accounts of a wide range of effects in the published face-recognition literature. For example, effects of associative and repetition priming (Burton et al., 1990), covert recognition in prosopagnosia (Burton, et al., 1991), name retrieval (Burton & Bruce, 1992), and name recognition (Burton & Bruce, 1993) all yield to simple explanations within this framework. The account of repetition priming is important in what follows, and so I review it briefly here.

Repetition priming in face recognition refers to the fact that familiar faces are recognized (as familiar) more quickly if they have already been seen in the experimental context. Face familiarity decisions are speeded if the same or a different picture of the person was seen earlier (Bruce & Valentine, 1985; A. Ellis, Young, Flude, & Hay, 1987). This phenomenon appears to be domain-specific: although faces prime faces, and names prime names, there is no repetition priming between faces and names in either direction. Burton et al. (1990) propose that this priming occurs as a result of strengthening connections within the IAC model. When a face is recognized, the FRU (coding the face) becomes active, as does the appropriate PIN (coding the person). Under a Hebbian update scheme, links connecting two simultaneously active units will be strengthened. If this occurs, the first presentation of a face will cause the link between the relevant FRU and PIN to become stronger. The second presentation of this face will therefore cause the PIN to become active faster and so be recognized more quickly. Note that this mechanism predicts no repetition priming between faces and names. Presentation of face will strengthen the link between an FRU and a PIN; there is no advantage conferred on the route between a *name input* and the relevant PIN (see Burton et al., 1990, for a fuller discussion and simulations). In this paper I aim to extend the IAC model to account for the processes of face learning. This is achieved using exactly the same mechanism as that proposed for repetition priming.

The IAC model as originally proposed incorporated a very simple front-end. In this conception, FRUs become active due to input from "features" pools. The simplistic assumption is that each face comprises a fixed set of parameters, which are computed by front-end processes from the visual image. Although one could label these parameters "nose", "mouth", and so on, it seems more likely that they represent dimensions that do not correspond to everyday labels such as these. However, it is simpler to describe these parameters in photofit-like terms, and so I continue the discussion using these terms, without in any way wanting to be committed to the actual parameter types that are used. In a later section I discuss realistic candidates for these parameters, which have arisen from work in vision. The essential point of the argument is that faces are recognized due to combinations of particular parameter values. Figure 2 shows an outline of this notion.

Under this scheme, there will be one input pool for "mouths", one for "noses", and so forth. The "mouth" pool (for example) will contain a number of units, each of which represents a value on that parameter—a particular kind of mouth, say. Each FRU is connected with a uni-directional excitatory link from exactly one feature unit from each feature pool. So, we can describe a face as consisting of a particular "mouth", a particular "nose", and so on. When the feature units corresponding to a known face are excited, activation will pass to the appropriate FRU. This is the purpose of the model. It must activate a specific representation of an individual face when presented with the components of that face. Furthermore, this must be achieved without too much interference. If one person's face has a similar "mouth" to certain other people, a similar "nose" to yet other people, and so on, the system should have no difficulties in retrieving the appropriate person from the particular feature input set. The problem then is how to activate the right representation from a particular combination of a small

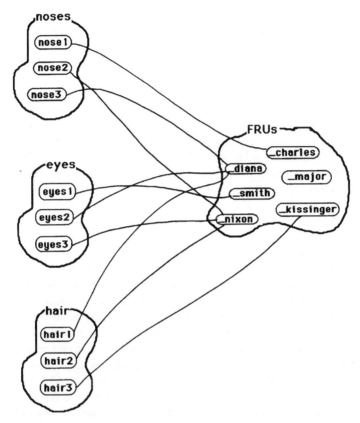

FIG. 2. Input of visual characteristics to face recognition units (FRUs). Within each pool, all units are connected with bi-directional inhibitory links. The links shown are uni-directional links from the input units (visual features) to the FRUs.

set of features. In fact, this is very simply achieved within an IAC model in which connections are hand-wired. It is more complex to imagine how appropriate connections may be formed in the first place.

Requirements of a Learning Mechanism for the IAC Model

Within the framework described above, the problem of learning a new face is one of detecting a new pattern of "feature" units and constructing a representation of this pattern. To carry any explanatory power, a mechanism to achieve this must have certain characteristics that we take to be true of human learners. First, the learning mechanism must be automatic. So, for example, it is simple to imagine how a "homuncular" process that explicitly examines patterns of input and compress them against a stored database of known faces might be implemented. If a pattern does not correspond to a known face, a new representation may be created. Although such a mechanism is trivial to implement, it is not particularly helpful. It seems unlikely that this "look-up" technique is used in human cognition. A more compelling mechanism would learn automatically. Exactly the same processes that lead to recognition of familiar faces should lead naturally to learning of new representations when necessary.

A second requirement for a useful learning mechanism is that it should allow gradual learning. For example, there should not be a simple discrete stage in which a new face becomes completely "known". Rather, the mechanism should allow different levels of familiarity and should display effects of familiarity that vary smoothly between unknown and very familiar faces.

The third requirement for the mechanism is that it should be tolerant of noise and incomplete data—*but not too tolerant*. Minor changes in "feature" sets should not produce radical changes in the representations that are learned or accessed. On the other hand, introduction of substantial noise should degrade response.

The final requirement of our learning mechanism is that it should itself be understandable. It should be possible at any time to describe the state of the system. This requirement is specific to those engaged in cognitive modelling. Engineers or other scientists may wish to investigate mechanisms that perform learning or other mappings on purely formal grounds. There are now a number of connectionist techniques that achieve impressive computational mappings without explicit representations of these mappings. For example, certain connectionist nets can perform arbitrary mappings between domains (Hinton, 1989), others approximate the Karhunen-Loève Transform (Sanger, 1989). However, in cognitive modelling, the model is assumed to represent some functional state. This being the case, it should be easy for researchers to translate any state of the model into the state they wish it to represent.

The first three requirements outlined above (automaticity, gradualism, and tolerance to noise) are characteristic of much contemporary work in connectionism. In particular, many applications using distributed representations provide these desirable properties. I will demonstrate that they are also achievable using local representations. It is important to point out that this is not a novel position. In their extensive review of distributed representations, Hinton, McClelland, and Rumelhart (1986) specifically cite IAC models as sharing many of the desirable properties of distributed representations.

The choice of local representations for the simulations presented in this paper is made on two grounds. (1) The existing IAC model of person recognition has a localist architecture. This model has already proved useful in providing accounts for a number of phenomena. It is, therefore, worthwhile to attempt to extend this model, rather than simply abandoning it and constructing an entirely new model to account for face learning. (2) Local representations provide easily interpretable states. As each concept is represented by a single unit, it is simple to interpret any particular state of the model. Although it is possible to interpret states in distributed representations, this often requires a second step; for example, using cluster analysis or dot product techniques. Models using local representations do not typically require these steps.

THE IACL MODEL

This section describes the extended IAC model, named IACL (IAC with Learning). The description is broken down into several subsections. The first section provides a general overview of the system. Then the details of the implemented program are described, and example simulations are given in the third section. Then a formal analysis of the model is described in which it is tested under different configurations. Finally, I relate the model to aspects of face learning in humans.

Overview

As with the model outlined above, the IACL architecture makes the assumption that faces are characterized as a set of features. The IACL model incorporates a number of feature pools and a pool of FRUs. The model is fully connected between feature pools and FRUs: links exist between every input (feature) unit and every FRU. These links vary in their strength. In its initial state, a sub-set of the FRUs is "known". This is intended to represent a particular point in an adult's history. The initial state is represented by the "known" FRUs receiving strong excitatory links from one and only one feature unit from every feature pool. Furthermore, there are strong inhibitory links from inappropriate feature units to these FRUs. The "unknown" units in the FRU pool each receive connections from all features with links of small weight, randomly distributed about zero. Figure 3 shows a schematic representation of the initial state in this model.

Input to the simulation is through excitation of feature units. In the case of a "known" face, appropriate features (one per pool) are activated by the experimenter. This leads to a rapid rise in excitation at the corresponding FRU and subsequent settling of unit activations. In the case of an "unknown" face, a set of feature units that does not correspond to a particular known face is excited. The patterns of connections between feature units and known faces prevents any "known" FRUs from rising above their resting level of activation. (Briefly, "known" faces usually receive at least as much inhibition from novel patterns as they receive excitation.) In this situation, one unused unit in the FRU pool rises in activation. After the unit activations settle, a simple Hebbian update function is applied to *all* between-pool links (as with the account of repetition priming). This Hebbian update tends to associate a novel input pattern with a new FRU. Subsequent presentations of this pattern increase the strengths of links until the new FRU has a similar pattern of connectivity as previously "known" faces— that is, it receives strong excitatory links from appropriate features and

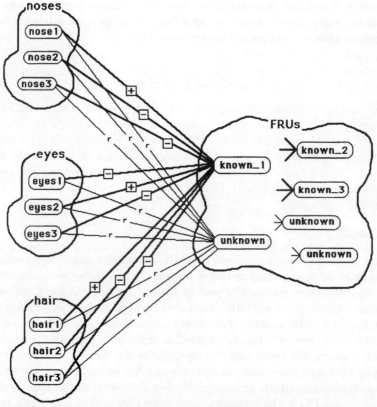

FIG. 3. Connectivity in the IACL model. Within each pool, all units are connected with bi-directional inhibitory links. The links shown are uni-directional links from the input units (visual features) to the FRUs. In contrast to Figure 2, the IACL model incorporates inhibitory as well as excitatory between-pool connections.

inhibitory links from inappropriate features. In the next section the particular implementation of this architecture is described in more detail.

Details of the Model

For the purpose of the simulations that follow, faces are (arbitrarily) represented as a combination of 12 parameters. That is, there are 12 input feature pools. Each of these parameters may take one of six values—i.e. there are six units within each of the twelve input feature pools. The possible nature of these parameters is discussed towards the end of this paper. However, for the time being it is simply assumed that early visual processing of a face delivers 12 parameter values. None of the results presented below appears to be dependent on this particular choice of the number of variables chosen. Results have been qualitatively unchanged across many variants on these numbers.

The pool of units representing FRUs comprises 100 units in this implementation. Although the possible number of feature combinations in this case is 6^{12} (around 2.1×10^9) there is not an FRU for each possible combination. In the first instance, 50 of these units have been chosen as "known" faces. A population of 50 faces was generated by choosing 12 parameters (one from each set) at random for each face. By chance, this will result in faces being more or similar to each other (in terms of how many parameter values they share).

Following previous work on an IAC model of face recognition, there are within-pool inhibitory connections in all pools. Within a pool, every unit inhibits every other unit by means of a negative link. These within-pool inhibitory links are unchanging in the present simulation.

There are also links between every feature and every FRU. In previous work (Burton et al., 1990), these links have been uni-directional—that is, activation may flow only from features to FRUs. This same pattern has been followed in the model presented here. However, in the simulations reported below, there appears to be little qualitative difference between a model in which links between features and FRUs are uni-directional or one where they are bi-directional. I will return to a discussion of this issue later in the paper.

In order to represent the "known" faces, each of the 50 FRUs from the population generated is connected with maximum positive (+1) excitatory links from each of the appropriate 12 features. Furthermore, the remaining 60 feature units for each known face are connected to the FRU with maximum negative (−1) inhibitory links. For each of the remaining, unused, 50 units in the FRU pool, there is a small connection between it and all 72 feature units. This is generated at random for each FRU and each feature and lies between −0.05 and +0.05. A starting state with random initial connection strengths is very common in connectionist architectures (e.g. multi-layer back-propagation nets—Rumelhart, Hinton, & Williams, 1986; competitive learning nets—Rumelhart & Zipser, 1985; self-organising feature nets—Kohonen, 1984).

All units have the same range of possible activations from a small negative value (-0.2 in this case) to a large positive value ($+1.0$ in this case). Furthermore, all units in the simulation start at the same, slightly negative resting activation (-0.1 in this case). Input to the network is made by maximally exciting a set of feature units (usually one from each pool, though see later for simulations in which only a subset of these 12 are activated). All unit activations are updated using a standard IAC update function (see Appendix). After a number of cycles, the unit activations tend to stabilize. After a certain number of cycles (sufficient for the network to stabilize), a modified Hebbian update rule is applied to all between-pool connection strengths within the model. A simple Hebbian update function results in connection strengths of arbitrary size. Here we ensure that the links approach a given maximum or minimum value (± 1), by an amount proportional to the product of the activations of units at each end of the link. The function used here is:

If $a_i a_j > 0,$ $\Delta w_{ij} = \lambda a_i a_j \ (1 - w_{ij})$

If $a_i a_j \leq 0,$ $\Delta w_{ij} = \lambda a_i a_j \ (1 + w_{ij})$

where a_i and a_j are the activations of units i and j, w_{ij} is the strength of the connection between units i and j, and λ is a global learning rate parameter used in all functions of this type.

Note that this architecture is a modification of some well-known networks. In particular, it differs from IAC models (McClelland, 1981) in that these models do not incorporate a learning mechanism. Furthermore, IAC models typically represent structure by use only of between-pool excitatory links, whereas the present model introduces between-pool inhibitory links. It is also important to note that this architecture is not the same as the competitive learning mechanism reported by Rumelhart and Zipser (1985). That architecture includes an extra constraint to the one described here (and hence reduces the degrees of freedom in the model). Importantly, Rumelhart and Zipser constrain the sum of connection strengths to any particular unit. Each unit has a fixed total of "connective strength" that is shared among links of feeding units. This extra constraint aids the learning. In the IACL architecture, there is no such global constraint. All the connection strengths are updated in strictly local fashion, and so updating a particular link has no automatic effect on any other links.

The model was implemented in C using the Rochester Connectionist Simulator (Goddard, Lynne, Mintz, & Bukys, 1989) and run on a Sun SPARCStation. Details of all the parameters used in the following simulations are given in the Appendix.

Simulations with the Model: A Demonstration

The first simulation demonstrates the simple effects of input to the model using the features associated with "known" faces. Figure 4 shows the pattern of activity at a particular FRU when all 12 of the appropriate features are activated (Figure 4a), and when only half of the appropriate features are activated (Figure 4b). It is clear from the figure that, as expected, the input of 12 veridical features causes activation of the FRU to rise very rapidly, and to asymptote after only a few cycles. When presented with only half of the appropriate feature units for this FRU, the figure shows a slower rise in activation. However, the decline in performance is not catastrophic. It seems that the appropriate FRU may become active through only a (relatively small) subset of its full complement of features. In this particular case, no other units in the FRU pool gain in activation (as there are 99 other units, they are not shown on the graph). Occasionally, presentation of a radical subset of an FRU's features causes a "similar" FRU to gain *some* activation (though not as much as the veridical FRU). This situation is discussed further below.

This simulation demonstrates the rather obvious fact that appropriate feature inputs will cause a rise in activation in the FRUs to which they are connected. It

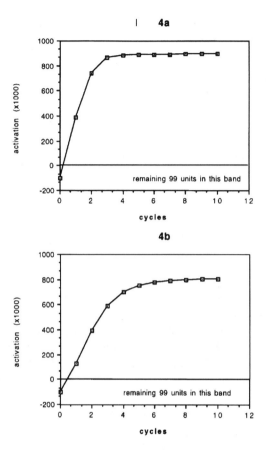

FIG. 4.   Activation of a known FRU following presentation of feature units associated with that FRU. a: FRU response after presentation of all 12 features; b: FRU response after presentation of only 6 features.

also demonstrates a simple property of part to whole completion in this network—that is, the FRU is activated by partial input. The next simulation demonstrates learning through recruitment of previously unused units.

Figure 5 shows the development of an FRU (note the difference in horizontal scale with Figure 4). A novel set of features was excited, one from each pool. Figure 5a shows the activation of all units in the FRU pool that ever take on positive activation (recall that all units have a slightly negative resting activation). FRUs are labelled from 1 to 100, such that FRUs 1 to 50 represent the "known" population and FRUs 51 to 100 are those that start as "unused". In this simulation, three units in the FRU pool achieve positive activations. The remaining 97 units in the FRU pool (including all 50 "known" FRUs) remain below zero activation during this simulation. After 35 cycles the units have stabilised and the

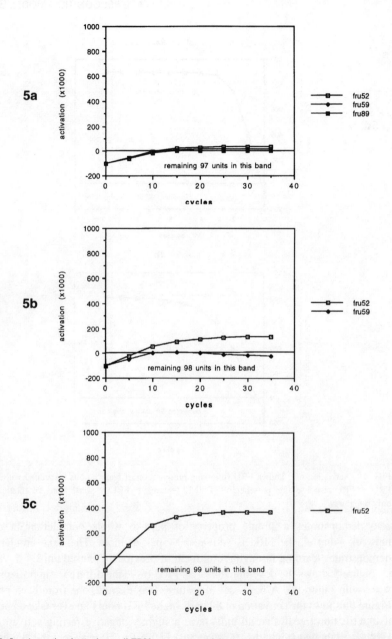

FIG. 5.   A previously "unknown" FRU comes to specialise on a pattern of features. a: response of all FRUs that achieve above-zero activation following presentation of a novel set of features. Hebbian updates occur after 35 cycles. b-e: effect of subsequent presentations of the same pattern of features.

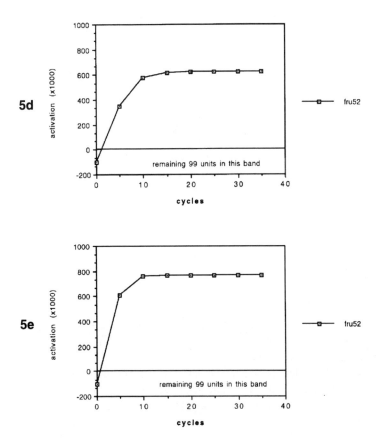

FIG. 5. Continued.

Hebb modification is made to all between-pool links in the model. Figure 5b shows the second presentation of this set of feature units. During this presentation, only two units from the FRU pool become active (above zero), and one of these quickly falls below zero. Once again, the Hebb modification is made after 35 cycles. Figures 5c, 5d, and 5e show subsequent presentations of the same pattern of feature unit activations. What is happening here is that a previously unused unit in the FRU pool is beginning to specialize on this particular pattern of input features. After several presentations of this pattern, the unit comes to have the same characteristics as previously "known" faces—that is, it develops strong excitatory links from relevant feature units, and strong inhibitory links from irrelevant feature units.

Figure 5 shows one particular instance of the development of an FRU. However, this is the common pattern. On presentation of a new set of features, several unused FRUs gain somewhat in activation. After Hebb modification, one particular FRU tends to win the competition and is finally recruited as a new "known" unit.

To understand why only "unknown" FRUs typically respond to novel patterns, one must consider the nature of the between-pool links. Recall that "known" FRUs receive links from *all* features. For appropriate features these links are excitatory, whereas for inappropriate features they are inhibitory. This pattern of connection is consistent with the intuition that *wrong* features should reduce the amount of activation received by a known FRU. So, activation of a *wrong* feature-value should be more deleterious to FRU activation than omission of that feature-value. One side-effect of this connectivity is that a novel set of features will typically send more inhibition to a "known" FRU than it will send excitation. It is for this reason that novel patterns generally do not excite known FRUs.

This section has provided a demonstration of learning within the IACL architecture. In the next section, a more formal test of the model's performance is presented.

Testing the model

Having described the general IACL architecture, it is necessary to ask how well it will perform. Given a novel pattern of feature units, how reliably will the model classify this pattern as a new face?

The essential problem for the model is to find a previously unused FRU that can come to specialize on a new feature set. Given that "unknown" FRUs are all initially connected with small random weights to all feature units, the architecture exploits the fact that by chance, some "unknown" FRUs will initially respond positively to the new pattern. Hebbian update is applied after each run of the model. The effect of this is to strengthen connections between feature units and responding FRUs. If several of the unknown FRUs respond positively, the model relies on within-pool inhibition to create a "winner", which will subsequently come to code that pattern of input. After a varying number of presentation-strengthen steps, a single FRU will respond to the new pattern. Subsequent presentations serve only to strengthen links between the pattern and the FRU, and eventually the new unit will come to have the same pattern of connectivity as the "known" units. Figure 5 provides an example of this development.

There are several ways in which the model can fail. (1) It can confuse a new pattern for a "known" face. On presentation of the pattern, an existing FRU may become active. This is likely to happen when a new pattern shares many features in common with a known face. (2) The model may fail to recruit a new FRU altogether. It is possible, given the random connectivity, that a new pattern will not cause any unit to rise above zero activation. (3) The model may recruit more than one new FRU. Under these circumstances, several unused FRUs may have very similar patterns of connectivity to a particular pattern of feature inputs. This class of failure is not catastrophic, as the new pattern is learned. However, it is wasteful, as spare unused units are used up unnecessarily.

There are several factors that are likely to affect the performance of the model. (1) It should perform well when there are many units in each feature pool. This is because the chances of a new pattern overlapping with an existing known pattern should be reduced. (2) The model should perform better when there are a large number of unknown units. This is because there is an increased chance of a new pattern having a good match to a randomly connected unit. (3) The model should perform well when there are many feature pools. Once again, this is because the increased variability between patterns should allow easier separation of one pattern from another. In the tests described in this paper, the number of known and unknown FRUs is kept constant, as is the number of feature pools. Experiment 1 demonstrates the ability of the model to learn a single new pattern. Two versions of IACL are examined in this experiment: a version with 6 units per feature pool, and a version with 10 units per feature pool. Experiment 2 demonstrates the ability of the model to learn sets of 10 new patterns, and Experiment 3 demonstrates its ability to learn sets of 25 new patterns.

General Method

Two versions of the IACL model were implemented. Each model contained 100 FRUs, 50 of which would be designated as "known" and 50 as "unknown". Each model had 12 feature pools. In one version, each feature pool contained 6 units, and in the other each feature pool contained 10 units. For each model, a known population of 50 "faces" was generated. This was done by randomly selecting one feature per pool for each face. Having generated the known population, known FRUs were connected to features as described above: appropriate features had links of strength $+1$ to FRUs, and inappropriate features had links of strength -1 to FRUs. The remaining 50 FRUs (the unknown set) were connected to all feature units with strengths randomly chosen between -0.05 and $+0.05$.

To test these models, a further set of 50 patterns was generated for each version. These new patterns were generated in identical fashion to the known faces—that is, for each "face" one feature unit was chosen at random from each pool. The models were tested by presenting each novel pattern to the network. In all the experiments, global parameters were set exactly as with the demonstration provided above (see Figure 5). These parameter values are listed in the Appendix.

EXPERIMENT 1

In Experiment 1, the model was given the task of learning one novel pattern. Starting in the state where the network has 50 "known" FRUs and 50 unused FRUs, the task is to find one unused FRU that can come to code the novel pattern. The model was tested in this way for each of the 50 novel patterns generated for these experiments, as described above.

The exact procedure was as follows. For each novel pattern:

1. Initialize the links in the network, such that there are 50 "known" FRUs and 50 "unknown" FRUs.
2. Set the activation of all units (features and FRUs) to their resting level.
3. Present the novel pattern by activating only those feature units contained in the pattern.
4. Run the model for 35 cycles.
5. If any "known" FRU has above zero activation, stop. The model has confused the new pattern for an existing pattern.
   If only one "unused" FRU has above zero activation, stop. The model has learned a pattern and subsequent presentations will only strengthen the links to improve the response of the FRU to this pattern.
   If more than one "unused" FRU reaches above zero activation, apply the Hebbian update to all links, and go to step 2.
   If no FRU reaches above zero activation, stop. The model will fail to learn this pattern.

The decision to use step sizes of 35 cycles was made on inspection of previous simulations. When configured with this number of units, the model appears to require 20 and 30 cycles for all unit activations to stabilize. No theoretical claims are made on the basis of this number—it is important only that one uses a step size sufficiently large for activation to have passed fully from features to FRUs.

Results

Table 1 shows the results of these simulations. Both versions perform reasonably well. In the version with only 6 units per feature pool, 40/50 new patterns produce unambiguous responses. A further two patterns are learned by the model, but recruit two rather than one novel FRU. As described above, this is not a catastrophic failure, but it is wasteful of unused units. In 8 cases, the model either fails to learn the pattern altogether or confuses it with an existing known pattern. On subsequent inspection, each of the 5 "misrecognized" patterns shared at least 7/12 features in common with a known pattern.

As expected, the version with 10 features per pool performs better. All new patterns are learned by the model, and there are no misrecognitions. However,

TABLE 1
Ability of the Model to Learn Individual Patterns in a Net with 50
"Known"and 50 "Unused" FRUs

	6 feature units per pool	10 feature units per pool
patterns learned with unique novel FRUs	40	45
patterns learned with duplicate novel FRUs	2	5
patterns confused with "known" FRUs	5	0
patterns for which no FRU rises above zero	3	0

Note: Performance was tested in two versions: 6 units per feature pool and 10 units per feature pool.

on 5 occasions the model recruits two rather than one novel FRUs to encode a pattern.

On the basis of these results, it appears that the IACL architecture is capable of learning individual new patterns. In the larger version of the model, all of the randomly generated test set were learned without confusion with the existing set. We now ask whether the model can learn sets of new faces.

EXPERIMENT 2

In Experiment 2, the model was given the task of learning ten novel patterns. Starting in the state where the network has 50 "known" FRUs and 50 unused FRUs, the task is to find ten unused FRUs that can come to code the novel patterns. To perform this experiment, the novel population generated above was divided into 5 sets of 10 patterns. Within each set, patterns were taught individually and in sequence. So, the first pattern was presented for several steps (25 in this case), each step being followed with Hebbian update. This was then repeated for the second pattern, and so on. From Experiment 1, it is evident that the model with 10 features per pool performs best, and so only this version was examined in Experiment 2.

The exact procedure was as follows. For each set of 10 novel patterns:

1. Initialize the links in the network such that there are 50 "known" FRUs and 50 "unknown" FRUs.
2. Repeat 25 times:
   2a. Set the activation of all units (features and FRUs) to their resting level.
   2b. Present the first novel pattern by activating only those feature units contained in the pattern.
   2c. Run the model for 35 cycles.
   2d. apply the Hebbian update to all links.
3. Go to step 2, but this time present the next novel pattern.

TABLE 2
Ability of the Model to Learn Sets of 10 Novel Patterns in a Net with
50 "Known" and 50 Unused FRUs.

	Novel Patterns to Learn				
	1–10	11–20	21–30	31–40	41–50
patterns learned with unique novel FRUs	9	10	10	9	10
patterns learned with duplicate novel FRUs	0	0	0	1	0
patterns confused with "known" FRUs	0	0	0	0	0
patterns for which no FRU rises above zero	1	0	0	0	0

Results

Table 2 shows the results of these simulations. For three of the sets, the model was able to recruit unused FRUs for all 10 novel patterns. One set contained a pattern that was never learned, and one contained a pattern that, though learned, recruited two unused FRUs. In no case was a novel pattern confused for a "known" FRU.

This performance is encouraging. It appears that the model can come to learn sets of patterns. Of course, it is the essence of the architecture that there are unused FRUs available to code novel patterns. Teaching new patterns early in the set reduces the number of unused FRUs available for later patterns. However, it seems that for set sizes of 10 new patterns, this does not harm performance. In Experiment 5, the set size is increased to 25, hence reducing still further the number of unused FRUs available for patterns late in the set.

EXPERIMENT 3

In Experiment 3, the model was given the task of learning 25 novel patterns. Starting in the state where the network has 50 "known" FRUs and 50 unused FRUs, the task is to find 25 unused FRUs that can come to code the novel patterns. To perform this experiment, the novel population generated above was divided into 2 sets of 25 patterns. Within each set, patterns were taught individually and in sequence, exactly as described in Experiment 2. Once again, only the version with 10 units per feature pool was tested.

Results

Table 3 shows the results of these simulations. Increasing the set size has increased the number of patterns that cannot be learned (two patterns in one set of 25 and three in the other). Each set contained one pattern that, though learned, recruited two novel FRUs. The remaining patterns (22 and 21 out of 25) were learned with a unique novel FRU. Once again, there were no cases in which a novel pattern was confused with a "known" FRU.

TABLE 3
Ability of the Model to Learn Sets of 25 Novel Patterns in a Net with
50 "Known" and 50 Unused FRUs.

	Novel Patterns to Learn	
	1–25	*26–50*
patterns learned with unique novel FRUs	22	21
patterns learned with duplicate novel FRUs	1	1
patterns confused with "known" FRUs	0	0
patterns for which no FRU rises above zero	2	3

Although the performance of the model decreases with a larger set size, it is nevertheless learning a substantial number of novel patterns. Even in the case where available unused FRUs are being eliminated, it is possible to learn the great majority of patterns within each set.

DISCUSSION

The tests above show that the IACL architecture is capable of learning novel patterns. Experiment 1 showed that when taught individual novel patterns, the model learns almost perfectly in the configuration with 10 units per feature pool. Experiments 2 and 3 show that the architecture is capable of learning sets of faces. As the number of available unused FRUs is reduced there is a slight reduction in performance (Experiment 3), though this is not catastrophic.

The aim of implementing a learning component for an IAC architecture has therefore been achieved. Furthermore, as described in this and the previous section, the mechanism appears to meet the requirements set out in the introduction: it is automatic, gradualist (Figure 5), tolerant of incomplete data (Figure 4b) and, due to its simplicity, easy to interpret.

Although the formal properties of the IACL architecture are attractive, its relation to human learning remains speculative. There are several aspects of the simulations that cannot be tied to human performance at present. As an example, consider the presentation of patterns within a set. In Experiments 2 and 3, each new pattern was presented for several steps (and hence learned well) before presentation of the subsequent pattern. This "blocked" manner of presentation achieves good results. However, it remains unspecified how many link-update steps correspond to a single viewing of a pattern for human subjects. There is certainly no attempt in the above to suggest that one step corresponds to one "instance" of a face presentation in a psychological experiment. The literature on connectionist stimulation contains models in which several link updates represent a psychological "instance" (e.g. McClelland & Rumelhart, 1985), and also models in which a single step corresponds to an "instance" (e.g. Burgess & Hitch, 1992). In the absence of any strong reason to tie particular formal aspects of the model to psychological processes, one must leave these issues open. Despite these problems, there appear to be some psychological effects that are echoed in the performance of IACL, and these are the subject of the next section.

THE IACL MODEL AND HUMAN FACE LEARNING

The model of automatic learning of new patterns described is achieved with a local representation scheme, through a mechanism that recruits unused units. Demonstrations of this phenomenon show how a simple local Hebb modification may be used to code novel representations with a network. The main aim of this paper has been to demonstrate that such learning is possible within a simple localist net. As the motivation for this work comes from an existing model of face recognition, we must now ask how such a model could relate to human data on learning new faces.

There are two reasons why it is difficult to relate this particular implementation directly to human data on face learning. The first is that it is severely under-specified as a cognitive model. In the above demonstrations it is simply assumed that visual processing delivers a set of parameters to the system, which are then used to individuate faces. So far, the nature of these parameters has been left unspecified. The aim here is simply to demonstrate that learning is *possible* in an IAC-like architecture. In the discussion I list a number of plausible candidate prameterisations that may feed this model, but so far it has not been possible to establish what are the primitives of face recognition.

The second reason for the difficulty in relating IACL to human learning is that there is rather little experimental work in this field reported in the literature. It is a commonplace that we can learn new faces when presented with them. However, the factors influencing this ability are not well understood. In common with other stimuli, exposure duration to a face increases one's ability to recognize it. This seems to be captured in the gradual development of FRU specialization demonstrated in Figure 5. However, the exact circumstances leading to good or poor learning are not known.

Given these problems, it would clearly be premature to attempt quantitative simulations of human face learning. Nevertheless, there are some effects reported in the literature that appear to be reflected in properties of the IACL model. In this section I list some of these effects and offer some observations derived from simulations. In most cases, these observations must remain speculative. However, they do offer hope that the IACL model will eventually be able to provide accounts of data from human learning.

Combinations of Known Faces

In the simulations presented above, novel faces (patterns) were constructed at random from the available feature set. It may be interesting to observe the behaviour of the model when it is presented with novel patterns constructed by combining features from known faces. Below, I present data from a simulation in which the input comprises half the features from one known pattern, together with half the features from a second known pattern. The motivation for presenting two "half faces" comes from a demonstration by Young, Hellawell, and Hay (1987). The authors showed that when the top half of one well-known face is aligned with the bottom half of another, the perceptual experience is of an entirely new face. When the two halves are misaligned, subjects are able easily to identify the two people. However, this ability is radically reduced by alignment. It would appear, then, that faces are *recognized* in a holistic fashion, rather than on a part-by-part componential match. So, mixing components of known faces does not produce recognition of a "mixed" person, but of a new person altogether.

Of course it would be naive to claim that presentation of half the features of a face in this model corresponds to the real situation of seeing only half a face. It is quite possible that the "features" are themselves global and cross the top-bottom divide (see the final section for a discussion of candidates for these features). The important point of the following demonstration is that a new face may be formed that has considerable overlaps with known faces.

Figure 6 shows the effects of presenting two halves of known faces. The data come from the version of the model with 6 units per feature pool, and all parameters were the same as used in previous simulations (see Appendix). Figure 6a shows the activation in the FRU pool when only the first 6 features of Face 3 are input. The FRU for the (known) Face 3 becomes active quickly. Two further FRUs (representing faces 14 and 34 in this case) also rise in activation somewhat. This is because Faces 14 and 34 happen to share four of their first six feature units with Face 3. All the remaining 97 units in the FRU pool remained below zero activation during the period of input. A similar pattern is shown in Figure 6b. Here, the units corresponding to Features 7 to 12 for Face 4 are input. Once again, FRU 4 rises in activation quickly. In addition, the FRU representing Face 41 gains some activation. Face 41 shares four of its last 6 units with Face 4.

Figures 6c to 6g show the effects at FRUs of simultaneously activating the first six features of Face 3 and the last six features of Face 4. On the first presentation, 6c, 3 of the 100 units in the FRU pool achieve positive activation. Importantly, none of these 3 units is a "known" FRU. In particular, Faces 3 and 4 (or any of the other faces that share features) do not become active during this presentation.

After the presentations shown in 6c, the Hebbian update function is applied, Figure 6d shows the activation in the FRU pool on the next presentation of this combination of features. Now only one unit achieves positive activation. Figures 6e to 6g show subsequent presentations of this pattern, each followed by a Hebbian update of *all* links between pools. As with Figure 5, we can see the development of a new FRU, specializing on this pattern.

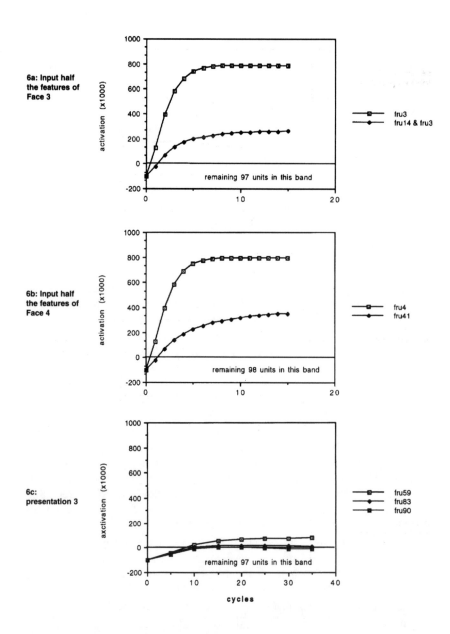

6a: Input half the features of Face 3

activation (x1000)

remaining 97 units in this band

fru3
fru14 & fru3

6b: Input half the features of Face 4

activation (x1000)

remaining 98 units in this band

fru4
fru41

6c: presentation 3

axctivation (x1000)

remaining 97 units in this band

cycles

fru59
fru83
fru90

FIG. 6. A previously unused FRU comes to specialize on a pattern created using half the features from one known face, and half the features from another known face. a–b: response of the network when presented with (a) half the features of face 3, and (b) half the features of face 4. c–g: response from the net when presented with these two "half faces" simultaneously. Hebbian updates occur after 35 cycles.

334

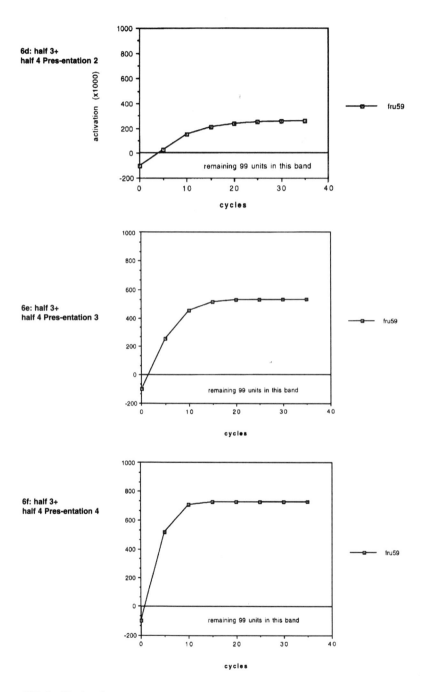

FIG. 6. Continued

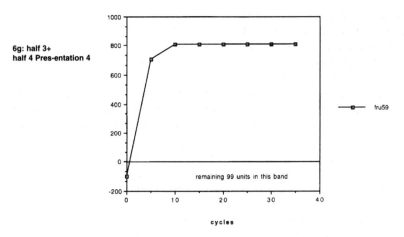

FIG. 6. Continued

The effect of combining faces, as demonstrated here, does not produce a new representation in every case. When two faces share many features in common, a composite is sometimes "misidentified" as a known face. For example, it is possible for two faces to share features such that the first six features of Face A and the second six features of Face B actually produce a composite that has 10 features from Face A (because of overlap between A and B). In this case, a new FRU is not recruited. Rather, the new combination produces activation in the FRU appropriate to Face A. It would appear that the network encodes a transition in its response from perfect input of a known face to input that preserves only some aspects of a known face. This appears to be analogous to the human case. A certain amount of distortion in input is tolerable. However, severe distortion (as in the case of combining two half faces) produces a novel representation.

Part to Whole Completion

Face recognition is robust under quite severe masking of the stimulus. We do not need to see (for example) complete full-face photographs of people in order to recognize them. The model described above clearly provides some part-to-whole completion properties. Figures 4 and 6 show that one does not need to present the entire veridical feature set in order to achieve high activation in the appropriate FRU. For example, Figure 4b shows that on presentation of only half the appropriate features, the FRU rises to a level only very slightly below that achieved on presentation of the full feature set (Fig 4a). However, it takes somewhat longer (more cycles) for this activation to be achieved. In particular, it is *not* the case that presentation of only half the feature set provides only half the FRU response.

Brunas, Young, and Ellis (1990) have demonstrated some interesting effects of presenting partial facial inputs to subjects. They observed repetition priming on a face familiarity task using part of the face as a prime, and the whole face as the stimulus. Priming onto the whole face was observed equally from the whole face, internal features only, and external features only. (Internal features here were generated by cutting out part of the face to include eyes, nose, and mouth. External features here means what is left of the face after cutting this portion out.) This equivalence of priming also holds when the primes and stimuli are constructed from different photographs. This appears to indicate that the priming is occurring beyond the stage of the initial stimulus, i.e. it is not due only to particular visual characteristics of the stimuli. Instead, the effect must be happening within the face recognition system itself. Burton et al. (1990) locate repetition priming between the FRUs and the PINs (see Figure 1), and this is consistent with the account offered here. Briefly, a presentation of the partial stimulus set will be sufficient to activate the FRU, and hence PIN. As Figure 4b shows no catastrophic decrement in FRU activation due to a partial stimulus set, repetition priming should be observed both for partial and complete presentations.

There is a further aspect of part-to-whole completion that is of interest here. The model as presented has only uni-directional links between feature pools and FRUs. As mentioned above, it makes no qualitative difference in the present implementation whether the links are uni- or bi-directional (though of course the absolute values of unit activations are different). However, if bi-directional links are used, a natural consequence follows. When the model is presented with a subset of the features appropriate for one face, the FRU rises as before. Furthermore, due to back-activation, the missing *features* also gain in activation: a subset of the features can cause re-instatement of the complimentary features. Whether or not this is desirable is dependent entirely on how one conceptualizes the features, and we will shortly come to a discussion of some candidates. The important point to note is that the desirable property of part-to-whole completion can mean two things in this situation. (1) It may mean that the outcome of a partial set is "recognizable" on a level comparable to the full set. (2) It may mean that a *partial input* can re-instate a legal *whole input*. For the purposes of the present model, the former criterion has been adopted. It is possible that the latter would be more desirable, for example to help construct a model of mental imagery of a face. As no such account is offered here, the simpler uni-directional configuration has been chosen. It is worth noting that future work may require a reconfiguration.

Internal and External Features

As mentioned above, there is little empirical evidence on the processes by which faces become familiar. However, one robust finding is that recognition tends to be focussed on internal features (eyes, nose, mouth) for very familiar faces rather than external features (e.g. hair, global face shape) (Ellis, Shepherd, & Davies, 1979). The standard explanation for this is that external features are more variable between people, but also more changeable for any particular person, than are internal features. So, as one recognizes someone many times, it is likely that the person will have a variety of hair-styles and varying global face shapes according to their age, state of health, and so forth. It is therefore strategically sensible to concentrate on the relatively constant aspects of the face and reinforce these aspects in the stored representation.

This account is very easily assimilable by the IACL model. Using the Hebbian update approach, the link between a feature and an FRU will be stronger if it is seen more often. Constant features will tend to be more highly associated with FRUs than transient features. Although this is simply a re-statement of existing accounts, it appears to be quite consistent with the current implementation.

Excitation and Inhibition

The configuration of the model is that units have a smaller negative range than positive range (consistent with other IAC models). In this implementation, units have a resting activation of -0.1, a minimum activation of -0.2 and a maximum activation of 1.0 (see Appendix). This has certain implications for the workings of the model. When a novel pattern of features is presented, the feature units are given their maximum activation. As with all input, irrelevant feature units are simply ignored—that is, they start with their resting activation. On presentation, an FRU starts to specialize on this pattern. Now, the Hebbian update on the links connecting features to FRUs is proportional to the product of the activations of units at each end of the link. As the activation on relevant features is 1.0 but activation on irrelevant features is -0.1, this means that excitatory links to the FRU are learned much faster than inhibitory links from features to FRUs.

It is not clear whether this corresponds to the real situation. However, there is a consequence of the architecture that seems to suggest that it might. The relative slowness in development of inhibitory feature to FRU links means that a brand-new pattern is much more likely to be falsely identified as a poorly known person (with whom it shares some features) than it is to be mis-identified as a well-known person. This will continue to happen long after the recognition speed (in terms of cycles for FRUs to reach some threshold) for old faces and relatively new faces have become the same. The present configuration implies that relatively recent faces are recognized with more tolerance to noise, or change of features, than very well-known faces. Furthermore, it is more difficult to make discriminations between very similar faces when these faces are not very familiar. This appears to be intuitively reasonable. One might very well mistake two similar but relatively unfamiliar faces. The point is that this difference between highly familiar and relatively unfamiliar faces will continue to be evident in the pattern of mis-identifications long after the response to veridical feature inputs becomes equivalent. This prediction will be the subject of future empirical investigations.

Learning Models and Developmental Models

The IACL model is intended to capture the processes of learning new faces when one already has a large store of known faces. The simulation addresses the situation in which adults find themselves: how to add a new face to an existing database. This is not the developmental problem. The problem addressed above is not how one moves from knowing no faces to knowing one face, but how one moves from knowing many faces to knowing one more.

In many PDP models the issues of learning and development are taken to be equivalent. Models that move from no knowledge to complete knowledge are shown. This is partly because a developmental model is often rather easier to demonstrate. For example, in back-propagation models the first few representations are learned relatively simply. However, these original representations are subsequently lost if the models are not constantly re-trained with old as well as new patterns (McCloskey & Cohen, 1989; Ratcliff, 1990). This is not the case with the present IACL model. Learning a new pattern has very little effect on the encoding of existing patterns.

It is important to note that IACL is explicitly not offered as a developmental model. The architecture assumes an existing "feature set" from which novel faces can be constructed. It seems unlikely that this feature set is originally finely tuned in children and simply waiting for input. A proper developmental model would therefore require a much more subtle approach than the one offered here.

DISCUSSION

Having described some observations with this simulation, I will now return to theoretical issues related to the IACL model. The assumption throughout the above is that early visual processing of a facial image delivers a small set of parameter values ("features"), the co-occurrence of which defines a face. The nature of these features has been left unspecified. It is now important to consider what these features *might* be.

There have been several different (but related) approaches to object recognition that rely on the idea of stored object-centred descriptions that can mediate recognition across many views (see Humphreys & Bruce, 1989; Bruce & Humphreys, this issue, for reviews). In many accounts these descriptions are taken to comprise combinations of low-level components (primitives). The nature of these components has been the subject of dispute, but some influential examples are generalized cones (Marr & Nishihara, 1978), superquadrics (Pentland, 1986), and geons (Biederman, 1987).

Could the IACL architecture form a basis for learning in general object recognition? It is possible to imagine that (for example) feature pools in an IACL model correspond to geons, and that units within a pool correspond to parametric values of these geons. Although superficially attractive, this approach hides a difficulty. It is not clear how such a model could capture the large number of different combinations and spatial relations of the small number of component parts of an object. Hummel and Biederman (1992) discuss this issue and produce a model that solves the *binding problem*, allowing individual components and their spatial relations to be bound temporarily for the purposes of object recognition. Solution to this problem requires a level of sophistication (notably a model of time) beyond that of the model presented here.

Although the IACL architecture will not clearly solve the binding problem, its use in a model of face recognition means that it may not have to. Object recognition is generally conceived as a problem of how to distinguish between objects made up of different parts, or of the same parts in different configurations. The problem in face recognition is how to distinguish between objects that all have the same basic arrangement. Diamond and Carey (1986) propose the term "second-order relational features" to describe the relations among the components of objects that all share the same basic configuration. In the face recognition domain, all objects have the same basic layout: eyes over nose over mouth. What differs between faces is the spatial relation of these components.

It is now rather easier to see how an IACL architecture could code faces. If some of the feature pools actually correspond to second-order relational features, there is no need to solve the binding problem. We assume that a model of this type is only for use on stimuli for which basic level object recognition has already been performed. Once this has been done, the "features" are known, and so the only remaining issue is to extract the parametric values of these features.

So far, I have assumed that the primitives of object recognition are geon-like volumetric descriptions. However, there are also a number of attempts to characterize objects in terms of parameterized *surface-based* primitives. These parameterizations use surface-types to capture descriptions of objects that are invariant over viewing angle (e.g. Brady, Ponce, Yuille, & Asada, 1985). Recently Coombes and her colleagues have used a surface coding scheme specifically to characterize faces (Coombes et al., 1990; Coombes, Moss, Linney, & Richards, 1991; Coombes et al., 1992). These researchers use 3-D descriptions of real faces measured using a laser scanner (Moss, Linney, Grinrod, & Mosse, 1989). At each point on the surface it is possible to measure mean curvature and Gaussian curvature. Using a simple threshold technique, the two types of curvature are given categorical values of positive, zero, and negative. Combining the two types of curvature, this gives nine possible "surface types" at each point in the surface. In fact, one of the nine combinations is impossible. This leaves 8 surface types, which can be labelled quite simply as "ridge", "peak", "trough", "valley", and so on.

Using this technique, Coombes et al. have shown that a face may be described as a combination of regions of different surface types. For example, there will be a patch of "peak" at the end of the nose, patches of "valley" to the side of the nose, and so forth. This scheme has proved sufficiently robust to aid the understanding of facial change as a result of surgery (Coombes et al, 1991). It is also possible to compare the faces of different people: e.g. faces have more or less peak at one location, more or less valley at another (Bruce, Coombes, & Richards, 1993). Parameterized surface types and their arrangements could form the basis for input to an IACL model.

In the discussion above I have listed some plausible candidates for features that might feed an architecture of the IACL type. All of these are "parts-based": they assume that faces are made up of smaller components, each locally defined. However, there is a growing body of evidence that faces may be recognized in more holistic fashion (see Bruce and Humphreys, this issue). The technique of Principal Components Analysis, or PCA (Kirby & Sirovich, 1990; Turk & Pentland, 1991), seems to offer a computational handle on this suggestion. In this method a set of eigenvectors (principal components) is derived from a set of facial images. The individual eigenvectors (labelled "eigenfaces" by Turk and Pentland) do not correspond to facial features such as eyes and noses but, rather, to a vector of pixel values of the same dimension as the original images. If one is using images of size 256×256, each image can be represented as a vector of 65,536 dimensions. A set of these images can be reduced to their principal components. Each component (eigenvector) will be 65,536 elements long and can be displayed as a 256×256 image. Using this method, faces are then characterized as a weighted sum across the eigenvectors. Each face is stored simply as a list of parameters (eigenvalues). In order to identify a particular face, one only needs to establish its weight on each of these eigenfaces and compare these wights to a stored database. This technique has the advantage that faces can be stored and compared in a very economical form. Furthermore, the eigenvector extraction can be implemented in a simple connectionist network. There have already been some attempts to examine the psychological plausibility of PCA methods applied to face recognition. For example O'Toole, Deffenbacher, Abdi, and Bartlett (1991) showed that PCA provided a natural account of the cross-race effect in face recognition.

The main problem with this pixel-based approach is that the principal components derived from a set of images describe regularities in the original *images* rather than in the original *faces*. So, background information contributes to the PCA. Furthermore, because the analysis is performed at the image level, changes of size or orientation of a face have radical effects on the overall characteristics of the image. Recently, Craw and Cameron (1991) have described a method that overcomes these difficulties. These researchers describe an automatic technique by which images of faces may be standardized by size and viewing angle. When these standardized images are subject to PCA, the resulting eigenfaces represent image characteristics of the face itself. Craw (1992) used this technique to represent 50 faces, each originally comprising 5000 bytes of raw image. He found that the first 20 eigenvectors sufficed to make subtle individuating discriminations between the faces. So, the PCA method provides a way of characterizing a complex facial image as a simple list of 20 parameters.

The principal components derived from studies such as these seem to be good candidates for the "features" described above. Using this method, a "feature" does not correspond to some simple measurement within the face, but to a complex pattern across the whole face. Eigenvalues are equivalent here to the particular units within a feature (eigenface) pool. There is, however, one problem with the analogy. Eigenvalues have continuous parametric properties, whereas the units in each of the feature pools are currently represented categorically: There is no internal organization within a pool of units. I will return to this issue below.

Although the IACL model as presented is not committed to any *particular* parameterization of faces, the important point is that there are a number of plausible options in addition to the simple "photofit" conception. Each of the techniques described above transforms raw data (either visual or surface) into a parameterized description. The IACL model shows how a novel representation (an FRU) may be formed as a result of the input of such parameters. Of course, this does not necessarily mean that the IACL model will produce human-like performance if interfaced with any of the parameterizations mentioned here. The potential benefit of marrying any of these schemes with the IACL model is that this now becomes an empirical issue. Future work will address the issue of how to combine perceptual and cognitive aspects of face recognition.

Further Work

The work presented here describes a very simple, automatic way in which new faces may be learned. Furthermore, this is consistent with previous work on modelling cognitive aspects of face recognition. In particular, the process by which faces are learned in this model is exactly the same as the process that gives rise to repetition priming in the IAC model of face recognition. It is central to the account of learning that front-end processing of faces delivers a set of visual parameters to the cognitive system. These parameters are not specified. However, a number of candidates have been proposed, each of which reflects current work in image processing and appears plausible. In short, the *idea* of parameterized faces seems to be consistent across a wide range of research.

Although the simple account presented here appears to offer some hope, there are clearly problems remaining. In this final section I consider three potential developments of the model: (1) A development to incorporate feature values with metric properties; (2) the integration of this model into the larger IAC model of face recognition; (3) the extension of the IACL architecture into other domains.

Properties of Feature Units

The nature of the feature units *within* pools in IACL may be problematic. Most of the candidate feature types discussed above offer numerical parameters rather than categorical parameters. The IACL account, on the other hand, treats the parameter values (e.g. 6 per "feature") as mutually independent categories. In this way, it is more akin to a photofit-like system in which one chooses different *types* of nose, rather than a value on a continuously varying dimension.

A potential development of this model would incorporate an ordering of these variables. Preliminary explorations of this type of architecture have suggested a technique for achieving this quite simply. As with the present system, each FRU is strongly associated with one feature from each pool. However, the degree of association between the FRU and neighbouring features dissipates gradually, rather than radically falling to a strong inhibitory value. Using a Mexican hat operator, it appears to be possible to encourage a (slightly) coarser coding of the mappings between features and FRUs. So, the main feature value excites the FRU maximally, neighbouring values excite it somewhat less, and distant values inhibit it. This introduces an implicit ordering of feature values within a pool and allows a more generalized mapping from features to FRUs. It is also consistent with the possibility that front-end processes do not always deliver exactly the same feature value on each encounter with the face but may be subject to noise across, say, different viewing conditions. Experiments with such an architecture will form the basis of future work.

An Integrated Model of Face Recognition

The IACL system described attempts to capture only a very small part of the person recognition system. Figure 1 shows core aspects of the IAC model that tie together face recognition units, person identity nodes (PINs), and semantic information. More recent versions of this model also incorporate mechanisms for person recognition through other routes (notably names) and for lexical output (Burton & Bruce, 1993). In the simulations described above, only the very early parts of the system are implemented. The simulations only capture how new FRUs can come to be formed. They do not address how new "people" can be represented by integrating FRUs, PINs, semantic information, and possibly other input modalities.

There are several reasons to proceed with the difficult task of integrating the IACL architecture with a model of the rest of the person recognition system. (1) If we are to capture psychological aspects of face learning, it is clearly necessary to describe how knowledge of a person comes to be integrated with our knowledge of other people. (2) It is possible that an integrated system will actually perform more efficiently than the isolated system described here.

The system implemented here models one of the most difficult aspects of face recognition: how can we see a novel face and recognize it as novel in the absence of other information? The system works in an entirely unsupervised way, and there are no mechanisms to provide feedback when mistakes are made. In fact, we generally learn about people in a multi-modal fashion—from names, voices, semantic cues, and so on. When introduced to someone, we are generally told their name and some further information; we are not simply shown the person's face. If we see somebody new on television, this person appears in a context that provides extra information. These extra pieces of information may support the processes that give rise to the development of a new representation for this person. If the new person looks similar to somebody we know, we can often use context to resolve the problem. For example, one would not expect to see a colleague in a TV play.

In an integrated model of person recognition and learning, all modalities could be used to resolve any ambiguous input. Furthermore, it may be possible to examine any top-down effects on face learning. In sum, the integration of these models is attractive not only to give completion, but also because the integration itself may provide properties not available either in the IACL model described here, or in the IAC model of face recognition developed elsewhere.

Other Interactive Activation Models

The mechanism described may prove useful in domains other than face recognition. The interactive activation architecture, or variations on it, have been used with some success in both word recognition and object recognition research. For example, the model proposed by McClelland and Rumelhart (1981) continues to attract attention from researchers (e.g. Jacobs & Grainger, 1992).

There are some properties of the IACL architecture that suggest that it may be useful in other domains. In a model of word recognition, the essential problem is to create a new vocabulary item. Although the present model has not been used to simulate vocabulary acquisition, it may be suited to the task. Words are clearly made up of component parts (letters). Furthermore, there is only a small number of options available for each part (letter). One could imagine constructing a model in which feature pools (representing horizontal and vertical lines, etc.) activate pools containing one unit for each letter of the alphabet. These may, in turn, activate word pools containing unused units that could be recruited on presentation of a new vocabulary item.

The exact arrangement of pools within an IACL model of word recognition is not straightforward, and the success of such a model may depend on its integration into a larger model of reading (see the previous section). Although there are some grounds for optimism, it remains to be seen whether the architecture described in this paper can be used to good effect in domains other than face recognition.

REFERENCES

Biederman, I. (1987). Recognition by components: A theory of human image understanding. *Psychological Review, 94*, 115–145.

Brady, M., Ponce, J., Yuille, A., & Asada, H. (1985). Describing surfaces. *Computer Vision, Graphics and Image Processing, 32*, 1–28.

Bruce, V. (1988). *Recognising faces*. Hove: Lawrence Erlbaum Associates Ltd.

Bruce, V., Burton, A.M., & Craw, I. (1992). Modelling face recognition. *Philosophical Transactions of The Royal Society of London: B, 335*, 121–128.

Bruce, V., Coombes, A.M., & Richards, R. (1993). Describing the shapes of faces using surface primitives. *Image and Vision Computing, 11*, 353–363.

Bruce, V., & Valentine, T. (1985). Identity priming in the recognition of familiar faces. *British Journal of Psychology, 76*, 373–383.

Bruce, V., & Young, A.W. (1986). Understanding face recognition. British Journal of Psychology, 77, 305–327.

Brunas, J., Young, A.W., & Ellis, A.W. (1990). Repetition priming from incomplete faces: Evidence for part to whole completion. *British Journal of Psychology, 81*, 43–56.

Burgess, N., & Hitch, G.J. (1992). Toward a network model of the articulatory loop. *Journal of Memory and Language, 31*, 429–460.

Burton, A.M., & Bruce, V. (1992). I recognize your face but I can't remember your name: A simple explanation? *British Journal of Psychology, 83*, 45–60.

Burton, A.M., & Bruce, V. (1993). Naming faces and naming names: Exploring an interactive activation model of face recognition. *Memory, 1*, 457–480.

Burton, A.M., Bruce, V., & Johnston, R.A. (1990). Understanding face recognition with an interactive activation model. *British Journal of Psychology, 81*, 361–380.

Burton, A.M., Young, A.W., Bruce, V., Johnston, R.A., & Ellis, A.W. (1991). Understanding covert recognition. *Cognition, 39*, 129–166.

Coombes, A.M., Linney, A.D., Grinrod, S.R., Mosse, C.A., & Moss, J.P. (1990). 3D Measurement of the face for the simulation of facial surgery. In H. Neugebauer & G. Windischbauer (Eds.), *Proceedings of the 5th International Symposium on Surface Tomography and Body Deformity*. Vienna: Gustav Fischer Verlag.

Coombes, A.M., Moss, J.P., Linney, A.D., & Richards, R. (1991). A mathematical method for the comparison of three dimensional changes in the facial surface. *European Journal of Orthodontics, 13*, 95–110.

Coombes, A., Richards, R., Linney, A., Hanna, E., & Bruce, V. (1992). Shape-based description of the facial surface. *IEE Colloquium on Machine Storage and Recognition of Faces. Digest 1992/017*, 9/1–9/4.

Craw, I. (1992). Recognizing face features and faces. *IEE Colloquium on Machine Storage and Recognition of Faces. Digest 1992/017*, 9/1–9/4.

Craw, I., & Cameron, P. (1991). Parameterising images for recognition and reconstruction. In P. Mowforth (Ed.), *Proceedings of the British Machine Vision Conference, 1991*. Berlin: Springer Verlag.

Diamond, R., & Carey, S. (1986). Why faces are and are not special: An effect of expertise. *Journal of Experimental Psychology: General, 115*, 105–117.

Ellis, A.W., Young, A.W., Flude, B.M., & Hay, D.C. (1987). Repetition priming of face recognition. *Quarterly Journal of Experimental Psychology, 39A*, 193–210.

Ellis, H.D., Shepherd, J.W., & Davies, G.M. (1979). Identification of familiar and unfamiliar faces from internal and external features: Some implications for theories of face recognition. *Perception, 8,* 431–439.

Goddard, N.H., Lynne, K.J., Mintz, T., & Bukys, L. (1989). *Rochester connectionist simulator.* Technical Report 233 (Revised), Department of Computer Science, New York: University of Rochester.

Hinton, G.E. (1989). Connectionist learning procedures. *Artificial Intelligence, 40,* 185–234.

Hinton, G.E., McClelland, J.L., & Rumelhart, D.E. (1986). Distributed representations. In D.E. Rumelhart, J.L. McClelland, & the PDP Research Group (Eds.), *Parallel Distributed Processing: Explorations in the Microstructure of Cognition. Volume 1: Foundations.* Cambridge, MA: MIT Press.

Hummel, J.E., & Biederman, I. (1992). Dynamic binding in a neural network for shape recognition. *Psychological Review, 99,* 480–517.

Humphreys, G.W., & Bruce, V. (1989). *Visual Cognition: Computational, experimental and neuropsychological perspectives.* Hove: Lawrence Erlbaum Associates Ltd.

Jacobs, A.M., & Grainger, J. (1992). Testing a semistochastic variant of the interactive activation model in different word recognition experiments. *Journal of Experimental Psychology: Human Perception and Performance, 18,* 1174–1188.

Kirby, M., & Sirovich, L. (1990). Applications of the Karhunen-Loeve procedure for the characterisation of human faces. *IEEE: Transactions on Pattern Analysis and Machine Intelligence, 12,* 103–108.

Kohonen, T. (1984). *Self-organisation and associate memory.* Berlin: Springer Verlag.

Marr, D., & Nishihara, H.K. (1978). Representations and recognition of the spatial organisation of three-dimensional shapes. *Proceedings of the Royal Society of London B, 200,* 269–294.

McClelland, J.L. (1981). Retrieving general and specific information from stored knowledge of specifics. *Proceedings of the Third Annual Meeting of the Cognitive Science Society,* 170–172.

McClelland, J.L. & Rumelhart, D.E. (1981). An interactive activation model of context effects in letter perception: Part 1. An account of basic findings. *Psychological Review, 88,* 375–407.

McClelland, J.L. & Rumelhart, D.E. (1985). Distributed memory and the representation of general and specific information. *Journal of Experimental Psychology: General, 114,* 159–188.

McClelland, J.L. & Rumelhart, D.E. (1988). *Explorations in parallel distributed processing.* Cambridge, MA: Bradford Books.

McCloskey, M., & Cohen, N.J. (1989). Catastrophic interference in connectionist networks: The sequential learning problem. In G. Bower (Ed.) *The psychology of learning and motivation, Vol 24.* San Diego, CA: Academic Press.

Moss, J.P., Linney, A.D., Grinrod, S.R., & Mosse, C.A. (1989). A laser scanning system for the measurement of facial surface morphology. *Optics and Lasers in Engineering, 10,* 179–190.

O'Toole, A.J., Deffenbacher, K.A., Abdi, H., & Bartlett, J.C. (1991). Simulating the "other-race" effect as a problem in perceptual learning. *Connection Science: Journal of Neural Computing, Artificial Intelligence and Cognitive Research, 3,* 163–178.

Pentland, A. (1986). Perceptual organisation and the representation of natural form. *Artificial Intelligence, 28,* 293–331.

Ratcliff, R. (1990). Connectionist models of recognition memory. Constraints imposed by learning and forgetting functions. *Psychological Review, 97,* 285–308.

Rumelhart, D.E., Hinton, G.E., & Williams, R.J. (1986). Learning internal representations by error propagation. In D.E. Rumelhart, J.L. McClelland, & the PDP Research Group (Eds.), *Parallel Distributed Processing: Explorations in the Microstructure of Cognition. Vol 1: Foundations.* Cambridge MA: MIT Press.

Rumelhart, D.E., & Zipser, D. (1985). Competitive learning. *Cognitive Science, 9,* 75–112.

Sanger, T.D. (1989). Optimal unsupervised learning in a single-layer linear feedforward neural network. *Neural Networks, 2,* 459–473.

Turk, M., & Pentland, A. (1991). Eigenfaces for recognition. *Journal of Cognitive Neuroscience, 3,* 71–86.

Young, A.W., & Bruce, V. (1991). Perceptual categories and the computation of grandmother. *European Journal of Cognitive Psychology, 3,* 5–49.

Young, A.W., Hellawell, D., & Hay, D.C. (1987). Configural information in face perception. *Perception, 16,* 747–759.

Revised manuscript received 1 May 1994

APPENDIX

All simulations reported here were run using standard IAC unit update functions (see McClelland & Rumelhart, 1988).

Unit Update Functions

Net input to unit i (net_i) is calculated as the sum of input from external and internal sources:

$$net_i = (\epsilon{\cdot}extinput_i) + (\alpha{\cdot}intinput_i)$$

where ϵ and α are global strength parameters, and *extinput* is the external activation given to the unit by the experimenter.
The internal input *(intinput)* is calculated as:

$$intinput_i = \sum_j w_{ij} \cdot output_j$$

where w_{ij} is the weight of the connection from j to i, and $output_j$ is the output from unit j. Only units with positive output are entered into this sum (see McClelland & Rumelhart, 1988, p. 12).

Once the net input to a unit is calculated, change in activation is given by the equations:

If $(net_i > 0)$, $\quad \Delta a_i = (max - a_i)net_i - decay\,(a_i - rest)$

Otherwise, $\quad \Delta a_i = a_i - (min)net_i - decay\,(a_i - rest)$

where *max* and *min* are maximum and minimum values for all units, *rest* is the resting activation for all units, and *decay* is the global decay on all unit activations.

Link Update Functions

The Hebb-like link modification equations used in this model are

If $a_i a_j > 0$, $\Delta w_{ij} = \lambda a_i a_j (1 - w_{ij})$

Otherwise, $\Delta w_{ij} = \lambda a_i a_j (1 + w_{ij})$

where λ is a global learning rate parameter.

Global Parameter Values

The global parameters were set as follows for all simulations: $max = 1.0$, $min = -0.2$, $rest = -0.1$, $decay = 0.1$, $\epsilon = 0.4$, $\alpha = 0.1$, $\lambda = 0.5$.

In each of the simulations between-pool excitatory and inhibitory connections for known faces had weight 1.0 and -1.0 respectively; all within-pool inhibitory connections had weight -1.0; initial connections between features and unknown FRUs varied randomly between -0.05 and $+0.05$.

VISUAL COGNITION, 1994, *1* (2/3), 349–369

Segregated Processing of Facial Identity and Emotion in the Human Brain: A PET Study

Justine Sergent, Shinsuke Ohta, Brennan Macdonald, and Eric Zuck

Montreal Neurological Institute, McGill University, Montreal, Canada

The brain is organized into segregated areas of relative functional autonomy and specialization. This basic principle of cerebral organization is well documented for cognitive functions that differ drastically from one another, but less so for functions that belong to the same domain, such as face processing. Yet several sources of evidence point to a functional and structural dissociation of various aspects of face processing, as suggested by (1) an analysis of the perceptual and cognitive demands made by the processing of diverse properties conveyed by facial configurations, (2) selective impairment of aspects of face processing in brain-damaged patients, and (3) different localizations of face cells responsive to properties conveyed by faces such as identity and emotion in the monkey's brain. This study used positron emission tomography (PET) and magnetic resonance imaging (MRI) to delineate better the neurofunctional organization of face processing in the human brain, by measuring cerebral blood flow while subjects performed tasks involving the recognition of faces or the recognition of emotions expressed by faces. The results showed segregated processing of facial identity and facial emotion, with the former being performed predominantly in the ventro-mesial region of the right hemisphere including the limbic system, whereas the latter was

Requests for reprints should be sent to Brennan Macdonald, Department of Medical Physics, Montreal General Hospital, 1650 Cedar Avenue, Montreal, H3G 1A4, Canada.

Due to the untimely passing of Dr Sergent, principal author, this paper appears in its form as accepted for publication.

This research was supported by the National Institute of Mental Health, the Medical Research Council of Canada, and the EJLB Foundation. We thank Glyn Hymphreys, Andy Young, and an anonymous reviewer for their helpful suggestions on an earlier version of this article. We gratefully acknowledge the help and assistance of our colleagues at the McConnell Brain Imaging Center and the Neurochemistry Unit of the Montreal Neurological Institute, without whom this research would not have been carried out.

carried out predominantly in the latter part of the right hemisphere and the dorsal region of the limbic system. This structural organization allows the parallel processing of different information contained in physiognomies and underlies the high efficiency with which humans process faces.

The human face is the product of evolution, and it has been carved into a multi-purpose unit that serves a variety of biological and social functions. Biologically, it is a necessary passage for air, drink, and food intake, and it houses the major sensory organs and the speech apparatus. Socially, we look at faces to derive knowledge about the persons we encounter in order to adjust our interactions with them. Part of this knowledge is concerned with determining who a person is, as the uniqueness of each facial configuration provides a reliable index of individual identity. But a face also conveys categorical information about sex, age, race, and other personal characteristics, along with being a window into the inner feelings and moods of the individual through the rich facial musculature that constitutes an elaborate means of expressing emotion.

Such a diversity of information is perceptually derived from faces effort-lessly, and these apparently automatic perceptual operations testify to the high level of efficiency achieved by the cerebral structures underlying face processing. It was long believed that the processing of faces relied on a single mechanism capable of analyzing all the various types of facial information, but recent cognitive and neuropsychological studies of normal and brain-damaged subjects have led to a very different view of the functional and structural organ-ization of face processing. It is, indeed, now established that the different personal properties conveyed by a facial configuration are derived and processed through different perceptual and cognitive operations sustained by distinct cere-bral structures. Such a view is supported by a large number of findings of func-tional and structural dissociations showing that (cognitive or biological) factors affecting the processing of a specific facial property do not necessarily influence the processing of other properties. This has been demonstrated in normal subjects through reaction-time experiments (e.g. Bruce, Ellis, Gibling, & Young, 1987; Sergent, 1985), electro-encephalogram (EEG) recordings (e.g. Davidson, 1992), and positron emission tomography (PET) measurements of cerebral activity (e.g. Sergent, MacDonald & Zuck, 1994; Sergent, Ohta & MacDonald 1992), in brain-damaged patients either with prosopagnosia (e.g. Bruyer et al., 1983; Humphreys, Donnelly, & Riddoch, 1993; Tranel, Damasio, & Damasio, 1988) or without prosopagnosia (e.g. Borod, 1993; Bowers, Bauer, & Heilman, 1993; Young et al., 1993), and in demented patients (Kurucz & Feldmar, 1979).

Functional dissociations within the domain of face perception and recogni-tion thus result from the particular processing requirements associated with deriving each of the properties conveyed by a facial configuration, implying that these different requirements are met by distinct cerebral structures. Whereas this functional and structural fractionation of face processing conforms with basic principles of cerebral organization (e.g. Young, 1992; Zeki, 1993), the details and specifics of how the neural network sustaining face processing is organized and compartmented are still elusive. The purpose of this study is to contribute some clarification to one aspect of this issue, namely that concerned with the processing of facial identity and facial emotion. Three main sources of evidence point to distinct processing demands and neurobiological substrates underlying these two properties conveyed by faces.

Perceptual and Cognitive Requirements

From a perceptual standpoint, the relevant information about identity and emotion is embedded within different combinations of features that make up the facial configuration. Indeed, a facial configuration is a multi-informational structure that can be subjected to different processes that take specific combinations of features into consideration (Sergent, 1989). Access to identity requires the perceiver to detect in a face what is unique to it and to achieve a configurational representation that highlights the physical invariants of that particular face. Any change from a neutral stance that would distort the usual appearance of the facial features, and configuration must be corrected in order to succeed in matching the perceived face with the stored representation of the corresponding face. On the other hand, recognizing the emotion expressed by a face requires the perceiver to discard what is unique to that face, to detect a deviation from a resting or neutral configuration, and to determine, on the basis of the pattern of modified aspects of the face, the particular category of emotion momentarily expressed by the facial configuration. In addition, because expression of emotion is a form of communication and can be directed at someone in particular (in contrast to identity and other categories), the perceiver must also attend to head orientation and gaze direction in order to uncover in reaction to whom the emotion is expressed (obviously, I will not react in the same way if an angry-looking face stares at me or at the person standing next to me).

It must also be noted that, perceptually, emotion is easier to recognize than most other properties conveyed by a face (with the exception of race, perhaps). For one thing, because of the categorical nature of emotion (Etcoff & Magee, 1992) as opposed to the uniqueness of individual faces, there are relatively fewer facial configurations expressing the various emotions and blends of them than there are unique facial configurations. For another, as suggested by schematic drawings of faces, it is relatively easy to draw a face with a few lines that will reliably express a given emotion (e.g. McKelvie, 1973), whereas more complex drawings are needed to represent different sexes, different ages, or different individuals. This suggests that the facial information conveying emotion may be more salient and more readily accessible than the information that must be processed to derive most other properties from a face. In support of this suggestion, the recognition of emotion appears to be relatively more resilient to perceptual degradation such as low-pass filtering than is the processing of other facial properties (Sergent, unpublished observations). Nonetheless, the recognition of facial emotion requires that facial features be processed conjointly and interactively, as the same movement of a feature (e.g. the brows, cf. Ekman, 1979) may be part of the expression of different emotions, depending on the changes in other facial features. Although much remains to be done experimentally to understand the mechanisms underlying the perception of facial emotion, the foregoing illustrates the different perceptual demands made by the processing of identity and emotion.

The cognitive requirements associated with the processing of facial identity and emotion are also different. For a face to be recognized as that of a specific individual, pertinent memories related to that face must be reactivated, and this requires access to stored biographical information (Bruce & Young, 1986; Ellis, 1992). In contrast, no episodic or biographic memory as such is needed to ascertain the emotion expressed by a face. Thus, in as much as different sets of information, subjected to different processes, are required to make sense of different aspects of the perceived face, one should expect different underlying structures to be involved in the operations related to the processing of facial identity and emotion.

Evidence from Brain-damaged Patients

Findings of selective impairments within the domain of face processing have only been recently reported, but they include dissociations between facial identity and emotion (e.g. Bruyer et al., 1983; McCarthy & Warrington, 1990; Sergent & Villemure, 1989; Tranel et al., 1988; Young et al., 1993). Typically, some prosopagnosics who, by definition, fail to identify faces of known individuals, can nonetheless recognize the emotion expressed by a face; alternatively, some non-prosopagnosics are selectively impaired at recognizing the emotion expressed by a face. Whereas such dissociations are well established and conform with the different processing demands outlined earlier, it has not yet been possible to uncover the actual neurobiological substrates of facial emotion processing. However, at least by default and assuming universality in functional cerebral organization among right-handers, one may propose that these substrates do not comprise the ventro-medial occipito-temporal region of the right hemisphere. This region is typically disturbed in prosopagnosics and is activated in normal subjects performing face-recognition tasks (Sergent & Signoret, 1992); the existence of a dissociation between facial identity and facial emotion processing thus implies that this region is not indispensable for recognizing facial emotion. Consequently, lateral and/or dorsal cerebral structures must underlie the processing of facial emotion.

Unfortunately, neurological data from brain-damaged patients do not provide a clear answer to the issue of localization. Young et al. (1993), for instance, using stringent criteria of impaired performance on six face-processing tasks, found four patients with selectively impaired recognition of facial emotion. All four patients (as well as the 30 other patients tested in this study, who did not have selective impairment of emotion recognition) had parietal damage; each of these four patients had further injury to at least one other cortical lobe, but there was no consistency in the lobe actually damaged among them. Thus, these findings would suggest that damage to the parietal lobe is not sufficient to disrupt the recognition of facial emotion and that injury to any other lobe may contribute to the deficit, but these data do not bear on the issue of intra-hemisphere localization. Unexpectedly, the damage was restricted to the left hemisphere in Young et al.'s (1993) four patients, suggesting a special role of this hemisphere in aspects of processing that are specific to the recognition of facial emotion.

However, these findings depart from the results of a recent retrospective analysis of selective deficits in face processing by brain-damaged patients: Bowers et al. (1993) observed that 22% (7/32) of the right-hemisphere-damaged group could adequately match pictures of faces but were deficient in matching the affects displayed on those faces, whereas only 6% (2/32) of the left-hemisphere group showed this dissociation. Selective impairment of facial-emotion processing is therefore not exclusively observed after left-hemisphere damage, as Young et al.'s findings might have led one to conclude, and this leads to the further suggestion that there must be right-hemisphere structures that participate in the recognition of emotion but not of identity.

It must be noted that deficits in both identity and emotion are a more common occurrence than selective deficit of either one (cf. Bowers et al., 1993), but this may be due to the large volume of the underlying lesion and does not rule out the existence of dissociations. Nonetheless, given the well-established role of the right hemisphere in processing facial identity, such a frequent conjoint occurrence points to a contribution of the right hemisphere to the processing of facial emotion. In addition, not only can the processing of emotion be impaired when other aspects of face processing are spared, but different components of the emotion system (such as perception, expression, appraisal, arousal) can also be selectively affected (Borod, 1993; Bowers et al., 1993). The fact that impaired recognition of emotion is reported in patients with lesion in such diverse cerebral regions therefore suggests that several parts of the brain may be involved in processes that are more or less directly related to emotion.

Evidence from Electrophysiological Recordings in Monkeys

An additional source of evidence pointing to a dissociation between the processing of facial identity and emotion is suggested by findings from cell recordings in the monkey's brain. Neurons with responses related to facial expression are more likely to be found in the superior temporal sulcus, whereas neurons with activity related to facial identity are more likely to be found in the infero-temporal cortex (e.g. Hasselmo, Rolls, & Baylis, 1989; Perrett, Hietanen, Oram, & Benson, 1992; Rolls, 1992). In addition, face-responsive neurons activated when processing emotion do not necessarily respond when the processing of identity is involved, and vice-versa. These findings thus suggest that there exist neural cells that may be specialized for different aspects of face processing, and these cells are essentially located in different regions of the brain. However, two additional findings must be kept in mind in this respect: (1) even the most selective face-cells discharge to a variety of facial stimuli (Gross & Sergent, 1992) and (2) face-responsive neurons can be found over a large extent of the temporal cortex, suggesting that only large lesions would produce face-processing deficits (Rolls, 1992).

The foregoing brief outline provides both arguments for, and evidence of, distinct processing requirements and substrates in the processing of facial identity and emotion. It also points out a series of difficulties inherent in uncovering the neurofunctional organization of facial emotion processing. Indeed, on the basis of current empirical findings, it would be difficult to make any prediction regarding the cerebral areas involved in recognizing facial emotion. However, our current understanding of brain functions suggests that at least the posterior right hemisphere must play a role in the perceptual operations inherent in analysing the facial expression. In addition, it is established that the limbic system plays an essential role in the processing of emotional information (McLean, 1990), but which area of this system participates in the processing of facial emotion remains unknown. It is now well documented, however, that identity recognition engages the right parahippocampal gyrus, a cerebral structure that is part of the limbic system. Does this particular area also subserve the processing of facial emotion, or is another part of the limbic system involved in this function?

In this study, PET measurement of rCBF, with the subtraction method, was used to address this issue and to delineate better the neurobiological substrates of the recognition of facial emotion as opposed to the recognition of facial identity. This approach allows the functional isolation of the component operations underlying these distinct operations on facial information (e.g. Fox, Mintun, Reiman, & Raichle, 1988). In addition, a technique that combines the functional information derived from the PET with the anatomical information of the subjects' brains obtained by magnetic resonance imaging (MRI) was used to increase the precision of functional localizations.

Some limitations of this study need to be pointed out at the outset. (1) With respect to the processing of facial emotion, it must be acknowledged that the experimental design is concerned with only one aspect of such processing, specifically the recognition of static expressive faces, whereas the expression of emotion is typically a dynamic process. The fact that different patterns of results obtain depending on whether static or dynamic representations are used (Humphreys et al., 1993) indicates that only one aspect of the issue is being addressed here. (2) The ecological validity of the present task is obviously restricted, as subjects are merely required to appraise the type of emotion being expressed without having to react to that emotion; in other words, the task requires the subjects to recognize emotions from a cognitive standpoint, not to engage in emotional behaviour. (3) Because of the low temporal resolution of PET measurements of cerebral activity, many experimental trials are required, which compels one to mix different types of emotions within the same session; as a result, no distinction can be made in this study between emotions of different valence. (4) Although separate analysis of a single subject's data is an alternative procedure for deriving the pattern of activation associated with the realization of a given task in PET studies (e.g. Lueck et al., 1989), it was not used in the present experiment, for several reasons. When comparing an activation condition to a control condition with the subtraction method, responses appear as discrete foci of activity over a background of spatially random noise. This activity is typically less intense in cortical areas underlying cognitive operations than in those sustaining primary sensory or motor functions. With the ^{15}O water bolus technique used here, in order to improve the signal-to-noise ratio, it is necessary to include data from more than one set of observations, either by repeating an activation condition within the same subject or by testing several subjects on the same activation condition. Because of the risks associated with exposure to radiation and therefore the limited quantity of radioactive material that can be injected into a subject, the repetition of the same activation condition within a subject by necessity restricts the number of different tasks that can be carried out on each subject. Consequently, for the purpose of examining the neurofunctional anatomy of diverse aspects of face processing and to perform comparisons between them, the group-study approach was deemed preferable to the single-subject data analysis.

METHODS

Subjects

Eight male subjects between 21 and 35 years of age participated in the experiment. They were in good health, under no medication, and had no neurological or psychiatric disorders. They were right-handed, as assessed with Bryden's (1982) questionnaire, with no left-handers among their close relatives, and they had normal visual acuity and contrast sensitivity. They were fully informed of the risks associated with exposure to radioactive material, in accordance with the regulations of the Medical Research Council of Canada and the Control Board of Atomic Energy of Canada, and they read and signed consent forms for their participation. Their remuneration was $100.

Procedures and Equipment

The study comprised three phases, described in the order they took place.

Preparatory Phase. This phase consisted of preparing the subjects to the study, explaining the risks, obtaining their formal consent, testing their handedness and vision, and introducing them to the experimental tasks in order to lessen potential anxiety and to reduce hesitations during the experiment proper. Each experimental task was explained and run in conditions identical to those prevailing in the PET study, except that different stimuli were used. The subjects were also requested to fill in a questionnaire containing a list of 250 names of famous persons, and to indicate whether or not the name was familiar, and, if so, whether they could image a representation of the corresponding face and how clear this representation was. The faces used in the professional categorization condition of the PET study were selected from this list for each subject, using faces the subjects were able to "image" mentally.

PET Experiment. The PET study took place the day following the preparatory phase and consisted of measuring rCBF in 4 different conditions run at 15-min intervals, with a different order of conditions for each subject. The stimuli were presented in total darkness on a high-resolution Mitsubishi monitor, located 60 cm from the subject's eyes, positioned perpendicular to eye gaze, and driven by a PS/2 IBM computer. The computer also controlled the duration of stimulus presentation and the interstimulus interval and recorded the speed and accuracy of the subject's responses. The stimuli appeared in the centre of the screen, at a size of 8° in height and 6° in width. The spatial frequency of the gratings ranged from 0.5 to 16 cycles per degree of visual angle, and contrast was 0.5. In the grating condition and the two experimental conditions, a stimulus appeared for 1 sec every 3 sec, such that 20 stimuli were presented during scanning, preceded by 5 stimuli for practice.

The subjects were in a supine position, the head firmly held in a customized frame containing rapidly hardening self-inflating foamlike material and located in the centre of the tomograph scanner. Ears were occluded with wax, and an intravenous catheter was placed into the left brachial vein for injection of $H_2{}^{15}O$ (40 mCi per injection), which served as CBF tracer. In each experimental condition, stimulus presentation started conjointly with the injection of the radioactive solution, and the recording of the emission of positrons began 15 sec later and lasted for 60 sec. In 3 conditions, the subjects responded by pressing, with the index or middle finger of the right hand, 1 of 2 buttons of the computer "mouse", which was placed on their abdomen.

The study comprised 2 control conditions and 2 experimental conditions.

1. *Fixation.* The subject looked at a fixation point located in the centre of the screen and was required to concentrate on this point. The illuminated area of the screen was of the same size and average luminance as the faces and objects presented in the other conditions.

2. *Grating Discrimination.* The stimuli were sinusoidal gratings of varying spatial frequency, either horizontal or vertical. The subjects pressed one button

in response to vertically oriented gratings and the other button to horizontally oriented gratings.

3. *Face Professional Categorization.* The stimuli were black-and-white faces of famous persons, drawn from the list presented to the subject the day before, and they were therefore all known by the subjects. Half the faces were those of actors, and half were of other professional categories (politicians, sportsmen, newsmen, singers), and the subjects' task was to decide whether or not a face was that of an actor and to press one of the two buttons accordingly. The expression of the faces presented in this condition was neutral. It must be noted that, strictly speaking, a semantic categorization of a face does no require explicit identification of the individual; however, a semantic categorization cannot be performed unless the face is actually recognized (e.g. Sergent, 1985), and, as such, can be considered as involving the same processes as those inherent in face identification, except for the retrieval of the name.

4. *Face Emotional Categorization* The stimuli were black-and-white faces of unfamiliar individuals expressing emotion (Ekman & Friesen, 1976). The faces expressed either positive (happiness, contentment) or negative (sadness, disgust, fear) emotions, with an equal number of positive and negative emotions. The subject's task was to decide whether the emotion was positive or negative and to press 1 of the 2 buttons to indicate the response.

As already done in an earlier study (Sergent, Zuck, Lévesque, & MacDonald, 1992), in order to minimize the risk that subjects would be tempted to pronounce the name of the individual or verbalize their responses, subjects had to place their tongue between their teeth during the 1-min duration of each scanning.

MRI Study. This phase took place between 2 to 4 weeks after the PET study. It consisted of a MRI scan of each subject's brain, with a Philips Gyroscan (1.5 Tesla), using the same head-holder and the same orientation of the head as for the PET scan.

Considerations about the Experimental Design. Because the pattern of activation associated with a given task is uncovered through the subtraction method, the choice of the particular tasks to be compared is critical in the design of PET cognitive studies (see Sergeht, in press). There is no unique and perfect way of selecting the tasks to be contrasted, which makes it necessary to justify the selection of a grating discrimination task as baseline in the present study. This choice was made in order to control as much as possible for the peripheral aspects of the face-processing tasks, that is, early visual operations and manual response, such that the operations not specific to face processing would be uncovered. Thus, the selected gratings had the same average contrast as the faces, comprised the same range of spatial frequencies as that of the presented faces, and were of the same size as the faces. In addition, gratings do not carry with them any semantic information that could be implicitly or explicitly processed. Subtracting a grating task from the face-processing tasks thus gave the possibility to uncover the cerebral structures specifically involved in the processing of faces. Given the relative autonomy of face processing compared to the processing of other objects, any other category of meaningful stimuli would have engaged cerebral structures not called for by the processing of faces, which would have resulted in biased findings as operations not involved in the processing of faces would have been subtracted in comparing a control to an experimental task.

However, it could be argued that grating discrimination, as a subtracted task, may not be specific nor difficult enough to provide a precise picture of the actual cerebral structures underlying the processing of facial identity and emotion. This is not a major difficulty, for the following reasons. (1) The neurofunctional anatomy of face-identity processing has been examined through the PET methodology (Sergent, Ohta, et al., 1992), and the cerebral structures involved in identifying faces are already well documented and precisely delineated. (2) Sergent, Ohta, et al.'s (1992) findings concur with radiological evidence from prosopagnosic patients (Sergent & Signoret, 1992a) and have since been replicated in a PET study (Sergent et al., 1994), as well as with depth-electrodes in pre-surgical monitoring of epileptic patients (Allison et al., in press). (3) The present design provides the opportunity to make a direct comparison between face-identity and face-emotion processing as to "isolate" the cerebral structures specifically underlying the operations by which each of these two properties conveyed by faces is derived. Thus, the relative lack of specificity of the face-minus-grating subtraction is compensated for by the high specificity of the face emotion-minus-identity and the face identity-minus-identity and the face identity-minus-emotion subtractions.

It must be noted, nonetheless, that the comparison between identity and emotion cannot be symmetric. On the other hand, even though neutral faces are used in the face-identity task, a "neutral emotion" is still an expression, and subjects may not refrain from processing the expression of the face. Consequently, some operations involved in the recognition of emotions may be contained in the face-identity task, which could preclude all the cerebral structures engaged in the processing of facial emotion from being uncovered by comparing face-identity and face-emotion. However, the grating condition provides an appropriate control, and subtracting this condition from the face-identity and the face-emotion conditions can reveal any overlap that may underlie the processing of facial identity and emotion. On the other hand, the use of unfamiliar faces in the face-emotion condition should guarantee that no process specific to the recognition of faces will be present in this condition. The combination of the grating condition as a baseline, and of a reciprocal subtraction of identity and emotion conditions, therefore, provides a sound basis for uncovering the neurofunctional anatomy of the recognition of face identity and of face emotion.

Scanning and Analyses

PET scanning was performed by measuring rCBF using the intravenous ^{15}O water bolus technique (Raichle, et al., 1983) and a Scanditronix PC-2048 PET scanner with in-plane and spatial resolutions of 5-to 6-mm full width at half maximum. Fifteen slices with a centre-to-centre distance of 6.8 mm were simultaneously imaged, which could be further divided by bilinear interpolation to produce 80 transaxial slices. A rotating germanium-68 source was used to correct the images for attenuation of the gamma rays in the skull and brain tissue. The image planes were chosen parallel to the subject's glabella-inion line, which was aligned with the tomograph's laser reference line and transcribed onto the head-holder as a marker for the correlation of PET and MR imaging. The MR images were obtained at the same 15 planes as in the PET study. Slice registration was ensured using a thin $CuSO_4$-filled (5 mm) catheter attached to the side of the customized head-holder and visible in an MR image, coincident with the reference line identifying the PET scan reference plane (Evans, Marrett, Collins, & Peters, 1989).

The PET activation functional images were mapped onto the MR structural images using a PIXAR 3-D computer and landmark-matching software (Evans et al., 1989). Interactive 3-D image software was used to establish an orthogonal coordinate frame based on the anterior commissure-posterior commissure (AC-PC) line as identified in the MR image volume. These coordinates were used to apply a linear re-sampling of each matched pair of MRI and PET datasets into a standardized stereotactic coordinate system (Talairach & Tournoux, 1988). It must be noted that this mapping of PET data on MR images is performed for each subject and each condition separately before averaging group data, and anatomical landmarks are used to re-sample each dataset into a standardized 3-D coordinate system of the brain. This procedure makes it possible to correct for large individual differences in brain morphology and to allow the subsequent averaging to be performed on standardized data.

The next step in the analysis consisted of normalizing the PET images for global CBF and determining the difference between control and experimental conditions for each subject. The mean state-dependent change image volume was obtained by averaging across subjects (Fox, Perlmutter, & Raichle, 1985) and then converted to a t-statistic by dividing the mean state-dependent change by the mean standard deviation in normalized CBF for all intra-cerebral voxels, and by multiplying this quotient by the square root of N (number of subjects). Anatomical and functional images were merged to allow for direct localization on the MR images of t-statistic peaks and for the anatomical correlation of extended zones of activation not expressible in terms of isolated peaks. The peak distribution was searched for significant signals using change-distribution analysis and z-score thresholding (Evans, Beil, Marrett, & Hakim, 1988). No correction for the number of comparisons was performed (Fox, 1991), and peaks with significance levels of $z > 2.81$, $p < 0.005$ are reported.

RESULTS

A preliminary analysis was performed on accuracy and latency of the manual responses made during the PET scanning. The percentage of correct responses was better than 90% in the gratings, emotion, and identity tasks in all but one subject, whose accuracy was 85% in the identity task. This level of accuracy guarantees that the subjects performed the task as requested, and it can therefore be assumed that the cerebral blood flow measured during each of the tasks reflects the activity inherent in the intended perceptual and cognitive operations. Response latencies were significantly ($p < 0.001$) faster in the gratings (672 msec) than in the other two tasks, which did not significantly differ from another (identity: 882 msec; emotion; 869 msec; $p > 0.30$).

The results of the comparisons between control and experimental PET conditions, reflecting significant changes in rCBF, are presented in Table 1, expressed as peaks of activation in terms of Talairach and Tournoux (1988) stereotactic coordinates, of their location in Brodmann's classification, and of the common name of the activated area. The most significant foci of activation are shown in Figure 1, superimposed on a MR image of the brain.

The activation associated with the grating-discrimination task, obtained after subtracting the passive fixation condition, engaged striate and peri-striate areas in the occipital cortex. There was a large involvement of the right area 18, in the inferior occipital gyrus and in the cuneus, which are assumed to underlie the initial analysis of visual stimuli, a finding already reported (e.g. Sergent, Ohta, et al., 1992). Also significant was the activation of the left motor and premotor areas (Brodmann's areas 4 and 6, respectively) corresponding to the manual responses performed by the subjects during the scanning. The activity associated with the grating-discrimination task was subtracted from the activity recorded during the two experimental conditions in the subsequent analyses.

Beyond the striate and peri-striate areas activated during the grating-discrimination task, additional cerebral structures were recruited by the performance of the face identity and facial emotion tasks. As shown in Table 1 and in Figure 1 (see Plate 1), distinct cerebral structures participated in the realization of these two tasks. In the identity task, the processing of faces resulted in the activation of the right lingual gyrus (area 18) and the right fusiform gyrus (area 37). These two areas are located in the posterior ventro-mesial region of the brain, are implicated in the perceptual processing of facial configurations, and their destruction results in a perceptually based prosopagnosia (Sergent & Signoret, 1992a). Further activation during the face-identity task was observed in the parahippocampal gyrus (area 36), in an area that plays a pivotal role in reactivating semantic information related to the individual whose face is perceived, and the destruction of which results in a memory-based prosopagnosia (Sergent & Signoret, 1992a). These findings are consistent with earlier results obtained in similar experimental conditions (Sergent, Ohta, et al., 1992; Sergent et al., 1994), and there is therefore

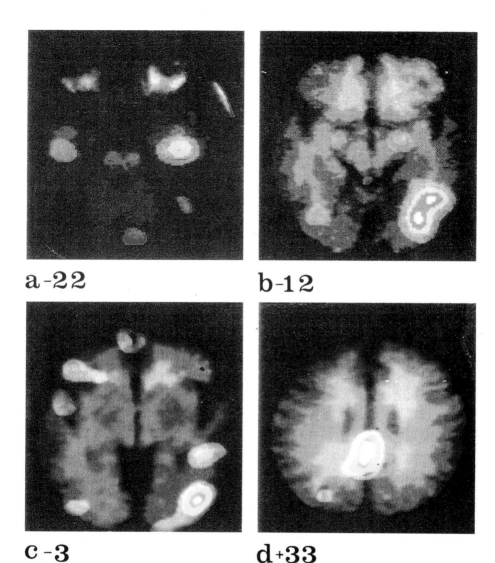

a-22   b-12

c-3   d+33

FIG. 1.   Foci of activation associated with the recognition of facial identity (a & b) and the recognition of facial emotion (c & d). The images were obtained after averaging from 8 subjects and subtracting the grating discrimination condition. The PET foci of activation are superimposed over MRI horizontal slices of the subjects' brains. The numbers below each image correspond to the level (in mm) of the slice on the ventrodorsal axis (Z axis in Table 1), and they suggest that the processing of facial identity takes place in more ventral areas than the processing of facial emotion. The two top slices illustrate the participation of the ventro-mesial areas of the right hemisphere in the processing of facial identity: in the parahippocampal gyrus (Slice a) and the lingual and fusiform gyri (Slice b). The two bottom slices show activation associated with the processing of facial emotion, in the right middle occipital gyrus (Slice c) and cingulate gyrus (Slice d).

Table 1
Significant Foci of Activation[a] derived by Paired Activation Subtraction

X	Y	Z	Brodmann's Area	Cortical Area
Gratings minus Baseline				
−5	−90	9	Area 17	Left striate cortex
−24	−83	−5	Area 18	Left inferior occipital gyrus
25	−93	−1	Area 18	Right inferior occipital gyrus
8	−94	6	Area 18	Right cuneus
−42	−18	60	Area 4	Left motor
−33	−4	58	Area 6	Left premotor
Facial identity minus Gratings				
29	−71	−8	Area 18	Right lingual gyrus
38	−54	−12	Area 37	Right fusiform gyrus
30	−22	−24	Area 36	Right parahippocampal gyrus
Facial emotion minus Gratings				
39	−80	−6	Area 19	Right middle occipital gyrus
−3	−50	33	Area 23	Left/Right cingulate gyrus
0	−40	29	Area 23	Left/Right cingulate gyrus
Facial identity minus facial emotion				
36	−51	−12	Area 37	Right fusiform gyrus
30	−25	−21	Area 36	Right parahippocampal gyrus
Facial emotion minus facial identity				
1	−48	35	Area 23	Cingulate gyrus
−2	−41	27	Area 23	Cingulate gyrus

[a] $p > 0.005$.

Note: Coordinates of peak activation are expressed in millimetres: X represents the medial-lateral axis (negative, left), Y the antero-posterior axis (negative, posterior), Z the dorsoventral axis (negative, ventral). The Brodmann's and cortical area corresponding to the coordinates are also shown.

strong evidence of their reliability and replicability. Indeed, the subtraction of grating discrimination from face identity in Sergent et al.'s (1992a) study resulted in significant CBF changes in the right fusiform gyrus (37, −55, −11) and the right parahippocampal gyrus (26, −17, −22), at locations that are almost identical to those obtained in the present study (cf. Table 1).

When emotion was the critical variable, different cortical areas from those involved in the processing of facial identity were recruited. The perceptual analysis of facial expression engaged the lateral part of the right occipital cortex, in the middle occipital gyrus (area 19). Activation was also found in the posterior region of the limbic system, essentially in the cingulate gyrus immediately above the corpus callosum (area 23). Despite the initial lateralization of facial-emotion processing in the right hemisphere, the activation observed in the limbic system did not seem to be lateralized, as the peaks were located on, or close to, the mesial regions of both hemispheres. The relatively low spatial resolution of the PET camera, however, prevents definite conclusions from being drawn from these findings with respect to cerebral lateralization.

The foregoing analyses involved the comparison of experimental conditions with the same control condition (grating-discrimination), and they led to the identification of peaks of activation associated with each experimental condition. However, finding that peaks of activation in two different conditions are located in distinct areas does not necessarily mean that the activated areas do not overlap or do not participate in the two tasks. In addition, a significant rCBF increase may obtain when compared to a control condition, but not when compared to another condition, even if the two conditions make different processing demands; a significant peak of activation obtained in a comparison between a control and an activation condition that would no longer be significant when comparing this activation condition to another activation condition would then suggest that the specialization of a given cerebral area is relative rather than absolute.

Accordingly, direct comparisons of activation between the two experimental conditions were carried out by subtracting one condition from the other. When the activation associated with the processing of facial emotion was subtracted from the face-identity condition, activation in the lingual gyrus (area 18) was no longer significant ($p = 0.12$), whereas the increases in rCBF that were also significant (right fusiform and parahippocampal gyri) in the initial analysis remained unchanged in this subsequent analysis (see Table 1). These findings suggest that the latter two areas do not significantly contribute to the processing of facial emotion, whereas the lingual gyrus might participate to some extent in the processing of facial emotion, even though this participation could not be demonstrated in the initial analysis. However, the latter suggestion needs corroboration from further investigation. Alternatively, subtracting the identity condition from the emotion condition resulted in the activation of the right middle occipital gyrus being no longer significant ($p = 0.19$), whereas the initially significant activation of the limbic system remained unchanged (see Table 1). These additional findings do not lend themselves to an unequivocal interpretation. They may suggest some overlap of the cerebral structures involved in the perceptual analysis of facial information with respect to identity and emotion properties, indicating that both the ventral and lateral regions of the right temporal cortex participate in the processing of identity and emotion information, from a perceptual standpoint; or they may indicate that subjects conjointly processed both identity and emotion information described in a facial configuration, in which case it is conceivable that the perceptual processing of identity and emotion is segregated and does not overlap.

DISCUSSION

The purpose of this study was to delineate better the neurobiological substrates of facial emotion processing and to determine the extent to which the different perceptual and cognitive processing demands inherent in recognizing faces and the emotions they express are sustained by distinct cerebral areas. As outlined in the introduction, there are both logical and empirical reasons for expecting a structural dissociation of these two functions given the different processing demands they make, the evidence of selective impairment of one or the other after brain damage, and the different localization of face cells responsive to identity and emotion in the monkey's brain.

The main results of this experiment conformed with this expectation and showed that the brain functionally and structurally dissociates the processing of facial identity and facial emotion. The recognition of a familiar face engaged cerebral structures that were distinct from those recruited for the recognition of facial emotion. This dissociation prevailed in two different regions of the cortex, assumed to perform different mental functions, as it was apparent in the posterior region of the right hemisphere and in the limbic system.

Dissociated Processing in the Posterior Cortex

One dissociation took place in the posterior cerebral areas underlying the analysis of the facial features and configuration that convey the relevant physical properties carrying specific information about an individual: the processing of facial identity resulted in the activation of the ventro-mesial, occipito-temporal region of the right hemisphere, whereas analysis of facial expression was predominantly performed in the lateral occipital region of the right hemisphere. The former finding replicates earlier results (Sergent et al., 1992; Sergent et al., 1994), and it provides a guarantee of the validity of the PET technique for uncovering the cerebral organization of mental functions along with offering strong evidence of the crucial role of the right fusiform gyrus in the analysis of the facial configurations in order to derive pertinent information about the identity of an individual.

The processing of facial emotion did not predominantly engage the ventromesial region of the right hemiphere, suggesting that this area is not devoted to the processing of faces as such but to specific perceptual operations on faces. Instead, the analysis of facial expression resulted in the activation of the right lateral occipital gyrus. Thus, even though the perceptual analysis of facial expressions requires the interactive processing of the facial features from which a given configuration emerges, as does the processing of facial identity, distinct cerebral areas were recruited to perform the analysis of these two types of configurations.

The present results are therefore essentially consistent with empirical evidence of a functional dissociation between facial identity and emotion processing. However, as indicated by the direct comparison between face identity and face emotion conditions, the results may not suggest an absolute dissociation. When the two experimental conditions were reciprocally subtracted from one another, changes of rCBF in the lingual gyrus during the identity task and in the lateral occipital cortex during the emotion task were no longer significant. Such a finding is consistent with an interpretation suggesting that these two areas participate, to a different extent, in the processing of both types of information, although it would not be possible at present to determine the actual contribution of each area to these processes. It is noteworthy that in prosopagnosic patients with conjoint deficit in facial emotion analysis (e.g. Sergent & Signoret, 1992b), the impairment is systematically more pronounced for identity than for emotion processing, as the patients are not completely unable to tell the emotion expressed by a face and usually succeed in recognizing happy faces and in telling positive from negative emotion. In addition, in studies reporting a deficit in the recognition of emotion in non-prosopagnosic patients, performance appears typically to be above chance (e.g. Young et al., 1993), which could suggest either that more than one cerebral area may normally contribute to the perceptual analysis of facial emotion or that disturbance in recognition of emotion following loss of the critical area may be more easily compensated for by the spared cortical areas than is the loss of facial identity processing (see Sergent & Signoret, 1992b, for further discussion of this question).

However, the present findings do not permit an unequivocal clarification of this issue. In fact, three somewhat different conclusions about perceptual processing of facial configurations could be drawn on the basis of the comparison between each experimental condition and the control condition: (1) distinct and specific cortical areas are devoted to the processing of identity and emotion, suggesting a clearly modular organization of the face-processing system in the human brain; (2) several areas—some more than others—conjointly contribute to the processing of each facial property, but only those areas that are predominantly involved in processing reached a reliable level of significance (the direct comparison of face identity and face emotion would give support to such a view); (3) there are individual differences in the functional organization of face processing (cf. Hellige, 1993), and, because of the averaging procedure used in this study, these differences were cancelled out, and the resulting pattern of results reflects the minimum common denominator to all subjects. Whereas the foregoing clearly points to the need for further experimental investigation, the results nonetheless provide evidence of a structural fractionation underlying a functional specialization of the perceptual operations performed on facial configurations.

Dissociated Processing in the Limbic Cortex

The segregation observed in perceptual operations was also present at subsequent levels of processing when the outcomes of these operations had to be interpreted and given meaning. As already reported, the processing of facial identity resulted in the activation of the right parahippocampal gyrus, whose role it is to reactivate pertinent memories associated with the perceived face (Sergent, Ohta, et al., 1992). This structure was not recruited during the recognition of emotion, and the direct comparison of activations in the two experimental conditions showed no functional overlap of this area with respect to the processing of emotion and identity. Instead, and unexpectedly, the recognition of emotion resulted in the activation of the parietal lobe, in the posterior and dorsal part of the limbic system. The neurological literature does not provide much indication that such a region of the cortex would be involved in the processing of facial emotion, and, to our knowledge, there is no report of specific deficit associated with damage to this area. This finding could thus be an artifact, resulting, for instance, from a deactivation of this area in the control condition used in the subtraction rather than from a genuine increase in rCBF in the facial emotion condition. However, if such were the case, it would follow that a significant rCBF increase should also have prevailed in the comparison between the face-identity condition and the control condition, but it did not. In addition, a comparison between the grating condition and the passive condition did not show any indication that this region of the limbic system was deactivated during the grating condition. There is, therefore, reason to believe that the present finding is not artifactual, and some empirical evidence in fact exists that links the recognition of facial emotion to the parietal cortex.

Indeed, Bauer (1984, 1986) has suggested that two distinct neural pathways linking the visual areas to the limbic structures are engaged in the processing of faces. One follows a ventro-medial route and is responsible for the processes underlying the overt recognition and identification of faces (e.g. Sergent, Ohta, et al., 1992); the other pathway follows a more dorsal route, initially involving the lateral temporal cortex and then projecting to the parietal cortex and the cingulate gyrus. As pointed out by Bauer (1986), a large body of behavioural and electrophysiological evidence implicates the dorsal pathways and its adjacent regions in emotional arousal and rapid selective orientation to stimuli that have motivational significance. The observed activation of the parietal cortex in face-emotion condition may thus be consistent with an involvement of the dorsal pathway in the processing of emotional information.

Whether this involvement is restricted to one hemisphere or engages both hemispheres cannot be unequivocally determined from the present findings. The peak of activation was located along the midline and slightly towards the left hemisphere, and, because of the relatively low spatial resolution of the PET camera, such a finding is inconclusive with respect to cerebral lateralization.

Given the initial predominant contribution of the right hemisphere in the perceptual aspects of processing of facial expression, one could have expected that further processing would be limited to the right hemisphere. On the other hand, on the basis of Young et al.'s (1993) recent results of an involvement of the parietal cortex of either hemisphere in patients presenting with a deficit in face-emotion processing, along with evidence from EEG recordings suggesting no posterior cerebral asymmetry in the processing of facial emotion (Davidson, 1992), one could have expected that parietal areas of both hemispheres would be recruited during face-emotion condition. Additional investigation is obviously needed to determine (1) whether there is unilateral or bilateral parietal involvement in the processing of facial emotion and (2) whether the present activation in the posterior limbic system is specific to the processing of *facial* emotion as such or to more general aspects of emotional processing.

Conclusions

Identity and emotion are both personal properties conveyed by the facial configuration, each property requiring specific perceptual operations to be accessed. By having these operations performed by distinct cerebral structures, the brain avoids potential interference in the processing of this information, and, at the same time, makes it possible to carry out simultaneously, in parallel, different operations on the same facial information. Such an organization underlies the remarkable proficiency with which faces are perceptually processed by the brain. On the other hand, identifying an individual and recognizing his or her emotion are two distinct functions subserved by two different regions of the limbic system, ventrally and dorsally, respectively. The present findings show a clear dissociation in the processing of identity and emotion beyond the visual perceptual areas, but only in the laboratory do we require subjects to focus on one property exclusive of the other. Social relations require not only to know the identity of the person one is dealing with but the intentions and emotional state of this person. Although these two regions of the limbic system may be distant from one another, they are part of a highly integrated system and have to work in close interaction.

REFERENCES

Allison, T., Ginter, H., McCarthy, G., Nobre, A.C., Puce, A., Luby, M., & Spencer, D.D. (in press). Face recognition in human extrastriate cortex. *Journal of Neurophysiology.*

Bauer, R.M. (1984). Autonomic recognition of names and faces in prosopagnosia: A neuropsychological application of the Guilty Knowledge Test. *Neuropsychologia, 22,* 457–469.

Bauer, R.M. (1986). The cognitive psychophysiology of prosopagnosia. In H.D. Ellis, M.A. Jeeves, F. Newcombe, & A.W. Young. (Eds.), *Aspects of Face Processing* (pp. 253–267). Dordrecht, Martinus Nijhoff.

Bowers, D., Bauer, R.M., & Heilman, K.M. (1993). The nonverbal affect lexicon: Theoretical perspectives from neuropsychological studies of affect perception. *Neuropsychology, 7*, 433–444.

Bruce, V. (1988). *Recognising faces.* Hove: Lawrence Erlbaum Associates Ltd.

Bruce, V., Ellis, H., Gibling, F., & Young, A. (1987). Parallel processing of the sex and familiarity of faces. *Canadian Journal of Psychology, 41,* 510–520.

Bruce, V., & Young, A.W. (1986). Understanding face recognition. *British Journal of Psychology, 77,* 305–327.

Bruyer, R., Laterre, C., Seron, X., Feyereisen, P., Strypstein, E., Pierrard, E., & Rectem, S. (1983). A case of prosopagnosia with preserved covert remembrance of familiar faces. *Brain and Cognition, 2,* 257–284.

Bryden, M.P. (1982). *Laterality.* New York: Academic Press.

Davidson, R.J. (1992). Anterior cerebral asymmetry and the nature of emotion. *Brain and Cognition, 20,* 125–151.

Ekman, P. (1979). About brows: Emotional and conversational signals. In M. von Cranach, F. Koppa, W. Lepenies, & D. Ploog (Eds.), *Human ethology.* London: Cambridge University Press.

Ekman, P., & Friesen, W.V. (1976). *Unmasking the face.* Englewood Cliffs, NJ: Prentice Hall.

Ellis, A.W. (1992). Cognitive mechanisms of face processing. *Philosophical Transactions of the Royal Society, London, Series B, 335,* 113–119.

Etcoff, N.L., & Magee, J.J. (1992). Categorical perception of facial expressions. *Cognition, 44,* 227–240.

Evans, A.C., Beil, C., Marrett, S., & Hakim, A. (1988). Anatomical functional correlation using an adjustable MRI-based region of interest atlas with positron emission tomography. *Journal of Cerebral Blood Flow and Metabolism, 8,* 513–530.

Evans, A., Marrett, S., Collins, L., & Peters, T.M. (1989). Anatomical-functional correlative analysis of the human brain using three-dimensional imaging systems. *Proceedings of the Society of Photographic and Optical Instrumentation and Engineering, 1092,* 264–274.

Fox, P.T. (1991). Physiological ROI definition by image subtraction. *Journal of Cerebral Blood Flow and Metabolism, 11,* A79–A82.

Fox, P.T., & Raichle, M.E. (1985). Stimulus rate determines regional blood flow in striate cortex. *Annals of Neurology, 17,* 303–305.

Fox, P.T., Perlmutter, J.S., & Raichle, M.E. (1985). A stereotactic method of anatomical localization for positron emission tomography. *Journal of Computer Assisted Tomography, 9,* 141–153.

Fox, P.T., Mintun, M.A., Reiman, E.M., & Raichle, M.E. (1988). Enhanced detection of focal brain responses using intersubject averaging and change-distribution analysis of subtracted PET images. *Journal of Cerebral Blood Flow and Metabolism, 8,* 642–653.

Gross, C.G. (1992). Representation of visual stimuli in inferior temporal cortex. *Philosophical Transactions of the Royal Society, London, Series B, 335,* 3–10.

Gross, C.G., & Sergent, J. (1992). Face recognition. *Current Opinion in Neurobiology, 2,* 156–161.

Hasselmo, M.E., Rolls, E.T., & Baylis, G.C. (1989). The role of expression and identity in the face-selective responses of neurons in the temporal visual cortex of the monkey. *Behavioural Brain Research, 32,* 203–218.

Hellige, J.B. (1993). *Hemispheric Asymmetry. What is left and what is right.* Cambridge, MA: Harvard University Press.

Humphreys, G.W., Donnelly, N., & Riddoch, M.J. (1993). Expression is computed separately from facial identity, and it is computed separately from moving and static faces: Neuropsychological Evidence. *Neuropsychologia, 31,* 173–181.

Kurucz, J., & Feldmar, G. (1979). Prosopo-affective agnosia as a symptom of cerebral organic disease. *Journal of the American Geriatric Society, 27,* 225–230.

Lueck, C.J., Zeki, S., Friston, K.J., Deiber, M.P., Cope, P., Cunningham, V.J., Lammertsma, A.A., Kennard, C., & Frackowiak, R.S.J. (1989). The colour center in the cerebral cortex of man. *Nature, 340,* 386–389.

McCarthy, R.A., & Warrington, E.K. (1990). *Cognitive neuropsychology. A clinical introduction.* London: Academic Press.

McKelvie, S. (1973). The meaningfulness and meaning of schematic faces. *Perception & Psychophysics, 14,* 343–348.

McLean, P.D. (1990). *The triune brain in evolution: Role in paleocerebral functions.* New York: Plenum.

Mintun, M., Fox, P.T., & Raichle, M.E. (1989). A highly accurate method of localizing neuronal activity in the human brain with positron emission tomography. *Journal of Cerebral Blood Flow and Metabolism, 9,* 96–103.

Perrett, D.I., Hietanen, J.K., Oram, M.W., & Benson, J. (1992). Organization and functions of cells responsive to faces in the temporal cortex. *Philosophical Transactions of the Royal Society, London, Series B, 335,* 23–30.

Raichle, M.E., Martin, W.R.W., Herscovitch, P., Mintun, M.A., & Markham, J. (1983). Brain blood flow measured with intravenous $H_2^{15}O$. II. Implementation and validation. *Journal of Nuclear Medicine, 24,* 790–798.

Rolls, E.T. (1992). Neurophysiological mechanisms underlying face processing within and beyond the temporal cortical visual areas. *Philosophical Transactions of the Royal Society, London, Series B, 335,* 11–21.

Sergent, J. (1985). Influence of task and input factors on hemispheric involvement in face processing. *Journal of Experimental Psychology: Human Perception and Performance, 11,* 846–861.

Sergent, J. (1989). Structural processing of faces. In A.W. Young & H.D. Ellis (Eds.), *Handbook of research on face processing* (pp. 57–91). Amsterdam: North Holland.

Sergent, J. (in press). Brain-imaging studies of cognitive function. *Trends in Neurosciences.*

Sergent, J., MacDonald, B., & Zuck, E. (1994). Structural and functional organization of knowledge about faces and proper names: A PET study. In C. Umiltà & M. Moscovitch (Eds.), *Attention and Performance, XV.* Hillsdale, NJ: Lwarence Erlbaum Associates, Inc.

Sergent, J., Ohta, S., & MacDonald, B. (1992). Functional neuroanatomy of face and object processing: A PET study. *Brain, 115,* 15–29.

Sergent, J., & Signoret, J.-L. (1992a). Functional and anatomical decomposition of face processing: Evidence from prosopagnosia and PET study of normal subjects. *Philosophical Transactions of the Royal Society, London, Series B, 335,* 55–62.

Sergent, J., & Signoret, J.L. (1992b). Varieties of functional deficits in prosopagnosia. *Cerebral Cortex, 2,* 375–388.

Sergent, J., Zuck, E., Lévesque, M., & MacDonald, B. (1992). Positron emission tomography study of letter and object processing: Empirical findings and methodological considerations. *Cerebral Cortex, 2,* 68–80.

Talairach, J., & Tournoux, P. (1988). *Co-planar stereotaxic atlas of the human brain. Three-dimensional proportional system: An approach to cerebral imaging.* Stuggart: Thieme.

Tranel, D., Damasio, A., & Damasio, H. (1988). Intact recognition of facial expression, gender, and age in patients with impaired recognition of face identity. *Neurology, 38,* 690–696.

Young, A.W. (1992). Face recognition impairments. *Philosophical Transactions of the Royal Society, London, Series B, 335,* 47–54.

Young, A., Newcombe, F., De Haan, E., Small, M., & Hay, D. (1993). Face perception after brain injury. Selective impairments affecting identity and expression. *Brain, 116,* 941–960.

Manuscript received 1 Novemver 1993

Subject Index